TWO RIVERS
OF THE
MIND

A SIMPLE AND FUN GUIDE
TO YOUR DESIRES IN LIFE

CHRISTOPHER J BOURG

TWO RIVERS OF THE MIND
A SIMPLE AND FUN GUIDE TO YOUR DESIRES IN LIFE

iUniverse books may be ordered through booksellers or by contacting:

iUniverse
1663 Liberty Drive
Bloomington, IN 47403
www.iuniverse.com
1-800-Authors (1-800-288-4677)

Because of the dynamic nature of the Internet, any web addresses or links contained in this book may have changed since publication and may no longer be valid. The views expressed in this work are solely those of the author and do not necessarily reflect the views of the publisher, and the publisher hereby disclaims any responsibility for them.

Any people depicted in stock imagery provided by Getty Images are models, and such images are being used for illustrative purposes only.
Certain stock imagery © Getty Images.

ISBN: 978-1-5320-7040-2 (sc)
ISBN: 978-1-5320-7042-6 (hc)
ISBN: 978-1-5320-7041-9 (e)

Library of Congress Control Number: 2019910860

Print information available on the last page.

iUniverse rev. date: 10/09/2019

To my two sons, Jake and Mason. Through their love and inspiration, I found the power to share these truths with them and the world.

Life Quote

Through the teachers of life's knowledge, I now believe that all people have the right to succeed in their ventures. I've shared these truths and systems to teach, guide, and inspire all to greatness. The greatest inspiration for the world can be found in the poem "Invictus" (which is Latin for *unconquered*) by William Ernest Henley, written in 1875:

> Out of the night that covers me, black as the pit from pole to pole, I thank whatever gods may be for my unconquerable soul.
>
> In the fell clutch of circumstance, I have not winced nor cried aloud. Under the bludgeoning of chance my head is bloody, but unbowed.
>
> Beyond this place of wrath and tears looms but the horror of the shade, and yet the menace of the years finds and shall find me unafraid.
>
> It matters not how straight the gate, how charged with punishment the scroll,
>
> *I am the Master of my Fate:*
>
> *I am the Captain of my Soul.*

I have put the last two lines of this great poem in italics in the hope that everyone who reads them understands their true meaning. I also hope everyone realizes that everything is possible. These lines from Henley lay the beginning of your voyage to wealth, freedom, love, and happiness in life.

CONTENTS

CHAPTER 1

CHOICE OF RIVERS FOR LIFE

IMAGINE YOURSELF GOING ON AN adventure that will take you down a river. Few people from the outside world have traveled this river. Some of these people's trips ended in devastation and others in unfulfilling adventure. But for a few, this was the adventure of a lifetime. These few people have seen things that others haven't and enjoyed the challenge the river brought them. At the end of the adventure, the first group wanted only to go home and hide, while the second group looked forward to what other rivers had in store for them.

Our lives and how we live them are like this river adventure. We are the adventurers on the river, and we must make the adventure fun. It's not the river's job to make us successful. Nor is it life's job to make us happy. What we make of every day is up to us. It's up to us whether we will face the challenges laid in front of us or stop halfway through the adventure and stay in one place.

So take this river adventure with me, and see if you have what it takes to pick the right path on the river and create the greatest adventure the world has seen. The choice is yours! I promise that if you are willing to try, this book will give you what you need to not only survive the adventure but also make it to the end as a successful and happy person.

So let's begin by meeting our main character Captain Bon.

INTRODUCING CAPTAIN BON

Hello there, I'm Captain Bon. I will be your guide through this book and will help you create a system to become successful in your adventures. We will travel over many lands and learn much together. Some of it will be fun, and some will be demanding work. As with anything in life, you will get out of this adventure what you put into it.

If you read my adventure passively, I'm sure it will be an entertaining story; but if you stop and think about the different things we discuss, you will learn a lot. You will have all the tools you need to better your life. Though that choice is yours, I hope you choose to learn and become better equipped for the adventure we call life.

Oh, sorry. I don't know where my manners went. I should have better introduced myself before telling you what you should do. As you know, I am Captain Bon. I am a real captain of a tugboat, and that has been my life for many years. At one time long ago, I was in the navy, but not as a captain. No, I was an ordinary enlisted man. My time in the navy taught me much about leadership and work ethic, but not much in the way of how to succeed in life.

After the navy, I married a beautiful lady named Theresa, and we had children. To me, my life's work was to support and raise my family. Along the way, I had dreams of taking adventures and becoming an explorer, but I didn't think that it was proper to run off and chase my dreams and possibly fail in supporting my family.

Theresa has been the greatest wife a man could ask to have in his life. She is a true partner and more. Not only is she a great mother to our children, but she operates her own business for accounting and tax services as well. She has two offices that she built from the ground up with only her hard work and determination. She has taught me as much as any book on becoming a success.

To educate myself over the years, I have studied many biographies of great people, stories about ancient societies, and self-help books. These books became my formal education and my hiding places from the world. I read everything I could get my hands on. In total, I have read more than seven hundred books. When you are on the tugboats, you have a lot of time to read or be lazy. I chose to read and learn, though I never really took action with the knowledge I had gained.

As I went through these self-help books, I found a lot of them had misleading information. I thought that many of these authors would lead people down the wrong road in life. It wasn't that the authors were trying to mislead their readers. It was they either had put the information together improperly or had only half the answer. Many were missing the essential parts needed for a road map to success.

Some authors, such as Napoleon Hill, came very close and developed a system that could work for people to become successful, but he lost many believers when he brought up the supernatural. Now I don't have a problem with using the supernatural. After all, I am from Louisiana, so I guess that's why his work resonated with me. Though even Napoleon Hill didn't give the driving points to help motivate me. I found the parts needed to motivate myself in other authors such as John Maxwell and Tony Robbins.

Along the way through all this reading, I started taking notes—at first to help remind me of the key points and then to compare what the different authors were saying. As I began to read biographies of great people like Abraham Lincoln, George Washington, Nelson Mandela, Gandhi, and others, I started seeing things in their lives that reflected points I had written down from the self-help books.

I found that many of these most successful people were using the main points I had found in the self-help and motivational books. But how did they apply them, and how did each learn to use almost the same system? Their systems intrigued me. It was like I had found the mystery of the Holy Grail. I had to understand better what was going on, so I looked at other successful people. What I found amazed me. Maybe others had been taught these lessons in school, but I hadn't gotten them. It was understandable if that was the case because I never paid much attention in school anyway.

As I dug deeper into the approaches of the different people, I could see that they were different but the system was the same. The better the people abided by a few of what I call "life truths" and the system to implement them, the more success they achieved.

I wondered whether others had found the same correlations I had found. Was this how these people became successful? Maybe, or maybe I was way off track. But I couldn't be off track. Each example lined up too perfectly.

After about a year of studying the system I had found, I decided it was time to put it into action. That action would be a desire I held deeply in my soul. My deepest desire was to go into the history books as an explorer. I didn't have to be the greatest explorer, but I had to find my way into those books. I also realized I would need the help, advice, and accountability of a mentor, but that will come later in my tale.

What You Will Discover in Our Hero's Story

In this book, we will look at the two rivers of our minds. You will have a choice of which river and boat you want to take. On one river, you will find the system and truths to a happy and wealthy life. On the other river, you will find the fears, acts, beliefs, and other things to avoid if you don't want to go over the waterfall and crash on the rocks below. You may also find in yourself the power to harness these truths or to set them aside and live life for whatever comes.

All things accomplished in life begin with desire and faith. In life, we choose to believe we can have our hearts' desires and act on those desires. Or we believe God has already written our story in heaven. The pages of time show the great people who chose to follow their desires with faith and plans of action and found a way to achieve those desires. And those who failed to follow these steps only found poverty and unhappiness at the bottom of the falls. However, the ones who found poverty and unhappiness were not necessarily poor in money. Many of the richest in money and material objects are haunted with poverty and unhappiness in their souls. Some of the most powerful people of the twentieth century led lonely, unloving lives behind closed doors and away from the public's eye. You see, you can be as rich as a Rockefeller but as poor as the poorest person in your heart. Now what kind of life is that? Who wants to live a life of riches but have no love in his or her life? You must have balance in your soul and your life. In the chapters to come, you will find the knowledge to help you create this balance and stop the inner conflict.

I want you to think back on the trips or adventures you have taken in life. Do you have the great memories of the trips you took alone? For most of us, it is the trips we shared with friends or loved ones that bring us the fondest memories. As humans, God made us to share our adventures with others. For many people, the planning of the adventure can be as fun as the adventure itself. Sharing your hopes, dreams, and goals with others helps you to not only prepare to go where you want to go but also solidify the adventure in your subconscious mind. After all, your subconscious mind is the part of you that controls you. Your subconscious is the hidden part of the mind that will get you whatever you convince it you should have in life. When you combine your subconscious with that of others and meld multiple subconscious minds together, anything is possible. Then not only will you have someone to share the adventure with, but together you will get further in the adventure than you can alone.

The truth and the system were taught to the most successful people throughout the ages. Historical figures such as Plato, Alexander the Great, Shakespeare, Roosevelt, Einstein, and many others throughout history understood and used these principles either through conscious or unconscious thoughts and actions. It took many of these people years to discover these truths and this system, and it took even longer to accept that it could be this easy. You see, each of us thinks it needs to be hard or only for the privileged in society.

This system has shown up under many names. The religions and governments of the world have this knowledge but fail to share it with the entire world in a way that can be understood by everyone. These ideas, systems, and beliefs are mostly put aside by people because they often don't believe that success could be so fun, simple, available to anyone, and reproducible on command.

Hard work is taught to us as the way to success, though this is not a completely true statement. And worse than not being a completely true statement, it creates false paths that do not take us to our desires.

Through these pages, you will receive first the truth about how to live your life like the 4 percent who have their desires, and then you will learn the process of repeating this throughout life with any desire. This process will work only as well as the person who applies it. As with everything in life, you only get out of the process what you put into it. And your desire, faith, self-suggestion, imagination, planning, and persistence will be the keys that will propel you.

Don't be worried that you can't do it. Anyone can do this process. And with very little effort and imagination, you will be successful, but more importantly, you will learn a lot about yourself. We will have to work, but we will make it fun.

In life, the most important thing is to find your bliss or passion. Your passion may lie in being a ditchdigger, a fireman, a nurse, a CEO of a *Fortune* 500 company, or the president of the United States. The truth is that you should do the work you love and love the work you do.

Wealth is so much more than your job, position in life, annual income, or whom you married. Wealth is the inner peace and love of oneself. The only person you must live with in life is yourself. So why not decide to be happy and do the things you love in life? Not every person in the world will want to own their own company or any of the other things in life that the world calls successful. True success and wealth is being able to wake in the morning, look in the mirror, and love the person you see without becoming self-absorbed. If you can find this truth in yourself, you will be richer than most of the richest people in the world.

Too often we judge our success by others' success in the world. I want you to think about this for a second. Would you judge the beauty of a rose by the standards for a violet? No way! We all know roses are red and violets are blue. But you may say, "That doesn't make sense. Those are just flowers." Well, yes, it does make sense. After all, we are just people. We are all in some way different and should not judge ourselves by any other person. We don't all want to be Einstein or Rockefeller. Nor should we strive to be those people. You can mirror some of their attributes, techniques, life examples, or behaviors to grow yourself. One way to grow is to model or emulate the attributes in successful people who serve as our heroes, but this does not mean adopting their entire styles. If we were not true to our goals, desires, and dreams, we would be resistant to our own identities.

As we go through the adventure of this book together, we will be watching a specific hero as he develops and uses the system to get to his desire. We will see some of the things that went wrong in his adventure and how he got beyond the troubles at hand.

Throughout the story, you will use your imagination, and you can replace Captain Bon with yourself. You will be modeling Captain Bon and learning how to use the system at the same time. How would you solve the problems? You will need to ask yourself questions at the end of each chapter to see how you would work through the issue or challenge at hand. How would you react? Did you have a better solution or plan than Captain Bon? Your plan may be different, but is it better?

Let's now visit more with our hero. His name is Captain Bon, and he has a desire to travel to Mount La Felicidad deep in the South American rain forest. He knows some have made the adventure, and he felt he could as well. He had dreamed about this adventure for years, but he never moved it from his imagination to paper to execute a plan of action. He always made the excuse that the time just wasn't right or that people would think he was crazy. He felt his family and friends wouldn't support this dream. He was right. They didn't understand the reason behind his desire to accomplish his dream. It wasn't their dream, and they didn't want him to be hurt when he failed. They also didn't want to see Captain Bon succeed. If he succeeded, what would be their excuse now for not going after their dreams?

Captain Bon had spent time studying the people who had been successful and the people who hadn't. He worked to prepare himself by learning all the knowledge of the potential pitfalls. He talked to many of both groups to get an even better understanding of what he was about to face. He also knew that the terrain had changed over the last year because of the weather and the construction of silver mines.

He also knew this was not an adventure he could do alone. He felt he needed at least one partner, but the group could be no more than four, including himself. These partners need to be adventurers. They would also need to be able to survive a harsh environment for up to a month.

Let's learn a little more about Captain Bon. Captain Bon is called captain because he operates a tugboat for his primary job and a shrimp boat as a hobby. He is forty-eight years old, and he has led a good life. He has enjoyed his life for the most part so far, but he felt he was missing something. He had many dreams throughout his life of doing something special, though he never acted on them. When he was a young man, he was in the navy and spent four years serving his country. He enjoyed his time and the relationships he made in the navy, but at the end of his enlistment, he felt there was more out there in the world for him. He was married shortly after leaving the navy, and he had children soon after that. He and Theresa, his wife, had one son and one daughter. With the birth of his children, he felt now he was responsible for his family and needed to work hard to provide for them.

Captain Bon knew Theresa would support him in whatever adventure he decided to go after just as he had supported her when she wanted to start her accounting and tax service business. Though she supported him going after his dreams, he hadn't decided to go forward and accomplish his dreams.

He still dreamed of one day taking an adventure that only a few had accomplished. He dreamed of working for himself and being his boss. While he had yet fulfilled his dream of the adventure, he had somewhat fulfilled his dream of being his own boss. He still worked for an industrial tugboat company, but now with his shrimp boat, he was at least the boss some of the time. However, it still nagged him that he hadn't taken the full plunge and become his boss or taken that adventure of a lifetime.

Like most people, he was afraid to leave his comfortable life for the risk of a greater reward. He couldn't overcome his fears of possible failure to move forward with his desires. There had been times when he was close to throwing caution to the wind and taking the chance. Like most people, he also shared his dreams with family members who meant well and cared for him, but they didn't want to see him fail. They advised him against taking the risk of leaving a secure job and becoming what he truly wanted.

But these family members were not Theresa. She believed he could accomplish whatever he put his mind to, but other family members couldn't see him making it. They would say, "If you were meant to do this, you would have done it before." Or they'd ask, "Do you know how many people have tried and failed to be their own boss?" His family and friends did believe in him, but they feared for his failure. Also, they feared for themselves. If he succeeded, why couldn't they? Why wouldn't they? Many just wanted to keep themselves and him safe. After all, they had decent lives. Wasn't that good enough?

His current life was no longer good enough for him. He had finally reached a place where he used the fear to drive himself to what he wanted. He turned the fear to his strength, and now he wouldn't let anything stand in his way. He would use everything he had studied and learned over the last fifteen years to help him succeed.

There's truth that many need to learn here. *What you resist persists.* If we persist in not being true to ourselves and the people we are at our cores, then the universe will come in and beat us back to our true selves. The universe does this for your own good to bring you to your success in life. But many of us keep pushing against the universe because we believe we know the best path to take. A better habit would be to watch for the doors the universe opens for us as paths come and then go through the doors instead of trying to go through walls where there are no doors. But now you understand that the choice is yours to make, and with the help of the universe, God, or whatever higher intelligence you believe in, you can become wealthy in your life.

In life, you are better served when you compete against yourself and no one else. If you ask yourself every day, "Am I doing the best I can do?" and then honestly answer yourself, you will go much further in life. There are many examples of successful people who do this every day. Two examples include Michael Jordan and Tiger Woods. While these two men compete against others in their sports, they compete more with themselves. The inner competition is what pushes them to practice daily, work out to keep their bodies in shape, and work to learn more about their performance through videos, trainers, and any other techniques available to them. They keep their minds focused on figuring out how they can be better, and this pushes them past the point where an opponent would push them.

Michael figured out a better way to train and then returned to basketball after his prime. Many of his critics said he couldn't do it; many were waiting for the great Michael Jordan to fail. Michael knew this, but he did not let it take hold of his mind. He was the master of his fate, the captain of his soul. Michael had a plan, and he believed in himself. He had to change his approach to training from when he was younger, and he developed a new way to work through the process to succeed. But Michael was no different than you—other than the fact that he had a plan and worked to make it happen. He believed in himself and changed his plan as he needed to get to his desires. And as important as anything, he could see himself succeeding. Can you see yourself succeeding?

Captain Bon's Seven Truths about Life

Now let's look at how we create the truth of a wealthy, happy, and joyous life. *The main truth is to live your life the way children live life until the world corrupts their minds with the dogma that tells them they can't do something.* Many have said, "I wish I had the energy that children have. I wish I had the faith in myself that my children have in themselves." Just watch children before the world fills them with its false dogma that suggests they can't do something, they will fail, or they will not be loved. Children truly believe that all the things they imagine are possible and that they can accomplish them.

If you question this as truth (and you should question all things), one only needs to read the life story of John D. Rockefeller Sr.. One of the richest men to have ever lived in modern times, he reportedly had a net value of 2 percent of all US currency. As a shrewd business tycoon, this man had a philosophy of working hard and playing hard that he got from his grandfather. He spent many hours bicycling and racing his children, playing games with them, and being a child too. Now that is a life of wealth.

The truth the world at large does not want you to know is that you can live life as a child with wonder. You need to only *ask* for it from yourself and the universe and truly have faith, and then you will receive this life. How great life would be if we only asked to live as children. But for most of us, this is too simple to be true. And the fear of looking dumb stops us from asking the questions that will help us grow. If you have ever spent time with children, you know they are the most inquisitive creatures on earth. They have no fear of looking dumb. Children only want to learn and grow in their world.

How hard is it? You must visualize in your mind with the feeling of having your desires. See yourself achieving your desire through your imagination. Believe with faith that a way of fulfilling those desires will come. Then you must take actions toward accomplishing your desire. And you must have fun on the journey. It's not very hard when you look at it that way.

So at this point, stop, close your eyes, and see your world through your inner child. Do not try to create the world you want to see. Let your inner child guide you through your desires and dreams like a ride at an amusement park. *See* and *feel* the fun you can have with your life. If you do this exercise, I promise you will enjoy the ride, and if you don't, it's your loss!

So Why Doesn't Everyone Know This?

Instead of living our lives like children, we surrender to fears in our imagination—the fear of failing, the fear of not having enough money, the fear of losing love, the fear of being branded as a failure instead of believing that the universe wants us to be loved, to succeed, and to live wealthy lives.

FDR said in his inauguration speech as president of the United States, "So, first of all, let me assert my firm belief that the only thing we have to fear is fear itself—nameless, unreasoning, unjustified terror which paralyzes needed efforts to convert retreat into advance." What FDR was telling the nation is that fear only has the power that we give it. It is when we focus on our fears that they come to be. If instead we were to focus on the positive things in our minds and push out fear, we could advance in our lives. Again, this is the law of attraction at work. When we focus on fear, it becomes what we truly want. As a result, fear is what we receive. Or to explain it a different way, we are focused on the problem, not the solution to the problem.

What Else Can I Do to Help My Inner Child Grow?

The best way to teach your inner child is to spend time with real children and play as they do. Spending time playing with your children, interacting with a family member's child, or volunteering as a big brother or sister to a child in need will help you grow your imagination more than anything else, and you will help create memories that these children will carry with them throughout their lives. If you go into this playtime with nothing more than the expectation to have fun and be a kid, you will also receive a memory to carry through your life. So go out and play "Pretty, pretty princess" or "The giant that protects the castle" and have fun, laugh, and grow your imagination.

The second truth in life is this: *If you think the same way as many of the people in the world, you will get the same life as them.* Remember the 96 percent of people who end up settling with what life brings them? But if you think on an extraordinary level, you will get an extraordinary life.

The third truth in life is as follows: *Don't play to win but refuse to lose at life.* This advice differs from what most people will tell you in life. And I am not one of those people who will tell you that if you *think positive*, you can have anything in life. Affirmation without action will not get you anywhere in life—other than becoming overweight and lazy, leeching off society. You will not get anything great out of life by being a leach.

You see, *playing to win* will let you down greatly when you do not win at every game in life. The truth is that you will not win every game. You are not the only person playing this game, and others have objectives in life that will cause you to take a different path or lose at times. As you go through life, you will have to change your approach from time to time. Things do not always go as we plan them in life. But you can change your direction or approach and still get to your desired campsite on the river of life. By *refusing to lose at life,* you will find the side currents that will help you down the river.

The fourth truth in life is as follows: *People need to grow and contribute in life to find happiness.* If you were to win the lottery tomorrow, what would you do for the rest of your life? Would you retire, take a long vacation, buy a new house, or go back to school? What would you do? Think about this and write it down.

Now, look at what you wrote down. How long would those things keep you happy before you got bored? One of the ironic things in life is that once we reach our goals or climb to the top of the mountain, we must find new mountains to climb. If we don't, we wither and die. As humans, we must have goals in life, but once we reach them, we must set higher goals. This way, we can continue to *grow and contribute* to the world around us. You may have seen people in your family and group of friends who have died within a year of retiring or losing their mates. Have you ever really wondered why that is? Most of the time, they have no one or nothing to contribute to, and so they lose their vitality for life.

So keep setting new goals in your life, do charity work, work with needy children, keep contributing to society, and you will keep your mind growing. If you are young, help at a retirement home. You will learn a lot from these people. They have lived the history you have only read. Find those people who have done what you want to do in life and spend time with them. Build relationships with them and learn what you need to know. They can help you with your plan and the real questions you need to ask yourself. By learning from the people that came before you, you can prevent yourself from falling over the waterfalls of life. And while you are growing, you will allow someone to contribute to the world. This way, both of you can find success and happiness in life.

The fifth truth in life is as follows: *You must create a plan and strategy in life to bring you happiness.* If you fail to create a plan and strategy for making yourself happy, I promise you will not spend most of your life happy. Life is hard and brings many challenges. You can create the path to your happiness. You must create your plan and change it as you need to.

Furthermore, you must have faith that you can do this anytime you are not happy or whenever life is too hard. You will use the system outlined in the "Desire" part of this book. You will use this system to get to any desire you want in life. Do this, and you will reach your true potential in life.

The sixth truth in life is as follows: *You need to smile more.* Unless you are the 2 to 3 percent of people who smile all the time, you probably don't smile enough for a wealthy life. Now we are not talking about what physiologist call the Pan Am smile but rather a true face-lifting, ear-to-ear, eye-wrinkling smile. This kind of smile releases endorphins in the brain; this is the feel-good natural drug for the brain and body.

Smiles make you happier and make others feel welcome, happy, and appreciated when in your company. Smiles are also less work than frowning. There are many other reasons in life to smile. We should barely ever have a reason not to smile.

If you are having trouble finding a reason to smile, then maybe you should smile to be contrary to your nature. If you do this often enough, you may create reasons to smile. You may feel as if you are smiling at yourself, you look foolish, or you have lost your mind. Enjoy life and smile. I promise, the frown police will not come and arrest you for your smiles!

The seventh truth in life is as follows: *Nothing in life is impossible.* Many of the things we take for granted today in our world were once thought to be impossible. Now the technology may not be available today for your desire, but that does not make it impossible. People would be well served to take the word *impossible* out of their vocabulary. It is just an excuse for procrastination in your life. Where would we be today if Albert Einstein had thought it impossible to violate Newton's law of absolute time? We would not have received the building blocks to many of today's technologies, including lasers, atomic energy, GPS, and many other inventions that found their roots in Einstein's theories.

You need to change your inner communication. Instead of thinking, *This is impossible*, you can say to yourself, "I presently struggle with a particular thing." You may look at this as just a simple redirection of your mind, and it is. This change in direction will change your outlook on things and keep you striving to improve daily. A view of possibility needs to be your view of life, whether it is in your exercise program, education, relationships, or business ventures. With faith in yourself and the universe, nothing is impossible.

CHAPTER 2

OUR THOUGHTS AND OUR MIND

FOR MANY YEARS, CAPTAIN BON held a desire/dream about making the trip up either the Vida or Larga Vida River to Mount La Felicidad. He had read about other people who had taken the journey, and he admired them for their courage. He was also jealous that they could conquer the river. La Felicidad was a special mountain. It held animals and plant life that hadn't been seen or touched for most of the life of the planet. La Felicidad was a rare area in the world.

The outside world had not visited this area because of the dense forest that surrounded the two parallel rivers that traveled from the populated village of Negombo to the mountain. These rivers both had their dangers and challenges, but there were some advantages too.

The Vida River was more than twice the distance of the Larga Vida River. Vida's was, for the most part, easier than the Larga Vida to travel on, but it had its pitfalls. One could use a larger boat for the adventure because of the width of the Vida River. That meant he could carry twice the supplies if he traveled on this river instead of the other. Captain Bon felt that carrying twice the supplies would make life easier during the adventure.

However, taking the Vida River meant traveling through an area populated by a hostile primitive village that did not take kindly to adventurers traveling through their territory, which was dangerous. There were other dangers, and as he thought about them, he considered how each could play a vital role in derailing the adventure. This river also had many deviating channels that either went around and circled back to the river or went to dead ends, and even others went to a couple of waterfalls that were not visible until the adventurer was right upon them. The river had not been mapped very well because of the extended travel time, so there could be areas where they didn't even understand the dangers. However, the Vida River had one less danger than the Larga Vida, and that was rapids. Rapids could destroy the boat and even possibly kill them on the spot. If it didn't kill them there, it could make getting out of the jungle with fresh water and food almost impossible.

The Larga Vida River was half the distance of the Vida, so the time to make it from Negombo to the mountain was a lot less. Time would be very important since the food and water they would need for the trip would be much less. Because the Larga Vida was much narrower than the Vida River and it had rapids, the boat they would use couldn't be very large. There were friendly villages and mining camps along the Larga Vida River, but Captain Bon wasn't entirely sure if his group could buy or trade for food and water. He knew that the mining camps were tight on supplies and that it would be hard for them to give up their means of survival. He read that the villages would trade for certain items like clothing, blankets, and corn, but how could this smaller boat carry these items to a trade? If he had the room to carry these items, he could carry more food and water.

Then there were the rapids. Bon understood from the stories of other adventure teams that the rapids on Larga Vida were dangerous. Many had their dreams destroyed when they smashed on the rocks. Some had made it through. But what was their secret? Were they more experienced at white-water rapids? Did they pick the right time to traverse the rapids when the water was lower and calmer? He felt if he could find the answers to these questions, he could create a better plan. He knew he would need a person on his team with years of white-water rafting experience, someone who could develop a plan to survive and even thrive within the rapids.

Captain Bon felt he and his team could develop a plan that would allow them to use the Larga Vida River and arrive at their destination in half the time. Sure, there would be challenges to overcome on the Larga Vida, but compared to the Vida River, it would be worth the difficulties they would face.

There were so many things to think through and plan. The multiple details were why Bon hadn't moved on the dream before. Every time he thought about the adventure, too many pitfalls jumped in his way. The unknowns just built up a fear in him that he never seemed to be able to get past. But others had done it. So why couldn't he? The unknowns were what churned his stomach at night. He wanted this adventure. No, he needed this adventure. He wasn't getting any younger, and he knew with each passing day that he would get older and that the dream would eventually slip away from him as so many others had throughout his lifetime.

Captain Bon thought back to his childhood and remembered what his father had always told him. "There is no need to worry about the things you can't change. They will come, and you will figure out how to get around them or deal with them. Worry about the things you can control and how you will change them. And even the things you can control, there is no need to worry. Move forward and change them. Never let worry stand in the way of your desires."

At this point in his life, he was forty-eight years old, and he finally understood his father's lesson. A smile came to his face as he thought about how wise his father was and how his father had been successful in his endeavors because he had understood this lesson. Captain Bon also wondered why he hadn't understood the lesson until now. Was it that he was hardheaded and thought his father didn't understand? Finally, he realized that until he had decided to move toward his desires and dreams, he hadn't had the strength to understand the lesson. The strength came from wanting this adventure more than anything else in the world. Now he was prepared to endure the demanding work that would come along the road to achieving his desire, and he understood that he needed others to help to get to his goal. All these things now prepared him to accept his father's advice and to succeed in his adventure.

WHAT ARE THOUGHTS?

Science tells us everything is energy. Science also tells us through quantum physics that our thoughts are a form of energy. Any thought replayed, planned, acted upon, and believed with faith will become a physical being. At this time, many of you are saying, "I can't do that." Well, in the words of Henry Ford, "Whether you think you can or you can't, either way, you are right." As you can see in the lives of famous people and friends, when the belief and faith were present, all things were possible.

What are thoughts anyway? They are creations in our minds of what we want to have, what we want to create, who we want to be, what we do not want, what we are afraid of, and many other objects of our desires and fears. They can be either positive or negative. It is our choice if our thoughts will be positive or negative. We decide our state of mind (creative or destructive), and we have the power to change our state of mind through self-leverage. I know we have all said, "That person or situation put me in a negative state of mind or bad mood," but I am here to tell you they did not. It is your choice how you react and what you think. Now I am not saying we are going to decide every minute of the day to be happy and creative. The truth is that we will all have feelings of negativity and destruction, and we have the power to change our thinking through self-leverage. No one else but you has control over your mind.

The problem becomes that most people in the world would rather blame someone or something for their state of mind or their failures in life instead of choosing to put the negative person or situation in the rearview mirror and proceed with their positive lives. Also, many of us rely on other people or things to make us happy. And then we get upset when they get it wrong or the objects don't fulfill us. I am here to tell you no single object of your desire can make you happy.

Happiness must reside in you. You know the path, and you have the keys to your happiness if you look inside yourself. If you are not happy with what you are without tangible things, you will not be truly happy. We have all seen examples of famous people who had everything and then died from drug overdoses. That is not winning in life or wealth. Death is losing the game of life. I am here to tell you that they did not have everything in life. If they had, they would not have turned to drugs. They were missing the main source of happiness, and that is self-love. We all have things about ourselves we would like to change, such as our weight, wealth, focus, knowledge, looks, and the list goes on. However, we first need to find the things in ourselves we admire and love to build from there. This self-love and self-admiration is the base to building the greatest temple of all—the temple of you. If you are not happy with just being alone with yourself, you need to first work on you and your inner happiness. Self-love and inner happiness are one of the laws of the universe, and that is the law of attraction. If you do not love yourself, you will not attract love to you. If you do not see the power in your mind, how do you expect to attract intelligent people to you? If you were to look back at your life and be honest with yourself, you would see this to be a great truth. But again, for 96 percent of the world, it is easier to make an excuse than face the truth. The choice is yours, but if you want to be part of the 4 percent of people who live with all the wealth in the world, you must abide by and understand the law of attraction. Always remember that what you focus on will be attracted to you.

#

Let's see how Captain Bon is working with the energy of his thoughts and the law of attraction.

Captain Bon decided to go after his desire and dream of taking the adventure to Mount La Felicidad. He used his imagination to build the story of how it would feel when he reached the mountain and completed his adventure. During his meditation sessions in the morning and evening, he could see the mountain at the end of the river's edge, and a feeling of warm happiness would come over him. He used these thoughts to reinforce the fact that he could do it. Captain Bon created a dream board that he kept in his office, and he pinned up things he would see on the adventure. He also wrote down in his journal what the trip would look like, what things he would see, and how he would feel when he arrived at his desire.

Captain Bon was building reminders for himself. He wanted to remember why this was important to him. While he was doing it, these reminders became the energy of feelings and desire. Reminders were another way to keep him focused on his dream. Captain Bon had learned this through reading about successful people and what they did to stay focused. Maybe they hadn't done so in the exact way he was doing it, but they kept themselves focused on their reasons. The focus and a reminder system helped them push through the tough times.

Captain Bon added daily to the adventure reminders, building a fire to get to his dream. He understood that the fire in his belly needed all the fuel it could get if he were going to accomplish his desire.

Captain Bon also understood that if he did this, it would help him attract the people he needed to help him get the hidden desire. He had studied the law of attraction, and while he felt most people didn't use it, he could and would. He understood that when you have a desire and learn all you can about it, people are attracted to you. If your dream is strong enough, they attach themselves to you.

It was like having two magnets. If you put two magnets together, they would either attract or repel each other. It all depended if you were putting together the like or unlike poles. If you put like poles on a magnet together, they repel, but if you put opposite poles together, they attract. From that lesson, Captain Bon learned that you couldn't have a team of only "why" people. Captain Bon defined why people as the visionary people or those who have the dream that the team will accomplish. The second group of people was the "how" people or those who put together the processes and procedures to bring the dream to reality. Captain Bon understood you needed both why people and how people for a team that could accomplish a goal. That's how the why person's vision and dream can be carried out by the how people.

He knew that most people used the law of attraction in just the opposite way or that they believed if they just dreamed of the desire, it would come to them. Captain Bon had come to understand that the law of attraction required the attraction of people who had skills that differed from his but wanted to attain the same goal as him. He also understood that the law of attraction meant that you couldn't just dream your way to your goal. The law required that you work toward your goal. It required action. To Captain Bon, this meant he had to act. Every day he had to do something that brought him one step closer to his dream. Maybe some days, he could get two or three steps closer to his dream.

Captain Bon also knew he had to attract people who could help. He would need a team to go with him, a support team that stayed behind, and a team of investors that would back his dream. He understood that for these people to help him, he had to give them something back. Captain Bon hoped that he could offer each of the people he attracted something that they couldn't get from anywhere else, understanding that they couldn't and wouldn't help without something in return. What could he offer them? What would they get out of his dream?

Thinking about this next step, he came up with some answers. The reward others would gain from Bon's adventure was important because he also knew that everyone wanted to know what was in it for them before they helped. That was just how people operated. He knew he was the same way. He didn't care about the dreams of others if he wasn't going to get something out of the experiences.

That meant after explaining the reasons to prospective partners, he had to explain what was in it for them. This way, the dream would become their dream as well. Once the dream became theirs and they owned it, they would put in the work to make Captain Bon's dream a reality. He had to build in them what he had built inside himself. He had to build the fire that would get them on board and help them propel the dream. So what would be in it for them, and how could Captain Bon explain it to them in a way that they would buy?

He first needed a mentor, someone who could help him put together the pieces of knowledge he had learned over the years into a workable system. Captain Bon felt he knew all the necessary parts but didn't know how to get it into a repeatable system. He also knew he needed someone with more experience who could bring together people to accomplish this adventure, someone with even more life experience than he had.

He thought about the qualities that mentors of this quality would need. Where would he find them? Maybe Theresa knew someone who had the experience he was looking for and wanted to pass on the knowledge.

The more he thought about it, the more he couldn't think of anything he had to offer a mentor other than the opportunity to pass on knowledge. Sure, he could offer to pay mentors, or he could offer to do work for them in return for their advice. Maybe that would be enough, but he wasn't sure. He figured it was at least worth a shot. He would speak with Theresa and see if she had anyone in mind.

Next, he had to consider the partners who would come on the adventure with him. As he thought about what each adventure would bring, he realized many partners could reap the same benefits as him. They would first have the reward of enjoying something that only a few people had experienced. Second, they would learn from the experience and would have that knowledge for the rest of their lives to fall back on. They'd learn about the logistics of planning the adventure and the challenge of putting everything together, not to mention the real challenges they would face out on the river to the mountain.

He then thought about the people who would stay back and support the adventure. What would they get out of Captain Bon's dream? Their reward was harder for Captain Bon to consider because he had never been in their shoes. Or had he? He thought back to his days in the navy and the feeling of satisfaction he got after a successful mission. He had always been one of the people who worked in the background and helped see the mission through to success. What was it that he got out of being in the background? Captain Bon thought about it for a few minutes, and then it came to him. It was about being a part of a successful team, no matter how small a part he played. It was about giving his best when he wouldn't be the one in the spotlight and feeling good about himself. He liked the camaraderie that came from working with others to accomplish a goal. That is what the support team would get, and Captain Bon now knew how to explain it to them.

Now it was on to the investors. Why would someone put up money for his dream? Now he was stuck. Why would someone give him money to chase this dream? It wasn't like there would be a big payday at the end of the adventure. It wasn't like they were going after gold or something that would repay the investors. What could Captain Bon give them? He thought about it for about two hours and wrote down some of the things that would make it worth their while to invest in the adventure.

After two hours, Captain Bon had a plan together for the investors. He could first go to the extreme sports drink companies and pitch them on sponsoring him as the oldest extreme adventurer. He thought the drink companies could tap into an older market through him. It would help them reach both the adventurers and people of his age-group. He could paint their logos on his boat and wear clothes with the logos too.

He could then approach other corporate sponsors that sold boats, camping gear, and other items he would need on the adventure. Even if they didn't give cash, they might give him the supplies he would need. Yes, this would work. He was sure that he could visit these companies over the next six months and convince them that they would get twice the advertisement out of their money by sponsoring him.

With his initial plan for all three groups now written down, he felt more than ever that he could get the help he would need to complete the adventure or at least get out on the river and aim for the mountain. It would take some work on his part to refine his plans into a presentation he could present to each group, but he was up for the challenge. He knew he could recruit a friend of his to help him put each plan into a PowerPoint presentation. He also knew he would have to practice the presentations for hours so that he could deliver each presentation passionately to convince their respective audiences.

His efforts were now underway. It was time to put his dream into action. The first step was to create the PowerPoints and approach the people and organizations that would help him. Captain Bon felt so excited. He was doing it, but at that moment, the enemy to his dreams came out.

Señor Doubter jumped up on Bon's shoulder and started talking in his ear. It was the normal song Señor Doubter was singing. "You're too old! You're crazy if you think anyone will back this dream of yours. You are not an adventurer and have no experience. It's not going to happen, my friend. And why would you take a chance on such a crazy dream? What's in it for you?"

Captain Bon felt his stomach turning into knots as Señor Doubter whispered, and he almost put his dream aside again when something woke him up. As he looked over at his picture board, the vision of the adventure came to life and played the story of success he had seen during his meditation. It was enough to build a fire. He wasn't going to let anything stand in his way this time. He had allowed Señor Doubter's voice to stop him before, but this time was different. He knew the reward he was after. He had built the reward up in his mind and could see the outcome. He had the law of attraction on his side and understood how to use it. He would be successful. With that, Captain Bon brushed off Señor Doubter by jumping into work on his plan and presentation. He was committed, and now he owned his destiny.

WHAT HAVE WE LEARNED FROM CAPTAIN BON ABOUT BUILDING THE PASSIONATE DREAM?

When we examine Captain Bon's story, we learn that you must build in your imagination what the outcome will be. You must build it as real as you can. Looking at the goal with your mind's eye, you must see and feel it. Through imagination, you build the fire that will burn on the cold nights and keep you going.

Most people in the world have dreams but fail to feel them. When you have a desire or dream, you must imagine what it will feel like to realize that dream or desire. You must see yourself accomplishing the goal. If you can't see yourself doing it, how will anyone else? Would you follow people who couldn't see themselves succeeding? No, we don't follow people who say, "I will fail, but please come with me." We follow people who instill passion in us and who have a passion for what they are doing. Passion is infectious. It gathers people with like goals, and together, they can accomplish amazing things in this world.

Captain Bon even went as far as building visual reminders of his passion. He put together pictures that would help him stay focused on his dream. He put it in a place where he would see it and then think about what he had done that day to accomplish his dream.

Humans are visual learners. We learn more from seeing something done than reading about it. While writing your goals on paper cement them, having visuals of your goals call you to action. Making these helps you to develop your imagination. It propels you to your goals. It reminds you what is at the end of the rainbow and why you want to get there.

If you have an office or a room that you work in, create picture boards of your vision and what you will gain when you get there. Sort the board like a story. Arrange the pictures of what you will get along the way. That way, it acts as a sounding board as well. You can then see if you are on track or not, and if you are not on track, you can quickly figure out how to get back on track.

Things will often change, and the rewards may not come to you exactly as you laid them out in your plan or the picture board. Look at the entire journey and decide if you are still on track or not. If you aren't taking actions that will get you to the reward, change what you are doing.

If you find you are on track, update when you feel you will arrive at the reward. The process is fluid, and it will likely change. Sometimes life gets in the way. But the point is to help you go after your goal.

You can build passion. You can build that passion about anything. Lots of crazy people out there do things we don't understand; however, they have passion, and they infect others with their passion. You can do the same if you believe in your dream. That is up to you. I can't build the passion in you. Your family can't build the passion in you. The dream is your dream. You must build the passion. You must live your dream every day.

Now some days living your dream will mostly be in your head, but you will need to take some action. The action could be as simple as writing out your goal. Or it could involve recruiting people to help you realize your desire. There are so many small actions necessary to accomplish any dream. Why stop at one a day?

GAINING HELP FROM OTHERS

What else have we learned from Captain Bon? We learned that everyone needs help to get to their dream and that no one does it alone. But the funny thing is that you must have something to offer people before they help you. For most, it's a paycheck. Ninety-six percent of all people do what they do for a paycheck. It's a way for them to be comfortable. Some do it for other rewards like the feeling of contributing or winning. Companies do it for money in one shape or another. Some companies do it to help the world. These companies are called nonprofits, but someone is usually still making money.

You will have to give more than money to attract and keep the right people. Everyone needs money, but that's not why they stay. That's not why they give 110 percent. If it's just about money, you will only get what you pay for, and nowadays that's not much. But if you build a vision with passion and if people share that passion, they will do things you never thought possible.

Your dream pushes you toward some reward. You must show people that you share the same vision. You will have to infect them with your passion. You will have to show them what's in it for them. Do these things, and you will surely succeed. Don't do them, and you will surely fail.

But here is the good news. You can do it. The ability is in each of us. But first, you must build a fire within yourself. You must build the image of the rewards for succeeding.

LAW OF ATTRACTION

How Captain Bon used the law of attraction is an important lesson. Captain Bon understood the law of attraction better than most people. For much of the world, the law of attraction is about dreaming and wishing with faith. People then think the universe will send them what they desire. Captain Bon understood this was part of the law of attraction, but many of the important parts were being left out. Let's see how Captain Bon understood and used the law.

Captain Bon did use his imagination to see his desires, and he did visualize attaining his desires, but he didn't stop there. He needed to act for the law of attraction to work. Captain Bon wrote down his plan and built picture boards that showed his path to his dream. He took actions each day to accomplish his dream. His actions included meeting with people who had accomplished what he wanted to accomplish and learning about the challenges they faced. He worked to find people who wanted to accomplish the same goal. It was the law of attraction at work. He was putting out to the universe what he wanted and what his dream was by finding others and learning from them. Seeking help led him to people who would help him achieve his dream.

Captain Bon also understood that not everyone on the team could be the same. He understood that completely like poles repel just like magnets. Instead of attracting, they would fight until they were apart. He realized he needed how people. He had the vision and had the reason for his dream. He was the why person. He now needed people who would help create the how. He needed the people who understood how to put the systems in place so that his adventure is successful. He needed people who could look at his plan and not just punch holes in it but help fill the holes with what was needed. He needed logistic people, survivalists, navigators, and financial supporters.

With this understanding, he could use the law of attraction as the universe intended. He could build the team through the law to become successful. The law of attraction would help him get to his dream.

FIGHTING SEÑOR DOUBTER

Captain Bon had finally found a way to beat Señor Doubter. Señor Doubter had stopped Captain Bon's dream for more years than he could count, but that was no longer true. He had built a fire strongly in his belly, and it was a fire that would burn Señor Doubter to the core. Through his imagination, he made his dream real. Captain Bon could see his dream. He had lived it through his imagination, and he knew it was possible. He felt it in every part of his body like the sun on a warm day. He had beaten Señor Doubter through his imagination.

Captain Bon knew that Señor Doubter would be back. He knew that Señor Doubter never gave up. It just wasn't in his nature. He also knew that if he didn't guard himself with his imagination and belief, Señor Doubter would win and stop him from getting his desire. Captain Bon also knew that Señor Doubter had challenged everyone who had been successful. It wasn't personal. It was how the human mind worked.

Captain Bon now understood he could use Señor Doubter to hedge himself against pitfalls. You see, Señor Doubter shows up when you are entering unfamiliar territory. He would use the doubt to prepare a plan to succeed. He would use the doubt to check his progress. He would use the doubt to find people to help him succeed.

Each of us can use doubt the same way. Instead of being paralyzed and letting it stop you, you can use it to succeed. There is nothing wrong with healthy fear. There is no room though for paralyzing doubt. Push through and use the doubt to create a better plan. Use the doubt to warn against potential pitfalls. Do not allow doubt to keep you from achieving your dreams.

CHAPTER 3

BECOMING DESIGNER, ENGINEER, AND CEO OF YOUR LIFE

CAPTAIN BON HAD DECIDED ON the path he would take to his adventure. He did so with the understanding that he had to be the designer, engineer, and CEO of his life. He knew that he had to divide himself into three people to become successful and achieve his dreams and desires.

Captain Bon knew he would have to recruit people along the way to help him in his adventure, but for designing, executing, and building his life, he would need to be three people or three parts. He would become the designer, engineer, and CEO of his life.

The designer would start designing the life he wanted and the dreams he wanted to accomplish. He would have to create plans for the various parts of his life. These plans would come down to all the details that he could identify. In the beginning, the plan could be general, and they could resemble a statement of the dreams he wanted to achieve. He would design his life the way he wanted and not just drift through life. He wanted to think through the details of his life and then put those on paper.

At first, he would list his dreams, goals, and desires. Then the designer part of him would create the reason behind his dream. From that reason, he would design the plan to reach the dream. At this point, he would turn it over to the engineering part of him.

The engineer would put together the plan and refine the details as necessary. The engineer part of Captain Bon would oversee putting the systems and processes in place to accomplish his dreams. He would also continuously improve the systems and processes.

Captain Bon knew that any plan, system, or process needed improvement over time. The engineer would work systematically to review the feedback from others and the deliverables to determine what improvements were needed. He would also evaluate when failures occurred and decide what change of direction was needed to achieve the wanted results.

The engineer would have to work closely with both the designer and CEO to guide the plan. The engineer would be the middleman in the operation. He would be the glue that would hold the team and the overall plan together.

He would need input from the designer to ensure that the plan was meeting the overall design. After all, the designer was the visionary or the why person of the group. The designer owned the vision, and the engineer owned the process.

The engineer owned the creation and implementation of the plans, systems, and processes that would become Captain Bon's life. He would be the how member of the team. As the how person, he would gather the team, including the mastermind group needed to review and triangulate decisions and challenges.

A mastermind group is a group that works together in harmony to help one another to accomplish their desires in life, including learning, growing, solving problems, or brainstorming ideas. Some may be large think tanks, while others may be a simple study group of two or three. This mastermind group work together to help each member advance in the areas they are presently focused on obtaining.

The engineer would be led by and report to the CEO. He would give the CEO reports about the progress of Captain Bon's life and adventures. He would also advise the CEO on decisions to make so that Captain Bon would receive his desires. The things Captain Bon may give could be time and energy or sacrificing family time to complete a task. Though it could be as serious a cost as Bon's life, whatever the cost, the engineer would give the possibilities to the CEO to decide on the course of action.

The CEO would be the team leader. He would evaluate the plans and work with the designer and engineer as they developed Captain Bon's life. He would be the part of Captain Bon that was ultimately responsible for approvals and denials during the implementation of the adventure.

Like any other CEO, he would have advisers both internally and externally. He would have his internal team, which would consist of the designer and engineer as well as his mastermind group to advise him along the way. But he would be the final decision maker when the group couldn't agree on a decision.

The CEO would drive the process and procedure by advising the engineer on the dates when he would need to deliver results necessary to achieve the dream. The CEO understood that he would have to see *more* and see *before* others in the group. Captain Bon learned this concept from John Maxwell.

Seeing more and seeing before meant he would always be evaluating the deliverables and how the team and plan were progressing. He would look for the changes and work with the team to develop plans to deal with these changes.

He would also see more by elevating himself above the daily actions so that he could observe how the intricate parts were working together. He would observe the actions and outcomes, much like watching a large machine operating. He would look at how the parts interacted and keep an eye out for glitches in the machine. If he found glitches, he would work with the engineer to smooth out the machine.

Captain Bon understood that if he told anyone about his plan to split himself into three different people, they might think he was crazy. He figured many people lived their lives this way, even if they didn't label what they were doing. They couldn't succeed in any other way.

Splitting into three different people allowed Captain Bon to look subjectively at the other parts of himself as they created and executed the plan and adventure. He needed this separation to be subjective. Captain Bon understood above everything else that no one could judge themselves subjectively. Their evaluation of their plans or actions would be skewed and biased. To evaluate himself and the plan honestly, he would need the ability to rise above himself and the actions.

Captain Bon understood this was the advantage humans had over other animals. It was a gift from God so that humans could change their lives as they saw fit. Humans could change if they chose to rise above their situation. With this ability, humans were their masters.

In rising above the situation taking place, Captain Bon would view each moving part and how each player on the team reacted. It was also important to understand the emotions tied to each decision and action from each player and himself. The nonobjective view would give Captain Bon the objectivity he needed to make decisions and changes that he needed to succeed.

It would also give him separation from his failures so that he could learn from the mistakes and get overly emotional about any particular failure. This way, he could determine the changes that are required in the plan. Being able to separate himself from the plan in this way would allow Captain Bon to see the needed changes.

Captain Bon felt that he wouldn't just keep repeating the same mistakes with this method. He knew he needed a guard from "emotional ownership." He knew that many people guarded their plans like children through what he called emotions of ownership. Emotional ownership was nothing more than the parental feeling from creating something, whether it was a child or a plan. If he invested emotions in the plan, he would defend his actions, even when it wasn't working.

From studying many successful people, Captain Bon realized that they used the ability to rise above the situation and evaluate what was going on to change direction as needed without fighting themselves and others. By having three parts to himself, he could rise above and evaluate things from three different points of view.

Now Captain Bon could take himself out of situations to make decisions, review failures, or evaluate changes. He was giving himself feedback without involving his emotions on the changes to the plan.

Captain Bon felt that the designer could review the situation to determine if the change would stay congruent with his life plan. The designer could advise what changes were needed that wouldn't change the ultimate design. After all, the designer knew what Captain Bon wanted from life to determine if the change would keep him moving forward to his desired outcome or take him off route.

The engineer could evaluate the mechanics of the changes and determine if these proposed changes were viable and if they could work in sync with the rest of the plan. It would be important to evaluate the congruency of the changes. The changes had to be in line with the values and beliefs of Captain Bon.

If the changes weren't congruent with Captain Bon's beliefs and values, changes might be needed. After the engineer determined a change wasn't congruent, he would have to determine if the belief and value were serving Captain Bon. He would go through and determine if the belief needed to be changed or if a different approach or decision would be necessary.

If the belief and value didn't serve Captain Bon, he would work to change the belief and value to a new belief. Captain Bon had learned a system to change beliefs through NLP. The engineer would need the designer and CEO's help to develop the new belief.

If the belief and value served Captain Bon and shouldn't be changed, the engineer would have to help the team find an approach that would be congruent with Captain Bon's belief and value. It wouldn't be easy, but it would be necessary. The engineer understood that a belief and value that he had evaluated and found to serve the host positively shouldn't be changed. If the team worked hard, they could find another approach that would be congruent with the belief and value.

Captain Bon had his internal team, and they were hard at work, developing his new life to achieve his dreams and desires. They would help him gather the team he needed to implement his plan and begin his adventure. The three parts of Captain Bon would help guide him to settle the issues that would come up along the way. Along with Captain Bon's mastermind team, the designer, engineer, and CEO would work to accomplish the adventure.

PUTTING YOURSELF IN CAPTAIN BON'S SHOES

Now put yourself into Captain Bon's shoes. See yourself as Captain Bon. You have just decided that you must have your life's dream and desire. You have learned many systems and processes by studying what others have used to achieve their dreams and desires. And you realize that you must split yourself into three different people to go forward.

It's time to divide into your three parts and to assign them their responsibilities. Each part will have a comment on the others' work, but each part must work within their domain to help you start your adventure. Each part of you must stay open-minded and brutally honest with the other parts. By working individually and together, the three parts of you can accomplish more than one person alone.

The trick is to give each part the time to work. You must divide the time that you have to work on your adventure into three. You need first to develop what you want out of life and what the result will be when you arrive after the adventure.

Then your designer part gives the outcomes and design to the engineering part to develop the plan in detail, map out the logistics, and earmark the necessary resources. He will also develop the systems and processes that you will use along the way.

The engineer will also continuously work behind the scenes to evaluate how the systems and processes are working and if the outcomes are what is desired. If the outcomes are not as needed, the engineer will work with the team to change the approach.

Your CEO will lead the team through the adventure by *seeing more and seeing before* from the elevated view of the adventure. He will work with each member of the team to continuously improve the plan and their performance.

Your CEO is not a dictator but rather a leader who values the best idea and approach to decisions and challenges. He listens to outsiders' thoughts and ideas and triangulates the correct path to take through a weighted system. He knows to listen to his experts but to also evaluate others' thoughts and ideas for merit and substance.

Your CEO also understands that he must first care for others before they help him with his plans, dreams, and desires. Through this caring, he can build a team that can and will accomplish the adventure at hand.

It's now time to develop your three parts. You can do it. You may choose not to take this approach, and that is fine; however, you are missing out on help from other points of view. If you look at anything from just your point of view, you will be biased. Your point of view is only a look from your perspective. If you look at your life, dreams, and desires from the perspective of a designer, engineer, and CEO, you will see things differently.

Dividing yourself into three points of view makes it easier to detach from the goal, rise above the situation, and view it objectively. You no longer have ownership of the plan and how well it works. You are an adviser that is evaluating the outcomes from the actions. And as an adviser, you can advise the team of the changes that are needed. You will do this by hearing others' input and ideas. You can then triangulate the best decision for the path forward.

You will test the new path first with the members of the team and the mastermind group by explaining the path to them. You are not the owner of the path but only the adviser. Thus, if received with reluctance, you can question why others feel that this isn't the best path. You can revisit the new path with the feedback provided to determine if further changes are needed or if this is the best path to take nonetheless.

After all, it's easier to question the details if you don't own the plan and only want the best outcome. So now use your three parts to develop the best life you can.

Here is an example of a simple table you can use to start developing your plan so that you can achieve your desire. You can use this format or another. It doesn't matter what you use, only that you get the needed actions on paper so that you can check your needed actions.

The table is a simple system, but again, it is meant to hit the high point and keep you moving toward your goals. The system is called mind mapping. In later chapters, we will learn about more detailed planning, but for now, you only need forward momentum daily. Remember only to take one step at a time.

So let's put your designer, engineer, and CEO to work by developing your mind map. Remember, you are just breaking your pathway to your desire into manageable pieces.

Dream/Desire	Question	Actions	Feedback	New Actions
Adventure to Mount La Felicidad	What help will we need?	Develop a plan with the list.	Need defined resources.	Develop a grocery list of resources needed.
Mastermind Group	What qualities of members are needed?	Develop a list of qualities needed in the group.	List of qualities is perfect but evaluate later.	Recheck list periodically.
Financial	How do we acquire financial support?	Develop a plan and presentation to pitch to investors and supporters.	The plan/presentation needs to explain better what the investors will get in return.	Rewrite plan to include investor return.
Adventure Route	What river will we take, and where will we set up restocking of resources along that river?	Work with team and mastermind group to develop the route and support plan.	Need to get advice from past adventurers.	Request past adventurers of the river to review the plan.

CHAPTER 4

THE SYSTEMS TO GET YOU MOVING

AS CAPTAIN BON SITS AT his desk and writes out a list of pros and cons on why he should follow his dream and take the adventure, he notices his clock, which shows him that he has been working on this list for a few minutes, but in truth, he had been working on it in his head for years. As he thought over the pros and cons, he recalled all the things in his life he was grateful for having. Though he had not moved forward in accomplishing this large dream, he had accomplished other smaller dreams that showed he could achieve a desire. Thinking about the things he was grateful for having and accomplishing put him in a positive state of mind. It also showed him that once committed, he could accomplish his goals. How far of a leap was it really from the small dreams to this large one? Sure, it would take more work, and others would have to get involved to accomplish it; However, the accomplishment of this large dream would bring a greater reward, which he would be grateful for throughout the remainder of his life.

Captain Bon had toyed with the dream of striking out on the river to Mount La Felicidad to explore the jungle of Silvana for as long as he could remember. He had read a book when he was in the navy about different explorers who had taken the voyage. Some of them never made it to the mountain and just returned to Negombo. A few others had died trying to accomplish this adventure. A select few had made it to the mountain and spoke of the wonderful sights they had seen. They said the mountain was an untouched region that seemed lost in time. The plants and animals were different than any they had ever seen before.

Looking at his two-sided list, he wondered why it had taken him this long to write down the pros and cons of the potential adventure. Maybe it was that he didn't want to face the truth that he was scared to step out of the ordinary and that the fear of failure had held him back all these years.

As he thought about those fears, he wondered how many other people in the world had their dreams taken by fear. What if everyone went after their dreams and desires? How far ahead would the world be today?

He was thinking through the multitudes of people who allowed fear (or the famous Señor Doubter in Bon's case) to hold them back; the number was daunting. Why was fear so powerful? It came to him like a bolt of lightning—the need to be loved and respected led to the root of fear. Everyone wants to be loved, and everyone wants to be respected. It is in our human DNA. Failing meant that he would not be respected or, worse, he might risk losing love. That in itself would be enough to hold most people back.

But what about the people who had succeeded? We love and respect them, don't we? Sure, we do. But how do you process the chance of failure and the loss of love and respect?

As he was looking over his list, the answer came to him. He and others like him hadn't built up motivation to get moving toward their dreams and desires. He knew he hadn't spent the time necessary to define his pleasures and pains to accomplishing his goals, and he was sure this was the case for most people who never took the risk. He hadn't developed a list of what he was grateful for in life and why it would benefit him to go after his other life goals. Captain Bon was sure this was the case for others who had allowed their dreams to fade in time.

Captain Bon had learned through NLP (neurolinguistic programming) that he needed to look inward and find both the pain and pleasure to any goal he wanted to accomplish. The problem was he hadn't used what he had learned. He needed to develop a plan that he would use on himself to motivate and reprogram himself to accomplish his dream. He could use the pleasure to develop the why and the rewards that he would need, though he also knew using pain would be a greater motivator. He knew through his studies that the avoidance of pain was the greatest motivator.

It didn't even have to be a real pain. The expectation of pain worked too. He knew that humans would do almost anything to avoid pain. The anticipation of pain could drive people to accomplish anything.

Captain Bon went back to his list of pros and cons and added two more columns. In these columns, he put the pleasures and pains for each of the pros and cons. He dialed in on the pain portion. As one of the pros, he would accomplish his goal of exploring the river and making it to the mountain, and thus, he would go down in the history books with other explorers. As he thought about this, he realized the two greatest pains of accomplishing the dream and not accomplishing the dream. The first pain was the easy one. What if he tried and failed? Well, the worst that could happen is that he could die. The thought that he could die was a strong pain. It was a fear no one wanted to face, and thus, most would avoid it. So what pain could overcome the fear of dying? Though Captain Bon knew the answer, he was struggling with putting it on paper. He knew that once he wrote down this fear, this pain could put his life at risk.

He took a few moments to think about it. As he did, another one of his father's life lessons came back to him. He hadn't understood it over the years, but now the lesson was clear to him. The lesson kept ringing in his head. His father had said, "When you are at the end of your life and are on your deathbed, be sure that you can look back on life and know you lived every day to the fullest." To Captain Bon, for years, this statement meant that he should die without regrets. Now he still believed it had this meaning, but he also felt stronger that it meant he should make sure he could look back on life and know he did his best every day. Doing his best every day was a unique way to look at life. If he looked over his life until now, could he say he had lived his life to the best of his ability? The answer was no, he hadn't, and it was all because of the fear of failure. Now the fear of living a substandard life was greater than the fear of failure. Doing his best every day wasn't a tremendous change in perspective, but the change was large enough to drive him to go after his dream.

Now through self-diagnosis, he could find the weaknesses in himself and build a plan that would help him overcome his fears. By understanding what the greater pain would be at the end of his life, he could propel himself to greatness. Captain Bon had solved a problem in himself that most people in the world wouldn't. He knew that he had to be different from most people if he wanted to succeed. Now he had a key to being different.

Captain Bon knew that with the present focus he had on improving himself and getting past the fear of failure, he could succeed. He also understood that focus created energy and that energy was what got things done. *Energy goes where you place your focus in life.* The proper focus was another large accomplishment for Captain Bon. He was feeling pretty good about what he had just taught himself and the technique he was using.

Thinking back over his NLP training, he created a checklist to follow. He wanted to use this checklist to ensure his plan was solid, and if it wasn't, he could then find the holes he needed to plug. Thinking of the main points behind NLP, he created four areas to evaluate his plan. They would include rapport, sensory awareness, outcome thinking, and behavioral flexibility. Going through his plan, he found that he had outcome thinking and behavioral flexibility. He also felt his plan had sensory awareness, but he wasn't sure that he had the needed rapport.

So how did rapport relate to his plan anyway? His plan was contingent on many outside people. The success or failure to achieve his dream was contingent on these people, so it stood to reason that he needed to understand how he would develop a rapport with them to accomplish his dream. He felt this was a subcategory to his plan. He couldn't define it completely without figuring out who these people would be, but he could develop the outline that would be filled in later with the specifics for each person.

As he thought about it more, this was also outcome thinking and behavioral flexibility at its best. Yes, he was covering his bases and building the most successful plan he could. No one could cover all the what-ifs, but he had a good place to start by using NLP to review his plan.

Captain Bon looked over what he had accomplished and realized he had acted. After all, how do you eat an elephant? One bite at a time. He was eating his elephant of a dream one bite at a time. He was proud that he finally made progress. He was grateful that he had taken the time to learn and understand NLP because it was now helping him test his plan. He knew that he would soon get additional help from the team he was developing and that he would help them realize their dreams through rapport. He now understood that he could be successful on the river and reach the mountain. Whatever the future held, he knew he was capable of overcoming any challenge.

WHAT HAVE WE LEARNED FROM CAPTAIN BON?

As human beings and not animals, we have choices about what we want and what we become. We are not driven by our basic instinct. Well, at least most of us are not! We can choose to live in poverty or rise to wealth. It is our God-given right. I am not here to talk to you in a theological nature. When I use the word *God,* it is in the representative nature of your creator, the universe, or whatever you choose to believe. I am referring to the greater intelligence when I use one of these names. As said by Alexander Graham Bell, "What this power is I cannot say. All I know is that it exists," and so do my feelings.

We ask, "How do I get moving? What systems will I use to motivate myself to get to the place where I can do this anytime I need or want to?"

First, you need to sit down and write out a list of the things you are grateful for in life. If people truly put their minds to it, they will find hundreds of things they are grateful for in their lives. We need to start here to put our minds in a positive state. Gratitude will put you in a positive state of mind. You can and should review this list in the morning as soon as you wake up. If it does nothing else for you, it will put you in a positive state of mind. We all get to choose to look at our situations as positive or negative. By reviewing what I am grateful for in life every morning, I can at least start my day in a positive light.

This gratitude will help in creating the wealthy life you desire. This exercise should not be a chore in your daily life but a way to show you that remarkable things exist. By doing this, you will create energy and momentum in your life. As you gain energy and momentum with the feeling of self-love, you will easily be able to use the system to create the life you want and deserve. You *cannot* allow anything or anyone to kill your energy, momentum, or self-love. You can't get in your way if you want the wealth that life has to offer you. *Remember, energy flows where attention goes.*

To get moving on this path, we must first look at what makes us move either toward or away from anything. People are like magnets and will move toward pleasure and away from pain just as all animals do. The funny thing is that animals will only move away from true pain or toward true pleasure. Humans, on the other hand, move most of the time from what they perceive will be painful or to what they perceive will give them pleasure. As you understand this and learn more about yourself through self-evaluation, you will learn how to use your pain and pleasure to change anything in your life.

Let's make a list of our pleasures (the things in life you love doing) and our pains (the things in life we do not like doing or try to avoid). The list will be an important exercise for us in understanding our motivation. You will learn a lot about yourself and develop your knowledge base if you take the time to complete this exercise. After all, isn't that what we all want?

Here are some examples from my list:

Passions	Dislikes
Spending time with my family	Laundry
Weight lifting	Housework
Writing	Accounting
Inventing and building things	Arguing
Bicycling	Waiting in lines
Public speaking	Spending time with know-it-all people
Reading	Long, drawn-out meetings
Spending time in a think group	Flying in airplanes
Eating out	News
Fishing	People who are not themselves
Flying in helicopters	Hunger in the world
Going to the movies	People who waste their natural talents
Playing music	People who complain about their lives and do nothing to change their states

I am sure you have some of the same passions and dislikes and also some different ones. There are no right or wrong answers here. This is your list to create. And with this list, you will find the things in life you should be doing to reach your full potential. Moreover, on the dislike side, you will find some things you will have to do but need the motivation to get through. One of the systems that helps with this is NLP (neurolinguistic programming). Richard Binder and Dr. John Grinder developed and founded this system about how people communicated within their minds and with the world. It also shows that in every communication we have, whether internal or external, there is always more than one perspective of the communication.

The system can be used by you to examine your feelings. The system has been used most notably (along with the system Tony created) by Tony Robbins in training people on how to better their lives through their examination. One of the things discovered was that when people were thinking, their eyes moved to predictable areas. The eye movement can be useful to you in examining yourself and finding truth in your own life. Examples of these eye movements are as follows:

1. If they recalled memories or pictures in their minds, their eyes moved to the top left.
2. If they were creating pictures or thinking creatively, their eyes moved to the top right.
3. If they remembered sounds or conversations, their eyes moved horizontally to the left.
4. When they imagined what certain sounds would sound like, their eyes moved horizontally to the right.
5. When they accessed certain emotions, their eyes dropped down to the right.
6. When they had internal conversations, their eyes dropped down to the left.

They also found that this could change if the person was left-handed. By asking a few questions of certain people and watching their eyes, you can find out their patterns—whether it is as outlined or in reverse order because of their dominant hand.

I have tried this experiment both with others and myself, and I have found it to be truly profound and accurate. I have used it more on myself than on others in developing the self-knowledge of my inner communication. NLP has been one of the most profound systems I have found to develop my inner dialogue and determine whether what I was thinking was a true fear or an imaginary feeling that was holding me back.

As mentioned, the NLP system has four pillars. They are rapport, sensory awareness, outcome thinking, and behavioral flexibility.

Rapport is created by developing a feeling of like interest and goals. The fastest way to develop a rapport with another person is through caring and asking good questions to find things you have in common.

Sensory awareness is evaluating if what you are doing is working or not and learning how to change what you are doing to succeed.

Outcome thinking is a system of thinking of what you want your result to be and then working backward to develop a plan to get to the desire.

Behavioral flexibility is being flexible and resilient in your actions so that you can change direction and behaviors to get to your desires. The ability to change direction or behavior is very important in today's world and our ever-changing environment.

As we will learn through this book, Captain Bon worked with these four pillars as a sounding tool to check his plans and the plans of others. These four pillars help in finding areas we may have missed. If a plan doesn't stand on these four pillars it isn't as strong as it could be. Take a minute to reread the definitions of the four pillars. Think about how you can use them to check the plan you have. Okay, take the time now to read the definitions, and we will start again.

Do you understand the definitions? Read them again. I'm kidding. I know you read them a few times already. I bet a few of you overachievers even looked at one of your plans to see if it had all these elements— excellent job. So let's take a moment and look at each pillar.

RAPPORT

So how would you see if your plan has rapport? Well, almost every plan requires help from someone else to accomplish the goals. And we all know that no one helps unless there is something in it for them. You must show them what's in it for them. That's where rapport comes in. You must build the relationship. There must be common ground and respect. A relationship without rapport has a challenging time working out, but the stronger the rapport, the stronger the relationship. That's just the way the world works. So let's take a simple example and explore rapport deeper.

Let's say you want to lose weight and get in better shape. You would like someone to do this with you, but you are not sure who it should be. You may consider someone who wants the same thing as you, which is a wonderful place to start. Maybe it's a friend or perhaps your wife or husband. It could even be someone you met at the gym. Well, you must ask that person to work out with you, not as a coach but as someone who shares the same goal as you.

You have already started building rapport before you even ask them. You both have the same goal, and that is the beginning of building the necessary rapport. You're not sure how to ask for help, are you? Well, the next step to building rapport and gaining a partner to work out with is striking up a conversation. It could be as simple as asking how this person is doing or asking for help in figuring out what would be the best time to come to the gym. You don't necessarily need to know these answers, but it's a way to break the ice.

As a next step to building rapport, you must ask questions about the person. You may ask, "How long have you been working out?" Or you may ask, "How often do you work out?" You may be afraid to ask questions, but don't be. People love talking about themselves. Here's a word of caution though: be genuine. People can spot fakes who don't really care but only want something from them. If you can't be genuine, don't try to build rapport. If you get to know the person and don't care for him or her, then find someone else.

You have started some conversations and are enjoying getting to know people. Don't just jump out and scare them away by asking them to work out with you. Get to know them better. You will sense when you have built rapport in the relationship, and it's okay to ask them to work out with you.

This process is also the same when you are asking someone to mentor you. You must build a rapport. There should be a kinship between you and your prospective mentor. Remember that as you are building rapport with people, there has to be something in it for them. Hey, it could be that they want a new friend. They could want to give something to the next generation. But there must be something in it for the other people, and you have to understand what that something will be.

SENSORY AWARENESS

Let's now look at sensory awareness and how it works. To me, sensory awareness is the most important of the four pillars. Most people think they have it, but they don't. They don't because they would have to say, "I am wrong, and this isn't working. I have to change." At some point, we all get stuck in the trap of doing the same thing over and over again, hoping it will work next time. Doing the same thing over and over and expecting a different outcome is the definition of insanity. If you fail at something, you have to learn from it, change your approach, and try again. Changing your approach doesn't mean you will succeed the next time. But if you do, you can learn another way of how to not get the result you want.

If you take the time and analyze what went wrong and make proper changes, you will eventually succeed. That takes not giving up. Unfortunately, most people say, "I have tried everything." They haven't tried everything because trying does not end until you succeed. Saying you've tried everything is just a way to feel good about yourself when you quit.

Why quit? Use sensory awareness to learn. Don't place blame, rather learn from the mistakes. Placing blame does nothing to fix the problem; it just gives you another excuse.

When working with a team to accomplish a goal, sensory awareness is important, but the team must understand it's okay to fail if you learn from it. I have often witnessed people playing the blame game in business and have even taken part in it myself. That was before I understood that blaming doesn't help build a better team. With the blame game, you also end up resenting the people who made a mistake and maybe even kicking them off the team. You lose assets when you do this. You have spent time and money on these people. Now you must spend time and money on others.

Now I'm not saying there aren't times when some people just don't fit. I am advocating trying to help people learn. If they can't or will not learn, then the team is better without them. But first, you should see if you can salvage some good assets. If you spend the time helping them, which is also a part of building rapport, you will have stronger assets. And in today's economy, you need all the strong human assets you can find.

Outcome Thinking

Now let's discuss outcome thinking and how we accomplish it. Outcome thinking is about considering what you want for your outcome. Once you know that, you can work backward from the outcome. Most people claim to see the whole picture, but they don't. No one can see every part—it's just too much for your brain to comprehend, and it will shut down on you.

With outcome thinking, you can envision what you want the desired result to be, and then you can build your plan to get to the desired result one step at a time. First, as you are stepping backward, don't think of every part that has to happen to get to the result. Look for the larger parts and identify them. Then break each of the larger parts into smaller subparts, and if necessary, break those subparts into even smaller ones. You can have as many subparts as it takes. There isn't a subpart police that will come and arrest you. Break it down as small as you can.

Once you have broken it all down, you now have the basis on which to build your plan. Just remember that you will inevitably forget something, and that's okay. Once you have built your plan, you can now go back and use the four pillars and make sure it's sound. Again, this will help you find holes in the plan and help correct them. I know this sounds like a lot of work. Well, that's because it is a lot of work. Anything worth having is a lot of work. You need to want it bad enough. Oh, and here is a little surprise for you. The more you practice doing this, the easier it gets. The more you do anything, the easier it gets. If you practice this system with everything you do, one day it will be like driving your car. You will get in and drive. It's the same with outcome thinking and backward planning. One day it will all come naturally. The time it takes to move from the feeling that it's demanding work to the feeling that it's like driving a car is totally up to you. The harder you deliberately practice this technique, the faster you will get there. Drive it, like you stole it!

BEHAVIORAL FLEXIBILITY

Now we have come to the fourth and final pillar, namely behavioral flexibility. Behavioral flexibility often seems to be the hardest of the four pillars for most people. They have made plans, and they feel their plans are good. They have put a lot of time into their plans, and they can't see why they will not work out. However, they missed the fact that something in the environment changed and that they need to alter the plan. It's understandable why most people feel this way. After all, certain plans are their babies; they're like parts of them. Just as real babies grow and change, plans often need to as well. No, I'm not saying that you should throw the plan out at the first sign of trouble. Evaluate what the trouble is and revisit the plan. Honestly look for what changes you may need.

I couldn't count the times on both my hands and feet that I made this same mistake and scolded people for veering from my plan. Often I come back and realize that I should have been the first to say, "We need to look at the plan and make some adjustments." I teach these principles and still sometimes fail to see that behavioral flexibility is needed. However, I do often find my mistake and learn from it in the end.

The most important thing is to learn and to be willing to change, stay flexible with your plans, and avoid distractions. Also, be open to suggestions from others as they pertain to the plan. You may or may not take the advice, but if you are open, you could find a better and faster way to accomplish your goal.

If you find you must change course or abandon the plan for a new one while you are using behavioral flexibility, then you should step back, take yourself out of the ownership role of the plan, and see what needs to change. Evaluate the new plan the same way you did the original. Poke holes in it with the four pillars and make it better, then point your boat in the new direction, and head out on the river.

CHAPTER 5

THE TEN STROKES TO PADDLE THE RIVER OF SUCCESS

THROUGH CAPTAIN BON'S TRAINING AND study of self-help systems, he was able to outline ten success principles with the help of his mentor Dennis. These would help him achieve his goals and create a healthier life. These ten principles came from many different systems that he had learned from experts. Much of what he used had been adapted from Napoleon Hill's book *Think and Grow Rich*. Captain Bon had also taken best practices from others, such as Tony Robbins's version of NLP, Simon Sinek's book *Start with Why*, and John Maxwell's leadership books. He and Dennis combined these different systems by finding the areas where they were congruent.

Dennis and he found that no one source had all the checks necessary to create the system that would work for Captain Bon. By studying the different systems, they created a repeatable system. The system would give him a base to check him against his progress. It would also be a system that they could teach others. In addition to him using the system to succeed, all the people who worked with him could also use the system.

They took the ten principles and created ten pitfalls to success principles to avoid. These were the main ten barriers that prevented people from getting to their desires. As they worked on the ten principles, they broke them down into subcategories. That way, he could make it easier for others to learn the principles and create a process so that people could use the principles daily. They created a simple checklist that he could use to check on his progress. This way, he could stay focused and move forward each day.

He used this system on smaller dreams to work out all the bugs before he tried it out on his greatest dream. That would be the true test of their system. Could it keep him on track and help him reach Mount La Felicidad? Now Señor Doubter jumped on his shoulder and started screaming in his ear, "You will fail. How do you think the two of you are smart enough to build a system of success? You are just a subpar copy of great people who have come before you. And again, what makes you think you can accomplish your dream?"

For a second or two, Captain Bon gave in to Señor Doubter. He was about to put his dream on the shelf again, perhaps forever this time. Then he looked down at Dennis and his success principles and knew he would do it. He would accomplish his dream. He would also teach his system to others along the way so that they, too, could go after their dreams and succeed.

You see, Captain Bon understood that to be great at anything, you had to practice, but not practice in the way most of us think. It had to be deliberate practice. Deliberate practice required practicing a selected task, getting coaching from a teacher, and getting feedback on if what you were doing was working or not. This way, improvements could be made by the student to improve.

Captain Bon had practiced his system by using it every day and looking at what worked and what didn't work. He also had teachers in the books he studied and the seminars he had attended, not to mention a great mentor in Dennis. The seminars and Dennis gave him a place to get some feedback from others who had already traveled his path in life. But he had trouble getting daily feedback until he started doing three things.

First, after learning about the four pillars of NLP, he started checking his plans to see if they were consistent with the four pillars. He would question his plan to ensure the four pillars were supporting it and that he had built in the questions for the future. If something didn't line up with the four pillars, he would change his plan.

The second thing that Captain Bon needed to do was to build a system to receive daily feedback on his plans. This area was a little harder for

Captain Bon. He felt that if he shared his plans to achieve his desires, the team would judge him. He feared that if his plans failed, the judgment would be harsh. Judgment was hard for Captain Bon to get past. Like most people, he felt that the fear of being judged was a large hurdle for him to get over.

He did have Dennis to help review and poke holes in the plan, but he didn't think that was enough. As he thought about it, he concluded that maybe if he shared his plans with others, it would inspire them to do the same. If they were inspired to share their dreams and plans, he could create a mastermind group to help solve challenges.

That's when a lesson from Napoleon Hill came to Captain Bon. Napoleon Hill taught that by working with others in harmony, one could use other's education and experience to accomplish certain goals. The melding of the minds within the group would create what Napoleon called the third mind. The *third mind* is a combination of all the minds working together in harmony.

Captain Bon now knew he would have to build a team that would work together as a think tank, a group of individuals who would help one another develop their plans to accomplish desires they couldn't accomplish alone. This group could also use deliberate practice. It would be a group working on a specific skill, and participants would provide feedback on certain plans to the originators.

Captain Bon understood that it took time to be more than efficient at anything in a lifetime to practice what you wanted to be efficient at, time to gain experience, time to look at what you were doing through different eyes, and time to understand everything involved in the adventure.

Through studying and reading, Captain Bon learned that it took more than talent for a person to become great. It took hard work. It took deliberate practice. It would take a normal person ten thousand hours to become great. Through additional studying and experiments on musicians, chess players, and even business professionals, researchers found that these ten thousand hours were a mandate for someone to be great. They also found that innate talent wasn't the determining factor. The researchers couldn't rule out talent as part of the equation, but those who performed deliberate practice for ten thousand hours were better than anyone else in their fields.

If Captain Bon started working on his ten thousand hours to become a great planner and developer of his adventures, it would still take him ten years, calculated at Bon working at it for forty hours a week. The time seemed unrealistic to Captain Bon. It wasn't that he was afraid to put in the work or that he was lazy. But he didn't want to wait till he was fifty-eight years old to take the adventure to Mount La Felicidad. So how could he work to get more deliberate practice in and do it faster? That's when he came up with the idea that he could gain time faster by teaching his system to others and organizing a mastermind group.

Through working with others in the mastermind group and through teaching his system to both members of the mastermind group and others who wanted to better their lives, he could gain the needed practice and feedback faster. Also, working with these people would allow him to borrow from their education and life experiences, thus reducing the time needed to go out and learn on his own. Again, it wasn't that he didn't want to put in the work. After all, when everything was said and done, he would have worked harder than if he had done it on his own. But this would cut down the time frame of the ten-year investment. He would still be investing the ten thousand hours. It just wouldn't be only his time. Rather it would be the joint efforts of all the people in the mastermind group and the people he trained.

He also realized that he had done the planning for work through his life and that some of this time had been deliberate training. Those hours would count toward the ten thousand hours he needed to become an expert. He couldn't quantify how many hours it had been, but who kept track of the hours anyway? He wasn't sure it was a hard number. It was more of a general time frame that researchers used to characterize individuals who produced the greatest works.

He thought of all the reasons this wouldn't work. The main barrier he could see that would stand in the way of his success was himself. He knew that he was shy and that it would be a huge step to gather people together to create a mastermind group. It would take even more internal strength to put himself out there as a teacher of his system. Of course, Señor Doubter showed up again and listed all the ways that Captain Bon would fail. He wasn't attacking the mastermind group or the system. He understood Captain Bon had built defenses in his mind and could justify these two endeavors. He now attacked Captain Bon's ability to put himself out there in the world and gather the people he needed. He used Captain Bon's fears of insecurity against him. He played up the insecurity of meeting people and the insecurity of building rapport with them. Señor Doubter also used Captain Bon's main insecurity—the unknown.

Captain Bon had already stepped way outside of his comfort zone by building this system and planning his adventure to Mount La Felicidad. He had to push himself even further if he was going to be successful. Outside of Bon's comfort zone is where Señor Doubter kept attacking. Captain Bon fought back at every turn. He had built up his dream this time, and it was real to him. There was no way Señor Doubter would get in his way.

On Dennis's advice, Captain Bon went out and interviewed different people from his community who were involved in all aspects of exploration. He also became a member of the local Toastmasters group to become more comfortable with speaking to groups of people. At work, he would train employees on his system of success. Every time he found the opportunity to share his system with anyone, he did. Doing this kept him focused on his dream and helped him refine his skills.

When people were negative toward him or the system, he would ask them questions to figure out why they thought it wouldn't work. He found that some were scared to dream and get their hopes up only to fail in the end. He understood this way of thinking all too well. After all, that was his attitude at one time. He wouldn't give up on trying to help these people. He would only change his approach. In the end, he was able to help some people, but others couldn't be help because they weren't ready to change. He understood their reluctance and felt bad for them.

He also built his mastermind group. It was a group of five members, including Captain Bon. They came from all walks of life. Captain Bon had met two of the members at the Toastmasters meetings. They were highly educated. One was an investment banker named Aaron, and the other was a graphic designer named Kelly. The other two came from the blue-collar sector of the town. One was an elderly cattleman named Brice who had been friends with Captain Bon's father. The second was named Jimmy, and he owned a hardware store in town.

Captain Bon enjoyed the meetings of the mastermind group. They met twice a week for two hours. During the first few meetings, they got to know one another and talked about their experiences in life. Captain Bon allowed them to become comfortable with one another before working with them. After about the fourth meeting, he slowly introduced the notion of working together to solve problems. He allowed each of the other members to figure out the problems they wanted to solve before he ever brought up his plan.

While they were solving challenges, Captain Bon taught them his system of success, but he did it without laying it out as a plan for success. He would interject and say, "What if we ask this question here? How do you picture feeling when you are successful at the challenge?" Captain Bon was still shy and was just throwing out his system. He was worried it wasn't going to work. He had to teach them without the team knowing.

When they got to Captain Bon's plan, each of the members had great input. Many of the barriers Captain Bon was trying to get past were torn down in just hours. The investment banker helped Captain Bon figure out how to raise funds for the trip. The hardware store owner educated Captain Bon on how best to pack for the trip so that he would get the most supplies in the storage area he had. And the old farmer helped teach him ways he could plan the navigation of the trip.

To Captain Bon's surprise, the investment banker was an extreme sports athlete in his early twenties and wanted to take the adventure with Captain Bon. Aaron enjoyed being an investment banker, and he was successful at his career; however, like Captain Bon, he felt that he needed this adventure to make his life whole. Captain Bon was more than happy to take Aaron on his team to travel the rivers to Mount La Felicidad.

It all felt a lot easier than Captain Bon thought it would. It was still demanding work, and he had to give of himself; however, it wasn't as hard as he had feared it would be. Now he was building energy and was on his way to fulfilling his dream.

Time to Learn Captain Bon's Principles to a Successful Life

As you go through and read the story of Captain Bon's adventure, you will see how he uses the principle to succeed in his dream of an adventure to Mount La Felicidad. Captain Bon's story is a simple one, but if you take time to evaluate each of the parts, you will see how he used the system to complete his dream.

As you read the story, think about the principles as Captain Bon uses them. Also, consider yourself and evaluate how you can use these principles in your life's adventure. Now all this hinges on the fact that you use your imagination to envision Captain Bon on the road to his adventure. Some may have a tough time with this, but if you practice using your imagination, you are performing the deliberate practice. And as you will see, deliberate practice and using your imagination are two of the principles to a wealthy life.

I have taught people that their imaginations are their best assets on the road to success—that is, if they follow up with action. Imagination without action is only daydreaming, and we're here to learn and succeed, not to daydream. That's why I want you to put yourself in Captain Bon's shoes. Become Captain Bon for this time we are together. Think about what you feel as Captain Bon. Think about what you are learning by stretching yourself as Captain Bon. I promise if you put in the deliberate practice of being Captain Bon, you will understand the principles better and be able to use them in your life.

Too often each of us read self-help books or attend seminars and feel motivated to take on the world, and we feel that way until we get back to real life and stop doing what we have just learned. It happens to each of us. Unfortunately, we allow our daily routines to take over, and we put aside what we have just learned. When we put aside what we learned, it is because we haven't made the new system a habit. It takes deliberate practice to make anything a habit. For the normal person, this requires using your willpower for about the first twenty-one days. You must force yourself to practice the new system, but as the days pass, you will not have to force yourself as hard. When you get between day fourteen and twenty-one, you will find the system has now become a habit. After day twenty-one, you will feel as if something is missing whenever you don't practice your new habit. That's just how a habit works.

It doesn't matter to your mind if the habit is good or bad. Your mind feels that if you are doing it, it must be okay. Habits are simple to instill in your life, but they're practically impossible to delete. Habits never go away. A habit is a three-part system. (We will review habits later.)

First, there is the trigger (what causes you to practice the habit). Second comes the action that makes up the habit. And the third is the reward. Each habit in your life has these three parts. Many of us can see the habits, but we miss the triggers and rewards. Finding what triggers particular habits can be tough. It could be as simple as the alarm clock going off in the morning or as complicated as stress from a specific situation.

Sometimes it's even harder to understand the reward you are getting from a habit. Let's look at the rewards of smoking for example. Smoking is a bad habit and kills people, so why do so many people still smoke? It's because it's a habit with a reward. The trigger for most people is stress, then they smoke cigarettes. The reward is the feeling that the nicotine gives them. Cigarettes today also contain sugar, so the body thinks it has been fed food. Between the nicotine and sugar, the body and mind are getting huge rewards that outweigh the mind's understanding of the dangers of smoking cigarettes.

The same holds for other addictive drugs that people use in life. The chemical highs from drugs are huge rewards. With some drugs, however, the high is about escaping the reality of the person's world. The drug takes people to a euphoric state where they have no worries.

As I said, we will discuss habits and beliefs later in the book, but you can see how one can use them to motivate or stall people. We need to determine whether our habits and beliefs are motivating us to realize our dreams or stalling us and keeping us from achieving our goals.

THE SUCCESS PRINCIPLES

Ten principles make up the system that can lead one to a life of wealth. We will go through and review each of these principles and how they work to create a repeatable path to success anytime you have a desire or dream you want to achieve. We will also discuss the principles of failure that will cause you to fail on your path to success.

If you are like me, you do not want to wait to learn the list of principles or success pitfalls in the next hundred pages or so to come. I have listed the principles and the success pitfallprinciples in this chapter. That way, you can reflect on them before we move forward and explain each of the principles and success pitfalls in detail.

THE SYSTEM PARTS TO YOUR SUCCESS PRINCIPLES

1. Dreams, desires, and decisions
2. Imagination
3. Your subconscious mind, beliefs, and values
4. Planning and chunking
5. Organization of specialized knowledge
6. Think tank / mastermind group
7. Deliberate practice and persistence
8. Leverage and stretching yourself
9. Faith in yourself or self-confidence
10. Relationships with people, body, and spirit

SUCCESS PITFALLS PRINCIPLE

Here are the success pitfalls for the above ten parts of your success principles. This is not a complete list, but these are the main pitfalls that you need to guard yourself against taking:

1. Mediocrity, accepting what comes, spending time on unnecessary decisions, and indecision
2. Perceived reality
3. Beliefs and values instilled in you by the world and accepted as truth
4. Failure to plan or chunking
5. Unorganized knowledge, know-it-all personality, and being closed-minded

6. Thinking that you can do it alone or that others' success came without help
7. Idleness, hesitation, and self-sabotage
8. Laziness, fear, and unconfident
9. Fear of the unknown, lack of self-confidence, and doubt
10. Unhealthy habits, poor rapport building, poor health, nonspiritual, physically minded, and unspiritual

#

As we go through the explanation of each step of the system, you will see that items two through ten only work as the supporting legs for the skills you learn in step one. It is important to understand and implement each of the nine principles that follow the first principle. Just as any building has load-bearing walls that support the structure, these ten principles support you in achieving your desires. But are you ready, willing, and able? Most people in life are ready and able, but they are not willing to do what it takes to move to the next level in their lives—whether it is having a simple plan, getting partners, removing beliefs that do not serve them, or resolving conflicts in their lives. Here's one big conflict in many people's lives. They often say, "I want to start my own company, but I need security in my life." I hope you can see how this causes inner conflict that you must resolve. You must ask yourself, "Am I *willing* to do what it takes to navigate up the river of life to where I want to be?"

CAPTAIN BON ON WILLING

Captain Bon now understood that he was always ready and able to take the adventure up the river to Mount La Felicidad, but he wasn't willing. He wasn't willing to face his fears of failure. He was willing to put in the demanding work needed to accomplish his desire, but he hadn't found it in himself to face the fears that came with any adventure. He had lived his life thus far afraid of what people would think or say if he announced his desire to go after his dream. He was afraid to leave the security he had and find only failure and ruin.

But now with the help of Dennis, he had created his system of success, which would help him find a way to put his fears aside. Perhaps he couldn't set them aside completely, but he could keep them at bay while he moved forward at least. Captain Bon understood everyone had fears, but he knew fears could be good. He could use his fears to build a stronger plan. Or he could use them as an early warning system. He just couldn't let his fears control him any longer.

He had now built a system to make him willing. Through his imagination, the adventure was real. He had seen himself at Mount La Felicidad. He had seen in his imagination that it would be a treacherous journey, but it was one that he could complete. He imagined his feelings when he completed the adventure. He now felt the pride of success, and that was enough to break the chains of fear and doubt that had held him back before.

Past Accomplishments Exercise

Before we move on to learning the system, let's first complete an exercise that shows us the desires we had in the past that we successfully achieved. Past accomplishments will show you that you do, indeed, have the power to succeed. We will also use these past successes to help build the attitude of self-success. As we all know, hindsight is twenty-twenty. We will use these successes to train our minds so that we can ride our boats to the success and happiness camp. Think back to your childhood. Write every little success on a piece of paper. List the plans or paths you used. You do not have to remember every detail, but we need to examine the way we think now and in the past so that we know how to build our system going forward.

Here is an example for you to use as a guide.

Desire

Desire 1: I want to lose weight and live a healthier life. My true desire is to look great in a mirror.

Plan for Desire 1

A. I must define my desire. I want to look good in the mirror and also to live longer.

B. I must decide on a gym to join and get a trainer.

C. First, I must evaluate my present weight, measurements, and conditioning with a trainer.

D. I must decide how much weight I want to lose (forty pounds).

E. I must construct my timeline to meet the goal (180 days).

F. I must evaluate my eating habits. (Diet makes up 80 percent of weight loss.)

G. I must work with a trainer on exercises and diet.

H. I must track calories and macros. (I must work to maintain 1,800 calories with a makeup of 35 percent protein, 32 percent fats, and 33 percent carbs.)

I. I must track my workouts. (I must record the amount I do per month in hours and divide that into a percent of the time by cardio and resistance training. My goal is 30 percent cardio and 70 percent weight training with a minimum of fifteen hours of total training a month.)

J. I must evaluate progress every fourteen days through weight, measurements, and endurance.

K. I must adjust my training and diet as needed.

L. Once I'm at my weight and size goal, I must work with a trainer on a maintenance program.

As you can see from this first plan, we have hit the high points. Though it doesn't have every step I will take listed, it does give me a road map to succeeding. As with any other plan, it will need adjusting, but again, we have a road map to get us on our way.

Too often people spend too much time writing out a *perfect* plan. There is no such thing. All plans have flaws. They will always have flaws because of the ever-changing world. Remember to use sensory awareness and behavioral flexibility to gauge your plan against the result you are achieving. If you are not getting the results you want, consider changing your approach, but remember to give your plan time to work. Rome wasn't built in a day. Nor was it torn down in a day. Plans need time to grow, and you are the only one who can say if it is time to change.

OUTCOME TRACKER

Day 14: I lost five pounds and one inch in my waist. (I started at 235 pounds, and I'm down to 230. I'm learning to control diet.)

Day 28: I am down to 228 from 235 (Seven pounds), and my waist is down 1.5 inches. My diet is getting better, and my endurance is up.

Day 42: Today I am down to 220 from 235 (total of fifteen pounds lost). My waist is down 2.75 inches. My strength and endurance are better now, and I'm up to three miles of jogging without stopping. I am changing my resistance training (trainer advice).

Day 56: I am down to 218 from 235 (total of seventeen pounds lost), while my waist is down four inches. It still looks to me like I'm losing fat, even though my weight hasn't changed. My endurance is up, and I am jogging five miles in fifty-five minutes. My strength is still growing. I have been adjusting my diet to increase it to 2,300 calories a day.

Day 70: Today my weight is down to 211 from 235 (total of twenty pounds lost), while my waist is down a total of six inches. My new resistance workout is helping with my strength and flexibility. It's been somewhat of a struggle to get an average of 2,300 calories a day into my diet. My average has been 2,150 calories a day. I have been adding a protein drink before bed.

Day 84: Now my weight is down to 204 from 235 (total of thirty-one pounds lost), and my waist is down a total of 8.5 inches. My endurance is good, but I'm having some trouble with the motivation to get to the gym when my trainer is not present. I am working to find a workout partner to help with motivation.

Day 98: Today my weight is at 204 from 235 (no change in weight), but my waist is down a total of ten inches. It looks like I'm still losing fat. I am now able to see abdominal muscles. I have found a workout partner for the days that I'm without a trainer. My diet is now on track at 2,350 calories a day.

Day 112: My weight is now at 202 from 235 (down a total of thirty-three pounds), as my waist is still down a total of ten inches. I am working to change my resistance training to include Pilates, as well as adding in swimming once a week for cardio.

Day 126: Today my weight is at 198 from 235 (down a total of thirty-seven pounds), and my waist is down a total of eleven inches. I am pushing my daily calories to 2,500 per day.

Day 140: My weight is at 195 from 235 (down fourty pounds), while my waist is now down a total of 11.5 inches. I have met the goal I set in the beginning. I am now working on creating a maintenance program.

Day 154: My weight is now at 194 (down fourty-one pounds total), and my waist is down a total of twelve inches. I have increased my calories to 2,800 a day to maintain my current size. I have changed my training to 75 percent resistance and 25 percent cardio for fifteen hours a month of resistance training and five hours of cardio for a total of twenty hours a month at six days a week.

#

Did you do the exercise? Or did you just read over it without much thought? Doing the exercise will help you build your support system in more ways than you can imagine. It shows you that you have been successful in obtaining your desires before, no matter how small the accomplishment may have been. You are building your inner support system by doing the exercises. We all need this support system to fight Señor Doubter.

As you can see from the example, I met my goal and have been maintaining it now for six months. During those six months, I had to adjust my original plan to a maintenance plan, but it worked the same way. In accomplishing this goal, I once again proved to myself that with a plan, a timeline, and a tracking system, I could achieve whatever I want.

For some, this wouldn't be a great goal to achieve, but for someone like me who has struggled with weight and overeating for his whole life, it's like making it to the top of Mount Everest. It's another win in my folder of life—one that I can look to when I start doubting that I can accomplish a dream.

If you didn't do the exercise, please stop now and do it. I'll wait for you. Okay, so now that you have done the exercise, you can see that you can accomplish the goals you set. You may even have thought about how you drove past doubt and fear to get to where you achieved the dream you were after. Doing the exercise is building your can-do attitude, which will also help you accomplish your desires.

It's okay if you fall back into a doubtful state of mind; we all do. You can't stay there if you want to realize your dreams. You must push past the fears and doubts that have hindered you in the past. You must change your beliefs about what you are capable of accomplishing.

Beliefs can be changed. We will talk later about *how* to change a belief, but for now, know that you can change any belief structure you have. It's all about your perspective on the belief. You also need to understand that the power to change the belief lives in you and no one else.

If you have done the exercise, you may already be changing some of your beliefs. If you still think that you can't accomplish your dreams and desires, you are missing the point of the exercise. You prove to yourself that you have accomplished dreams before. Even if they were small dreams, you accomplished them.

Whether small or large, all dreams and desires have the same parts. There may be more parts in a large dream compared to a small one, but they still have the same makeup. If you break each dream down, you will find that their makeup is the same. When people look at large dreams such as taking an adventure to a faraway location compared to going to the grocery store down the street, their brains become overwhelmed. It's not that the larger trip is any harder, but there are more parts to consider.

We allow the unknown to make us think that we can't accomplish the dream. At one time in our lives, going to the grocery store down the street would have seemed just as daunting. Think back to the time when you were a small child. That child had never driven a car, and when going anywhere, you could only accomplish the task with the help of others. Friends or family members may have stepped in, but someone helped you get to the store.

The larger dream of adventure to a faraway land is no different. We will still need others help. We will still need to plan the route, and we will still need to decide what we need to take for the trip. It's that simple. To believe that we can accomplish the large dream, we only need to break it down into smaller parts. The process is called *chunking*. By dividing the tasks into smaller sections and dealing with one section at a time, you can accomplish any dream. It's that simple. Later we will look at how to accomplish chunking.

CHAPTER 6

DREAMS, DESIRES, AND DECISIONS
THE REASON TO START YOUR ADVENTURE

DREAMS AND THE ADVENTURE

For many years, Captain Bon held the dream of becoming a famous adventurer. It wasn't for the fame or the money. No, he wanted to leave a legacy of his life. He wanted a legacy written about him in the history books as a great adventurer. But like most people, he never acted on his dream. His beliefs didn't support him taking the necessary action. He put the dream away and didn't think of it much. He had decided that dreams were for children and the rich. He was just a normal man, and he needed to be comfortable in the life he had.

As he matured and entered his late thirties, he came upon a few books that would change his life. These books would make him reevaluate the possibility of accomplishing his dreams. He started to understand that the only thing holding him back from his dream was himself. Like most people, he resisted this notion. He would struggle with this idea. He didn't want to admit that he could change his life and fulfill his desires.

After reading the books, interviewing people who had come from nothing but chased down their dreams, and studying people like John Rockefeller, he understood the power was in him to make his dreams come true. So what was stopping him from realizing his dream? Why had he put it on the back burner when others hadn't? What would he do differently to achieve his dreams?

Captain Bon decided the first step would be to return to his main dream of being an adventurer and traveling the river to Mount La Felicidad. He would spend time each day for the next month making his dream a reality. He would build the fire of desire inside as he examined the barriers to his dream and then build solutions, not give excuses. Yes, this would be the first step.

His second step would be to set deliverable dates. He understood that it was part of the problem with a dream. Even if he were taking action daily, if he didn't set deadlines for himself to accomplish each part of the plan, his mind would only think of this adventure as a dream.

He might do some of the work out of willpower, but he wouldn't engage his subconscious, which could help him achieve his dream. The adventure wasn't going to be a preference. It was going to be a must, and he would engage his subconscious mind's help by setting hard dates.

By setting dates, he would also finally receive the feeling of achievement. When he met a date, no matter how minor, he would have a victory. He would have taken one more step toward his dream. The victories would create forward motion. He knew the more forward motion he could build through small accomplishments, the better the chance he would accomplish his dream. Confidence building was tough, and this was how it worked—he needed these small wins to keep his mind focused on the goal.

Captain Bon started creating a timeline of deliverables. The timeline would give him a measuring stick to see the progress he made along the way. The timeline would also engage his subconscious mind's help in getting to the next stop on his journey.

As he thought through the different accomplishments that he needed to start the adventure, Señor Doubter jumped on his shoulder as he always did. But this time, Señor Doubter didn't scream at him. He spoke in a soft, calm voice that sounded like the voice of reason and certainty.

Señor Doubter said to him, "Bon, I know you want to leave a legacy, but look at the hundred things you have written down already. How can we accomplish these tasks? Look, it's great to have dreams. I would love for us to go down in the history books as a great adventurer, but what happens if we fail? Let's be real here. We could die. Now, where does that leave Theresa and the kids?"

Captain Bon was now listening intently. There was nothing he loved more than Theresa and his kids. Theresa and his kids were his life, and bringing pain to them wasn't something he could bear.

Señor Doubter went on in his calm voice, "How will you pay your bills over the next six months to a year while you go off and play this game? Will Theresa have to support you and take from the money the both of you have put aside for retirement? How is that fair to her? She has worked so hard over the years."

His words raised doubt in Captain Bon. The words brought images of his family crying because he had died on the adventure. Tears welled up in his eyes at the images in his head. Maybe he was selfish. After all, how bad did he want this dream?

Looking down at the road map of things he would need to accomplish only stirred more doubt in him. There were so many things he would need to do to get to the starting point, and then it was still possible that he would fail.

All these thoughts ran through his mind, and it was just too much for him to handle. He had to get away and clear his mind. He knew he had to somehow push Señor Doubter out for a little while if only to gain a different perspective on the situation. Captain Bon decided he would put his list aside and go for a walk at the park near his home.

WHAT CAPTAIN BON LEARNED ABOUT DREAMS

Captain Bon learned that we must build our dreams in our minds and bodies. Our dreams must become real in us before they have a chance to become real in the physical world. Dreams are the start of a successful plan. We must build the desire for our dreams, but not just as preferences. It must become a must-have or a need for your life.

You see, most people state their dreams as preferences. They say, "I would like to have that car." Or they say, "I would like to start my own company." These are preference statements and will never call anyone to action. Once you turn your dream from a preference to a must-have, you will have what you want. It's that simple.

The change seems simple, and that's why most people miss it; however, the change is huge in your mind. The mind only understands what it is programmed to understand. When you state loose preferences, it just ignores them. It may use them to give you a little daydreaming fun, but it will not help you find a way to achieve your dreams.

Conversely, when you make the decision that you will realize the dream, you cut off all roads away except the road to success. Now I know many of you are thinking that this isn't true. I am here to tell you as many have before: it is all true. You can find a way to achieve your dream if you are focused on achieving your dream. It can't be a preference. It has to be a must-have. Once you decide it is a must-have, you will build the desire to keep it inside of you. Once you have done these two things, you will start finding people and systems that you can use to achieve your dreams.

I want you to take a second and think about Thomas Edison. Thomas Edison was a man who had a dream of inventing the light bulb to light the world. Light bulbs already existed, but they didn't last long. He was trying to invent something that was not in the world. He was trying to invent the bulb that could be powered by electricity but would not burn out in one use.

Now he understood the technology that came before his invention and why it did not last, so that gave him a start. He had built his dream of inventing the long-lasting light bulb into a desire that consumed him. It was all he focused on achieving. Did he succeed in creating the light bulb on the first try? No, he didn't even succeed on the one-hundredth attempt. But he learned each time and changed his approach. He didn't give up and say, "I've tried everything." He learned and built the dream stronger.

If you know anything about Edison and the invention of the light bulb, you most likely heard that it took more than a thousand failures before he succeeded. Now that's believing in a dream. That's believing in yourself. We all have that determination in us, but we have allowed doubt and excuses to take the determination away.

You may not succeed the first time you go after your dream. That's okay. Look at what went wrong, learn from it, build your dream and desire stronger, and go out and get it. I promise that if you want it badly enough, given enough time and persistence, you can have your dream.

Captain Bon also found that he would need to set a timeline. We must assign deadlines to accomplish our dreams. Now the dream may not be fully realized until ten years from now, but we must set a date. Your mind must have a timeline to associate with your dream. If not, then your dream will stay just that, a dream. It will never become a reality.

When you set a timeline with dates of deliverables, it holds your mind accountable and helps you with solutions. It also helps you focus on physical achievement. Your subconscious mind is working behind the scene, developing solutions to the roadblocks between you and your dream. Your subconscious is counting the days till your appointed date, and it knows when it must have a solution. If you gain the aid of your subconscious mind, it will help you with the needed solution, but you must set firm dates.

You can do this by looking at your plan and setting milestone dates. The dates shouldn't be arbitrary. They need to be realistic. If your dream was to walk on Mars and you are just starting planning, you wouldn't set a date of a year from now to arrive on Mars. Your subconscious mind would understand that this date wasn't realistic and would refuse to help. But now if you set a date of walking on Mars ten years from now, you could obtain that goal, and your subconscious mind would join in to help.

Another reason to set dates is to evaluate your progress in meeting the deadline. It will help you gain the needed willpower to keep moving forward. It will also help you determine the progress you have made. If your dream is to write a novel that must be ninety thousand words, you can look back after just a week and see how many words a day you have written. If you have done seven thousand words in seven days, you know it should take a total of ninety days to complete. If your due date is only sixty days out, then you know you must push it. But if you have written fourteen thousand words in seven days, you know you only need a total time of forty-five days and can push up your delivery date.

You can see from the previous paragraph how measuring can keep you motivated. You get to see your progress in real time, and that will help you gain your subconscious mind's help. Your momentum is like a snowball. If you get it rolling down a hill, it will grow and grow, but if you stop it in one place, it will melt until there is nothing left.

Having set dates and adjusting them as needed will help you reach your goals, and it will do it with a lot of force. Not setting deliverable dates will only compel you to come up with excuses so that you can take the day off and be lazy. Remember, things that are measured get done.

I want to share a little about my dream. I started this book about five years ago after I had a dream to help people. I didn't care so much about money or fame, though everyone wanted both. I wanted to help people. I had learned how to be successful, and I wanted to share how I used these principles to get where I was in life.

I spent about three months writing and putting what I had learned and what had worked for me on paper. Then I stopped. I allowed life to get in my way. I allowed my dreams to slip away. It nagged at me over the five years. I would write a few paragraphs sometimes; however, I never really reignited my fire, not unlike my character, Captain Bon.

After reading a book by Chris Fox titled *5,000 Words Per Hour: Write Faster, Write Smarter*, I realized I had abandoned my dream because I wasn't writing daily. (By the way, if you want to be a writer, Fox's book is a must-read.) I understood that it was about getting in the habit of putting words on paper each day. It wasn't about anything other than that. Some days it was editing, some days it was laying out the next section, but all days were about putting words on paper. It had to become a habit; I focused on it daily with no excuses. It didn't matter whether I wrote five thousand words today and tomorrow I wrote two hundred. It was about staying in the habit.

But I already knew all these things. So why wasn't I doing them? Well, it seemed that I didn't put the time aside to focus on my writing and that I hadn't made it into deliberate practice. These were two important parts that were missing. So I decided that for the next twenty-one days, I would set my alarm to get up at five in the morning and write. I would make it a deliberate practice, and I would get feedback daily through friends and family on what I wrote that day.

The day before I started, I sat down and thought about how it would feel to finish and publish this book. I even saw myself at a book signing. I could see the cover with the artwork, title, and my name. I turned the book over and saw a picture of me next to an author's bio. It was real. I had made it real in my mind.

When I awoke the next morning, I wasn't someone who was writing. I was a writer. I had the book published. Writing for the next twenty-one days wasn't easy. I hated to get up at five o'clock every morning, but it became easier. It even became something I looked forward to doing. Each day I pushed myself to write more and more, and around day twelve, the story was developing. The development of the story helped me get in front of my laptop and write more.

Knowing I needed feedback on my writing so that I could get better and solidify my habit, I asked a couple of friends if I could send them what I had written each day to read. They agreed and promised to give me honest feedback. These friends don't want to hurt me, but they do want to see me succeed. They provided me with constructive criticism that was vital to doing my best work. They became my mastermind group for this book. Their constructive criticism helped me create a book I couldn't have written alone. And this was a daily process. If I needed to make changes, I could make them that day.

Once the twenty-one days were over, I couldn't believe how my story had developed and how many words and pages I had written. In just twenty-one days, I had gone from twenty thousand words to more than fifty-two thousand words. But the greatest thing I had was the feeling of success. Now the book wasn't complete, but I was more than three-quarters done. I was also proud that I had come up with the story of Captain Bon to help portray the principles.

It still amazes me that I had learned and understood the principles, but even while teaching them, I missed using them on some of my dreams. I have a life that most people would dream of having. I have everything a man could want—great kids and a wife who is the love of my life. We have our dream house, and we take trips all over the world. But even though I have all these things and could be content, I still have dreams to fulfill. These principles have helped me fulfill many dreams and will help me fulfill the dream of publishing this book and hopefully help others fulfill their dreams too.

Always remember that memories are what we are and dreams are what we can become.

DESIRE

CAPTAIN BON'S SINCERE DESIRE TO BE REMEMBERED

As Captain Bon walked through the trails to clear his mind of Señor Doubter, he went through his dream. He looked at the dream and considered his sincere desire. What was he after? What would keep him up late at night working? What would carry him through the rough waters to come? What would keep Señor Doubter's voice from derailing him? He knew he had to understand what the one thing in this adventure for him was that nothing else in life would give him. So what was it?

It was the need to be remembered. Bon asked himself, "When my life is over, what do I want?" He wanted to be remembered throughout time and to have his name written in history books. That was the one desire that would push him to achieve his dream.

He would use this desire to build a fire in himself. It would become his life raft in the troubled waters of the river. It would be the one thing he held on to no matter what else he lost. The desire to be remembered was the strongest desire he had in his life. He knew he would leave a legacy for being a good husband and father, but that memory would fade from the world in only a generation or two; however, being a successful explorer could last forever. Leaving a legacy as an explorer was what he wanted more than anything else in his life.

He also knew that this was a desire that others would share with him. It would be a way to give them something in return for their help. They may not help him so that he could become famous, but they would do it so that they could become famous. This one desire aligned with Captain Bon's system. It would stand the test of his questions, and it was something he could give others.

With the thought of his true desire blazing in his body, Captain Bon hurried from the park to his home office. His feelings now supported him and had pushed Señor Doubter out. By finally understanding what he wanted, the plan seemed to be writing itself. He could see now how he would approach potential team members and ask them to join him. He now understood how to convince financial supporters to put up the capital needed to accomplish the adventure. It was all about being remembered throughout time.

Captain Bon now knew how to sell the adventure. It was so simple that he had missed it. Others would help him for the same reason he wanted to accomplish his dream. It would be to leave a legacy. Even if for only a short period, people would know who he and the others were and what they had accomplished.

Arriving at his office, he sat down and turned on his computer. The words of the plan flowed out of him. The desire to leave his legacy drove him. He was able to write most of his plan and the presentations in only four hours. The four hours passed so fast that Captain Bon hadn't even noticed the time. It wasn't until Theresa walked in and asked if he was hungry and what they should do for dinner.

Captain Bon looked up at his wife with the most joyful look she had seen in years.

"Bon, why are you so excited?" she asked.

"I know how to do it," he said.

"Do what?"

"How to accomplish the adventure to Mount La Felicidad."

"Really? That's great. What finally got you past the barricade?" she asked.

"I figured out what I want and the why behind my dream."

"Well, I thought you already knew the why behind taking the adventure."

"And what do you think my why is, my sweet wife?" he asked her.

"Well, that's easy. You want to leave a legacy of something great. We all know that's your why."

"Hmmm. It's great that everyone knew it before me!"

"Don't be upset, my love," she said. "You are a little slow!"

"You know you're not as funny as you think you are."

"Really? I think I'm pretty funny."

"Yes, my dear, you are funny, but not as funny as you are beautiful," he said.

"Well, thank you so much. Now, are you ready to eat?"

"Yeah, let me put these papers away, and I will meet you in five minutes."

"Okay," she said. "See you there."

WHAT IS DESIRE?

People get desire and dream confused and think they are the same. Desires and dreams are different. Dreams involve multiple people, while desire is purely about oneself. The distinction is important and one that must be understood for the principles to work for you. You must understand that it is your desire that will get you to your dream.

We will do a thousand times more for ourselves than we will do for others. That's the truth. Now many people will go out of their way to help others, but if they have a burning desire, they will go further for themselves. We spoke about it earlier, but let's talk a little more about why you will do more for yourself than others.

You get the benefit. It's oversimplified, but anything you do, you do for some payback. If you help others, it's because you get to feel better about yourself or you like how people see you when you help them. If you build a company and employ a thousand people, it's about the feeling you get from succeeding in building the company and not that you have given people a place to earn a living. Even having children falls into this theory. If you have children and raise them to be successful in the world, it's not all about the children. It's about your accomplishment as a parent.

I know many of you may not agree with these statements. As human beings, we want to think of ourselves as givers and not takers, especially when it comes to our children. But the deep truth is that if you didn't get something, you wouldn't do the work. We are all lazy, and the reward must outweigh the work. It's just that simple. So use it. Use your selfish trait to help propel you in the process of accomplishing your dream. I promise you will help others along the way, or at least you should if you fulfill one of their needs.

Now we need to talk about not using people and throwing them away to get to your dreams. People are our most valuable resource to get to our dreams and should be treated as such. You will cross paths with many people in your life, and you should treat them with the respect and courtesy that you would like someone to treat you. Stepping on people to get what you want and leaving them in the mud is not profitable to anyone.

You will start an adventure with some people but not finish the adventure with them, and that's okay. There will be people you only need for a brief time. That's okay. And there will be people you can't work with for one reason or another, and that's okay too. But through it all, treat all people you meet as valued assets. The better you treat others, the better you will be treated. When you want to say or ask anyone for something, first ask yourself, "Will this hurt or benefit this person?" If it hurts that person, don't do it. There is no reason to hurt people. If it benefits the person as well, go forward.

Now we all know life is not that black and white. It's easy to say that we shouldn't do something if it hurts someone or move ahead with the plan if it benefits someone, but often it may fall in the middle ground. When you're not sure if it will hurt or benefit a person, think about the other question we learned, What's in it for him or her? Asking this question will help with your decision to proceed or not.

The more you become known as the person who cares for people, the more you will attract people. John Maxwell has a saying that sums it up well. John Maxwell says, "People don't care what you know until they know you care." You can see how this helps with gaining people's help. But I turn the saying around and ask, "How do I care for people so that they care to know me?" Either one of these questions will lead you to the result that assures you treat people as assets.

Remember that what you do for others, you are doing for yourself. The universe has a way of bringing back to you what you put out there. The energy you put out is part of the law of attraction. If you send out negative waves into the universe by using people, that will eventually come back to you. You may not see it until you are very old, but I promise it will come back.

Some call it karma; others look to the Bible passage that says, "Whatever a man soweth, that shall he also reap." Whatever the name, it is all the same. If you put good out into the world, good will return to you. If you put negative actions into the universe, negative actions will eventually come back to you.

WHAT'S YOUR DESIRE?

What is your desire? What does it mean to you? Is it a big house in the country, a beautiful mate in life, a bodybuilder's body, a Porsche, or wisdom? Only you can decide. But is it the desire of your heart or just an object you can and will get if you go after your true-life desire? Many people focus so hard on the material things in life that they miss their earnest desires as they chase the material ones. All of us at one time or another are guilty of not considering our hearts' sincere desires. We spend too much time looking at what our loved ones, society, or the world thinks our desires should be.

The advertising industry is the best at doing this. Advertisement agents do it so cleverly that we don't even notice it happening. They play the music that comforts us or show us pictures that make our minds want the products (even if they do not show the products) and cause the subconscious mind to associate the products with being better people. These mind games show a true genius! Just listen to some of the drug advertisements. As the music plays and the beautiful pictures roll, they are quietly telling you that this drug may kill you. But they are so pleasant and inviting in their approach that we go to our doctors and ask for the drugs. Now if advertisers can do this to you, then why would you think you couldn't do the same thing to get your sincere desire?

Also, what many people do is concentrate on what they *do not* desire in life. And then wonder why it keeps coming to them. They forget about the law of attraction, or they think they are special and can outwit the law. They are so focused on what they don't want, that they have used all their energy on what they don't want. They waste their time, and they still get what they didn't want out of life. Consider the times when people focus on their debt. Now you may say, "But I am focused on getting out of debt." The person is still focusing on their debt, and by the law of attraction, the universe will bring you more debt. Do not focus on your debt. Set up a debt repayment program and forget about your debt. Then take the time you have been spending on focusing on getting out of debt to focus on how you can earn more money. Focusing on earning more will be a better use of your time and energy.

Now for those who would say there is no true proof of the law of attraction, a higher intelligence, or God, I ask, "What good can come of focusing all your energy on what you do not want in your life?" Most misunderstand this. You are focusing on the problem instead of focusing on workable solutions to your problems.

If you look at the richest people in the world, you will find they are problem solvers. They do not put their energy into worrying about the problem or what caused it. They put their energy and brainpower into finding the solutions. And they get paid for this so-called talent. So why not model your life and the way you use your energy after the successful people and not the unsuccessful ones? *Again, the choice is yours to make.* After all, a firing squad won't show up at your door if you choose to focus your energy on the problem.

HOW TO GET THAT DESIRE

So how do we go after our desires? The system you see in the following section will help you cement the desire in your subconscious mind. Many people will not admit to using this system or may not realize they have used it to become successful. But rest assured that they have used it in part or whole. The system is not a complicated system, but it will take a little faith and dedication of time on your part.

1. Get yourself in a peak state of mind—one filled with the possibilities available to you and with the feelings of self-love and faith in your ability to succeed. You can do so by using your past success as an anchor to gain motivation.
2. Fix in your mind the exact desire that you want to receive or accomplish.
3. Determine what you will give in return to gain your desire. As with anything in life, you have to give to get. Whether it is your time, a special service you have to offer, a specialized knowledge you possess, or your money, you will have to decide what you are willing to give up to get what you want.
4. Set a definite date by when you will achieve your desire.
5. Create a definite plan on how you will get your desire. Begin working on it at once. Do not wait until you have all the answers. If you wait, you will never have all the answers. If you start your plan and have faith in yourself and the universe, the parts of your plan will come to you. Be on the watch for opening doors and knowledge the universe will provide to you. These opportunities

will come to you. The only problem in most people's lives is that they think that their own will or thoughts must bring success instead of the will and thoughts of the universe.

6. Write out a clear, concise statement of your desire, what you will give in return, a definite date, and your plan. After you have done this, sign the statement at the bottom. By signing your statement, it will help in creating ownership of your statement.

7. Read your statement with a "feeling of already having your desire" at least twice daily, preferably in the morning before you start your day and at night before you go to sleep. More important than just reading the statement is the feeling of the specific desire. See in your mind what you will do as you travel to your desire. Who will be on the trip with you? So often people fail at this point because they reason that if they did not feel the desire, they will not be let down or become failures.

If you take these massive action steps in this system and use them to feel you have acquired your desire, you will find a way to gain your desire through yourself and the universe. The path will be laid out in front of you for the next step.

Just be cautious not to give up on yourself or the universe. Some desires are like a mushroom and will grow overnight, while others are like the great oak tree and may require twenty years to blossom. So many have given up one step short of the goal they were after. At that moment, the universe's seed may be about to break ground, but then you give up and say, "This does not work." Then the universe pulls the flower back into the seed. You have changed the desire that you asked the universe for, and it will give you your desire. It does not care that it was not your sincere desire. All the universe knows is the desire saying with feeling, "This does not work."

Again, for those that do not believe in a higher intelligence, once you let doubt into your mind about your ability to accomplish what you set out to do, it becomes a downward spiral—one that will surely not take you where you want to go in life but to the place you feared you would go.

DECISION

CAPTAIN BON'S TURNING POINT IN LIFE

Captain Bon's life had now changed, but he knew he wasn't yet committed. He had his dream and had put feeling behind it. He could see it happening. He understood that his most sincere desire was to leave a legacy and that this desire would resonate with others. He had used a system to cement the desire in his subconscious mind. But something was missing. He hadn't yet cut off all other options. Now was when he made a true-life decision.

He decided that he would become the adventurer who traveled through the river to Mount La Felicidad no matter what anyone else said or thought of him. He decided to act and create a plan to accomplish his dream. At this moment, his life changed. It wasn't that he knew exactly how he would do it, but there was no other path for him now. He could and most probably would fail along the way. It may take a hundred, maybe a thousand attempts, but he would fulfill his dream. He wouldn't abandon his dream because he had finally decided to have what he wanted most in life.

With this defined decision, Captain Bon began to write out his plan to accomplish his dream of traveling the river to Mount La Felicidad. He started what would be a complex plan by working backward from arriving at the mountain. At this point, he only wrote down the major points. He knew he would have to go into more detail later, but for now, this was action. It was the action that came from making a true decision.

Captain Bon also knew he needed to set a timeline to achieve his dream. He understood that he was moving toward attaining his dream and desire by starting his plan, but he needed to have specific dates. With specific dates to have the plan together, find a mentor, begin a mastermind group, gather a team, find financial backers, and embark on the adventure, his mind would help him deliver his dream.

To set this timeline, Captain Bon worked backward from when he would set out on the river to Mount La Felicidad. His journey would begin on the river fourteen months from this day. He felt that this was ample time to put all the other parts together.

He would also set dates for the other parts so that he had something to hold himself to and help himself stay motivated. He knew in the back of his mind that he might be off about some of the dates, but having these dates as his goal and convincing himself that he had no other options would force his mind to find a solution to achieve the dates.

He also knew that he had to have dates to keep the other people on the adventure with him focused. With these dates circled on a calendar, everyone would have goals to meet. They would add other dates for smaller deliverables, but these were the main dates that had to be achieved to reach the river and start the adventure in only fourteen months.

TRUE DECISIONS

What are the decisions? I have heard the answer put a million different ways. A decision is a choice/direction made in the mind that cuts off any other thought/direction on the subject. However, 96 percent of the people in the world don't define this as a decision. A decision to most is adopting an "I will try it" attitude or what most like to call a preference decision. Preference decision is not a true decision. Again, it is just a preference if the person does not have to work hard to make it happen.

Think back in your life when you were finally at the point with someone or something when you said to yourself, "Never again." If you made a true decision, then you would never do that again. If you went back and did it again after your so-called decision, then you made a preference decision. We have all made both types of decisions. Determining whether it was a life decision or a preference decision involves your beliefs and values. You must evaluate whether the decision aligned with or contradicted your beliefs and values.

Now at this point, you may doubt this to be true, but if the decisions we make are in contradiction to our beliefs and values, they will never take hold. We must look and see if we need to change the courses of our lives by changing our beliefs and values. Then we can determine if we want to forgo our decision and not change our lives. You see, when you make a life decision or even a preference decision, your mind either consciously or subconsciously reviews your beliefs and values to see if the decision is in line with them. Some decisions will only be preference decisions. Unless the decision comes because of great pain, your values and beliefs will override any decisions that are not in line with them. You see, the decision will conflict with the beliefs and values you have already programmed into your mind.

There's good news! Now you know when you cannot seem to decide on something. So too, you can change your beliefs and values by using pain and imagination. Again, as we have said previously, we can change anything that resides in our mind to benefit us. The power and knowledge are in you.

In later chapters, you will learn the techniques for changing your beliefs and values to those that propel you through the decisions on the river of life instead of ones that send you to the waterfalls.

Most people cannot even make a preference decision because of procrastination. They tell themselves (or lie to themselves) that no decision needs to be made, that the problem will take care of itself. They do this for many reasons (e.g., fears of looking stupid, being a failure, loss of love, etc.). But what they are doing is procrastinating and delaying the journey down the river of life toward their desires. Their fears are not real. They are made up in the people's minds, and they grow stronger because of the feelings they put behind their fears. The fears become real, and then the people procrastinate on making that life decision that will change their lives.

We need to make our own decisions in life and stop letting others make our decisions for us. Making our decisions is the only way to a wealthy life. Who in the world knows more about what you want better than you do? Then why trust the most important decisions you must make to others?

Some people think that others know what's best for them. It doesn't matter how much they care for you—whether parents or spouses. They can't know how you truly feel about anything. Even if you explained your feelings to a tee, they still wouldn't understand.

They may have more knowledge on the subject, and they may have more life experience. Use them as advisers, but don't allow them to make the decisions for you. That's your job. If the decision you make turns out to be good or bad, it still needs to be your decision. If it's a wrong decision, then learn from it. After all, you have an emotional connection with your decision, and you can learn why you felt the emotions you felt from the wrong decision.

When many of us are young, we make bad decisions with credit cards. We go out and charge up to our limits and then have trouble paying them back. Why do we do this? Well, it feels good to live like the Joneses for whatever time we can. But then the credit card bills come in, and we must struggle to pay them.

If you look at this from the outside, you would think yourself crazy. But that's just how we as humans learn. We make unwise decisions. Then those decisions become mistakes. Then we must face the consequences of those decisions. Finally, we work through the consequences.

If we are smart, between facing the consequences and working through them, we step outside of ourselves and see what happened. We evaluate what we did wrong and why it went so wrong. We also evaluate the feelings that lead us to the decision (chasing pleasure or avoiding pain). And then we evaluate the feelings of the consequences (feeling pleasure or feeling pain).

If we make this evaluation, we should learn. I say *should* because sometimes we miss part of the feeling portion and end up not fixing the why. Looking at the feelings is important. All decisions have feelings tied to them. Feelings are how we create habits. If you are not evaluating your feelings about a decision and changing them when needed, you will not change the habit. And remember, habits don't go away. They just lay dormant until you trigger them.

If we go back to our example of the overspending on credit cards, what feelings do we need to change so that we don't make the same mistake again? Well, we had the feeling of accomplishment that came with having the card. We got a greater feeling of accomplishment when we bought a bunch of material items. Now that's a great feeling, but it would be a better feeling if we weren't struggling later.

Now we need to look at the feeling of struggling to pay off the credit cards. We are nervous that creditors will sue us. We have anxiety that we can't meet our obligations. We worry how people will look at us if we don't meet the obligation and must file for bankruptcy. On top of all that, we're hiding the situation from family and friends.

With the understanding of the pleasure we received at the start and the pain it created after, we can change our habit. Remember, you will work harder to avoid pain than to gain pleasure. Now you can use the pain that the overspending caused to change how you look at using credit cards.

As you are making decisions to get your desire and realize your ultimate dream, remember to take time and look at what you are doing right and wrong. Learn from both good and bad decisions. Taking time out to review doesn't have to take days or weeks. You can do it in a few minutes or an hour. But do the work and evaluate the decision. Learn from both your successful decisions and the decisions that were failures.

I keep a notebook with a list of the decisions I make when it comes to planning or going after one of my desires. It has been helpful to me to learn and make corrections. Do I write down every decision? No, but I write down as many as I can. If I run into issues and look back and do not see the decision written down, I add it. I'm not sure when I got into this habit, but it has become invaluable to me.

Find your system to review your decisions or use mine. Whatever you use doesn't matter. Just evaluate your decisions. Like a scientist that is working on an experiment, you must take notes. How will you know where you went wrong without them?

In the end, if you let others make your decisions, you will not get to the place where you want to go. You will not be happy, and you will have missed out on the fun part of life—the journey! If the decisions are yours and they do not work out, what does it matter? Learn from the experience, change your approach, and make another decision to go forward. In other words, pick yourself up, dust yourself off, and get your butt moving forward. You have not failed. You have received an education. Now go out and create your dream, find your desire, and make decisions!

THE PITFALL PRINCIPLE TO DREAMS DESIRE, AND DECISIONS

Captain Bon spent most of his life trapped in the success pitfalls principle of accepting mediocrity and what life gave him. Bon struggled with indecision. Most of the time, he wasn't stuck between two decisions and ended up picking the wrong one. He just never made a decision that would change his life.

Like most people, Captain Bon just accepted what came to him. He thought dreams and desires were not for people like him. People who reached their desires were different from him in some way. They weren't going to allow the fear of failure to stand in the way of achieving their dreams. They pushed through the fears by deciding to have their deepest desires and created plans to achieve those desires.

When they did fail—and they did—they analyzed what did and didn't work so that they could adjust the plan and move forward again. Successful people didn't give up and say, "I can never do this." They kept their attitude positive and looked for solutions to succeed.

Now sometimes the solution meant recruiting others that could help with skills they didn't possess, and other times, it was just taking a different path than they had taken before. It depended on what they found didn't work from the first attempt and being honest with themselves.

Captain Bon realized that mediocrity had held him back for most of his life, but no more. He had educated himself through the books he had read about others' success, and he now understood how they had succeeded. He realized he had to have a plan that he owned to succeed. He would have to write his plan down step-by-step and create a timeline for the dates when he should complete each step. Then he would work toward his dream each day. Some days would produce greater results than others, but that wasn't the point. The point was to keep moving forward to the next milestone on the timeline.

The timeline would help keep him accountable so that he could attain his dream. He'd also be accountable to the others who were on the adventure with him. He knew there would be times when he would want to give up or when he wouldn't believe he could accomplish his dream. He would have to use the accomplishments to reassure himself he could indeed accomplish the adventure. It wouldn't be easy, but he thought that nothing worth having was ever really easy.

Thinking back over the biography of Bill Gates he had read, it struck him how everyone thought Gates was an overnight success with Microsoft. They hadn't realized that Gates had been working toward creating the Microsoft programming for a lifetime. They didn't understand that he had been logging time on computers since he was a teenager. They could only see the man who was now so rich and successful. With the thought of Gates and others who had succeeded, Captain Bon understood that it is not what we do in one day that makes us successful but what we do every day. To stop living a life of mediocrity and attain your dreams, you must work daily.

With this realization, Captain Bon took a hard look at his life and decided that he couldn't live like this anymore. He had to chase his dreams. He had to realize his destiny. He finally made a true decision, and by doing so, he cut mediocrity out of his life. No longer would he accept whatever came. He would make what would come. His life would now be what he made of it and not what anyone else chose for him.

Captain Bon knew that he would have to stay diligent in his system. He had many habits he would have to change, and some wouldn't be easy to alter. It would take a lot of work, and he would have to stretch himself beyond what he had done before.

Some days would test his will and determination. But he would have to push through if he wanted to realize his dream of making it to Mount La Felicidad. Doing this would take help, but he knew some people wanted the same dream he wanted and would help him get to his dream.

He also knew many people wouldn't support him, and others would want to see him fail; however, he couldn't worry himself with these people. He would do what he could to avoid confrontation with them, but he wouldn't back down either. He would objectively listen to them because he knew that what they had to say could contain knowledge or warnings. But he wouldn't allow them to kill his dream.

Captain Bon also knew that he needed help with decisions. He would need others involved with the adventurer who could make decisions. If he wanted to accomplish the adventure, he wouldn't be able to make every decision. That would take up too much of his time. Thinking through such things as white-water rafting was not in his wheelhouse. He would need someone with those skills who could make decisions. There were many other parts to the adventure that would only waste his time if he used his decision-making power on them. He knew that with an adventure of this size, they would have to decide on more than a million activities. If he tried to make each one, he would be sixty years old before he started the adventure.

The required work brought other thoughts to his mind. Could he trust these people to make the right decisions? Would a bad decision derail the entire adventure? Going over it in his mind, he determined that most organizations make more than a thousand decisions a day. And of the decisions made, the CEO does not make 99 percent of the decisions. Now the CEO may have input on 5 percent of these; however, he has to trust but also inspect the decisions of his or her people. If someone made a bad decision then they correct it, it becomes a learning opportunity. The company keeps pushing forward, and the CEO stays focused on the main 1 percent of decisions that needs his or her attention.

Captain Bon realized if he didn't allow the people on the adventure with him to make the decisions or if he tried to make every decision, the adventure would be doomed. He and his dream would get dragged down by the actions of daily activities. He had to be the captain and guide the ship. He had to trust the people on the adventure with him to make these decisions while he kept his eyes on the larger picture and made the decisions that were truly vital to the survival of the adventure.

Allowing others to make the decisions was all unfamiliar territory to Captain Bon, and his self-confidence still wasn't very high; however, he knew he could work through this fear and get to his dream. His reason and his imagination were his driving forces now. That was the best driving force anyone could have, and he had it.

WHAT YOU NEED TO KNOW ABOUT THIS SUCCESS PITFALLS PRINCIPLE

What you have in life today came from your decisions or lack of decisions. If your life isn't what you dreamed of as a child, it's because you chose to take the road of mediocrity. You may blame others for where you are in life, but you're just hiding behind excuses.

Life is what we make it. It may be demanding work to have more, but it isn't that much more work. You think it is because you are looking at it from the wrong perspective. You are looking at it as a big picture and not the small decisions that it takes to change your life.

If you find what you really desire and also find the why behind that desire, you are starting down the road out of mediocrity. Now you need to make the decision that will cut off every other option. Both small and large decisions get you where you want to be. Some of the decisions will not work out, and you will fail. If that's the case, decide to try one more time.

One thing you need to understand about the decision is that you don't have time in life to make every decision. Now that may seem to contradict what was said earlier, but it doesn't. People get confused in this area. They believe that they are moving forward if they are making every decision. That isn't the case. Busy work does not equal productive work. Busy equals lazy.

The decisions we are talking about are the decisions that change your life or the world. Sitting at your desk and reading every email or getting involved in every conversation will not change your life. It will only keep you busy. You need to focus your decision-making power on the important decisions that only you can make. Again, you may think that you need to make every decision, but that isn't the case.

Have you ever wondered why people like Steve Jobs or Mark Zuckerberg wore the same type and style of clothes each day? It's because they understand that we only have so much decision-making power in a day, and they didn't want to waste that thinking power on something as unimportant as the clothing they would wear each day.

To illustrate this point, I want you to think of a situation such as the death of a loved one. If you haven't gone through this experience, I'm sure you know people who have and can use their experiences for the exercise. Imagine all the decisions people had to make in just a day or two—who to call and tell, setting up the funeral, what clothing to put your loved one in for the last time, what to wear, what food to serve if you should serve food, and the list goes on and on. You may be making all these decisions. If so, how drained are you at the end of the day? Could you make a life decision at the end of this day? No, you couldn't. None of us could. Many people hide in their bedrooms and feel exhausted. You have used all your energy to make decisions, and you have no energy left to even function.

Now I'm not saying that you should avoid decisions such as these during a time like this. I'm saying you do not have to make all the decisions. I'm sure other family members can help and can make many of these decisions for you. They may not make the decision that you would make, but that doesn't make the decision wrong. It's just different. Of course, there are some decisions that only you should make. Make those decisions and leave the rest to someone else. Save some of your energy so that you can get through the day. You never know when that really important decision will come up, and you'll need the energy. Just as a champion sprinter keeps a little energy stored for the end of the race, you need to keep some of your decision-making energy stored for the end of the day.

The bottom line is that we have to make decisions to get to where we want to go in life. Just make sure they are the important decisions and don't accept what comes in life again. Make the life you want through your dreams, desires, and decisions.

CHAPTER 7

IMAGINATION
THE GREATEST GUIDE IN THE UNIVERSE AT YOUR DISPOSAL

CAPTION BON THINKS OVER HIS journey on the river and his destination to Mount La Felicidad. Through his mind and his notes on paper, he has identified his goals for the trip and the rewards of reaching Mount La Felicidad. He thinks about the happiness he will have when he reaches his goal. He also thinks about the twist in the river and the sights he is sure to see along the way, the views he will behold, and the exotic animals he will see for the first time. The thoughts brought a smile to his face. What an adventure he and his two partners Kelly and Aaron will find. What fun they will have and the challenges that will bring them closer as friends and partners.

As he is going through all the different possibilities, fear creeps into his mind. What if they smash the boat on the rocks in the middle of this vast jungle around the river? What if they underestimate the food they need? So many things could go wrong on this adventure, and if they did, it wouldn't only be his life at risk. He would also be risking the lives of his two partners.

Now he was willing to play with his own life. Well, not really. But was he willing to play with the lives of Aaron and Kelly? He wondered if they had the same thoughts and fears as he did. He knew they had talked over the possibilities of destruction and failure as a group. But did they have the same fears?

Then Bon thought, *This is my imagination, and it's not reality. I can make my imagination what I want it to be, and I can make it come true. Sure, I need to be cautious, and I need to plan this adventure out. But there is no way that I can know all the traps that lay out there on the river. Nor could Kelly and Aaron. We will have to prepare for the unknown the best we can. If we face something that we can't prepare for, such as the boat smashing on the rock, we will have to figure out our best plan B.* There was no way he could bring a second boat with him, or could he?

He then used his imagination to see the boat smashing on the rocks and sinking. What could they save? What should they try to save first? Well, that was easy. They needed to save as much of the food and water as they could gather.

What next? What else could he save? They could save the gun they would have with them, the ammunition for the gun, and maybe their sleeping bags and the tent. The more he imagined how to save things, the more he realized he could use his imagination to prepare better for disaster.

If he could do this, then why couldn't Kelly and Aaron do the same thing? He realized that he needed them to work with their imaginations and write down their thoughts. The three of them could use what they wrote down to create an even better plan. Using your imagination was the key. Use your imagination and tap into the universe for the answers. Don't allow your imagination to create obstacles for your goals. After all, it was *your* imagination, and you could change the scene if you wanted. You could make it what you want it to be.

Captain Bon gathered up Kelly and Aaron, and he explained that they can use their imaginations to create solutions. He also told them that he wouldn't scorn or make fun of any solutions. It wasn't about what answers they thought up but that they used their imaginations. They had to put themselves outside of the problem they presently faced to find the solution. It seemed a little strange to his two partners, but they were willing to give it a shot.

Through the practice of this technique, Kelly, Aaron, and Captain Bon found many ways to solve the issues facing them along the river. They also had fun doing it. It turned a stressful situation into a game. They could now become heroes in their lives and save the day. It wasn't stressful anymore to face problems. It was fun.

Kelly said to the group after considering what would happen if an issue with the water arose, "Go figure. What could have been disasters is now a game." It changed the team's attitude toward solving problems. And as Aaron once said, "Using your imagination takes the pain out of facing problems."

WHAT CAPTAIN BON UNDERSTOOD ABOUT IMAGINATION

It was best said by Walt Disney, "It is fun to see your imagination come to reality." Our imaginations are the greatest guides we can use to get us through the river of life. While most people do use their imaginations and dream of better lives, they let their fears and lack of self-confidence stop them from going after their dreams. Many people allow their imaginations to create all the rocks that will sink their boats. They allow the fears to take hold and never move forward. It doesn't enter their minds that they could use their imaginations to create solutions to the problems or that they could use a mastermind group to help them solve the problems. They give up on the adventure before it begins.

None of us have all the answers or training to be successful from the start. But that shouldn't mean that you don't start. If your adventure is worthwhile, if the rewards you receive are in your mind, you can and will find a way. Yes, you will fall along the way, and yes, family and friends may think you are crazy. Many great people were thought of this way and nonetheless succeeded in what they were trying to do. When you start to worry that you don't know enough, think to yourself, *I will leap and grow my wings during the fall.*

You will grow your wings as you fall. You will learn from your mistakes. Now if you put the blame on the outside world and don't analyze what went wrong, you will never grow your wings, and you will be a bloody mess on the concrete of life. We all make mistakes, but it's what we learn from our mistakes that makes us successful and great. It's that simple. However, most would make it more complicated so that they have an excuse not to move forward.

As in anything, you will need help along the way. You will need to seek out experts in their fields to help you get to your goals. But you must listen to them, and then you must decide if their advice is the best course of action. Having a mastermind group to work with comes in handy to gain expert advice. Why do you think large corporations have a board of directors and not just a CEO? Why are the board members normally from different walks of life? It's because each of these people brings a different perspective and various skills to the group. Now, does that mean that if you have a mastermind group, you will have success? Not by a long shot. You could still fail. With a mastermind group, however, your chances of success are greatly increased.

You are probably thinking, *Where do I gather this group? How do I decide whom to ask?* Again, you need to leap and grow your wings as you fall. You may have to change people in your mastermind group as you go. You may have to add people. Some people may decide to leave the mastermind group. These are not things that should worry you. Nor should you worry what people will think of you for asking them to be a part of your mastermind group. Now you may have to explain what a mastermind group is to them. You can say it's a group of people who come together to solve problems like a think tank. If you put it this way and ask them to be a part of a think tank, they may think differently about the group. Everyone wants to be known as smart, and now you are telling them that you think they are smart. It's funny how our minds work. If we think we are smart, we *are* smart. If we think we are dumb, we *are* dumb.

You need to make the people feel smart and work with them to solve the problems on the adventure. Together, all of you will learn, and each of you will gain satisfaction from the accomplishments you achieve. Using each of your imaginations, you will have a greater adventure than you thought possible.

Now you may have to work with them to use their imaginations. You may have to *train* them to imagine how they can work through solutions to various issues that may come up during the adventure. You may even have to work with some of them to be open with their thoughts and solutions. Many people fear speaking up and revealing their thoughts because they think that others will judge them unless they have a *great* solution. You see this situation starting in grade school and lasting throughout life with many people. They allow their fears to stop them from sharing what they know or what they think the right answer is. This fear comes from the external laughs from others or internal thoughts they think others have. So that will be a habit you will have to help them fight through.

Therefore, you will have to put a stop to any criticism that may come to others in the group. If you allow criticism to creep into your mastermind group, you are allowing the worst danger to productivity to grow in your garden. Once criticism takes root in a mastermind group, it's hard to get positive things accomplished. If you see the weed of criticism growing in your group, pull it out and burn it. If it grows back again, do the same as you have before. Ridding the group of criticism is a must. If it keeps coming from the same member of the group, pull him or her out. You have a bad blueberry in a package of blueberries. How long does it take for that bad blueberry to cause all the other blueberries to become bad? If you pull it out when you first find it, the other blueberries will be fine and never become rotten. The action may seem harsh, but it must be this way. Sure, you will not be popular with the bad blueberry, but the others will give you more for being a leader.

You can use your imagination as a guide and strategic partner to navigate your river of life. It can be the greatest guide to your true desires. As you take action, your imagination can help you solve the problems along the way.

One of the most useful tools in problem-solving is in NLP (neurolinguistic programming). Teaching yourself to step outside of yourself when you come to a fork in the river of life and not put limits on what you could do. Though you did not know the path to take or the answer to your problem, you looked at the problem and asked yourself, "What would my hero do in this situation?" The question points you in the direction you will need to go. You see, you did not put any limits on what you could accomplish, and thus, you were able to look at it outside of yourself. In life, we seem to have an easier time believing that our heroes can do things we can't do. The truth is that we are a lot more resilient than any hero. Thinking this way is a good trick to use to get out of your way. In using your imagination, you could see the two paths as if you had already traveled them, and thus, you knew where they would take you.

Now you may say, "How can that work? I have not traveled that waterway. There is no way I will know if one side has a waterfall." That is the whole point of this exercise. As you imagine the path, you can look for the pitfalls, rocks, rapids, and other dangers that you need to avoid. At the same time, you can imagine the people who can help you along the way. Look at what you would do to avoid the rapids. (Maybe you would walk on the bank of the river.) Think through all the other obstacles to help you avoid the rapids.

LET'S LOOK AT HOW CAPTAIN BON AND HIS MASTERMIND TEAM WOULD ACCOMPLISH THIS.

Captain Bon, Aaron, and Kelly had been on the adventure for fifteen days when they came to a fork in the river. They checked their map, but it didn't show this fork. Which way should they go? They got together and discussed the situation as they always did when faced with a new problem. Each gave their thoughts about why the fork wasn't on their map. Bon thought that maybe it was just a small runoff and that it would lead to a dead end, but Kelly wanted to know which one led to the dead end. Aaron said that the map they had could be out of date and that a canal may have been dug to support one of the mining villages that had popped up in the last year. One of these branches could circle to the main river upstream. They couldn't be sure.

Captain Bon said to his group, "What would the adventurers from the past do? Our heroes, what would they do?" The group thought about it, and each spoke out; however, Captain Bon then said to them, "Let's use our imaginations and find what they would do." Again, each stopped and played the situation out in their minds, but this time, they were not themselves, they were their heroes. As they went through the situation, they could see their heroes working out the problem.

Kelly's hero was Joan of Arc, who had faced the English on the battlefield. She had been fighting the English, and now they had retreated. She had come to a fork in the road following their retreat and had to decide which way to go. She knew they had split up and had a bad feeling one group was circling back to attack her from the rear, but which group went which way? It was a hard decision to make. She decided to get information from her generals and trackers before proceeding. They advised her on the trails and the English's tactics. That was the answer. Find someone on the river to advise them on which way to go. Even if it cost some time to do so, taking the wrong fork would cost more time in the end, and they could encounter hidden dangers.

Aaron did the same in his imagination, except he was the explorer Marco Polo. He envisioned himself marching through the Alps, looking for a new land path to China. Marco Polo had to have come to many forks in his adventure. Aaron had read many books on Marco Polo and knew this to be true. What did Marco do when he found himself in these situations? Well, he did a few things. He consulted with his fellow explorers on what they thought was the best path. He sent riders ahead and kept the main explorer party in camp to rest until they could gather more information, and sometimes he sent explorers in both directions with a return time they had agreed on. These plans helped him prevent the team from wasting time and energy. That was the answer. Send one person ahead while the other two stayed and set up camp. After all, they could take the small raft and explore one of the options in the couple of hours it would take to set up the tents and all the other equipment. It would cost them a few hours extra today, but it could save them a full day tomorrow.

Captain Bon also considered the situation in his imagination. Now Captain Bon had special heroes in mind. His were Lewis and Clark. He thought about their adventure for President Jefferson to explore the territory of the Louisiana Purchase and to try to find a water route from Missouri to the Pacific Ocean. He knew they had faced great difficulties in their two years of exploring. They must have come to this same sort of decision many times. How had they done it? Captain Bon considered this in his imagination and thought of himself not as Lewis or Clark but as one of the explorers with them. Watching each of their decisions could give him a clue about what to do in their present situation.

So how had Lewis and Clark explored such a vast land? How did they decide which direction to go? It came to him how they did it. They used the resources they had come across on the trip, including the native tribes. They asked about the road ahead as they passed through. They had scouts they would send ahead to look for the best path to take.

Then he realized that their team had not asked enough questions during their previous stops with the locals. Not asking more questions was a mistake he would not make again. But should they backtrack and ask questions now? Returning to the last village would mean losing two days. No, that wasn't the best plan, but there was a second option. They could send someone ahead to explore one side of the branch in the fork. One of them could quickly look this evening as the other two made camp.

Our three adventurers talked it over and decided to send someone ahead to investigate which path would be best; this was the best option they had. All three also agreed that they would ask more detailed questions as they came to different villages and met more people in the future. They now understood they couldn't fully rely on their maps for the latest information.

As they spoke, it seemed strange to them that all three had come to similar conclusions by using their imaginations. It also occurred to them that there was something strange in how the visions were so powerful. It was like their heroes were teaching them from the beyond. But they now had a plan to proceed, which excited them, and they had learned a lesson about what they needed to do better in the future. All this came from just using their imaginations to solve the problem at hand.

They decided that Aaron would be the one to take the small raft and explore the branch of the fork to the right. They also decided that he would travel up the branch for no more than two and a half hours before turning around. That way, he could be back before dark. Captain Bon and Kelly would set up camp and start cooking dinner while he was exploring.

Less than three hours later, Aaron returned to his partners with the news. He had traveled only an hour when he reached a small village. He spoke with the people there and learned that this new branch that was not on the map had been dug out within the last eighteen months. It now gave a roundabout to an area in the river where it was very rough and there were large rocks that could damage boats. It would add an extra four hours to their trip; however, the water was calm, and they could restock their supplies at the village. All three agreed that this was the path to take and that their imaginations had given them the answer they needed just when they needed it.

What Have You Learned from the Story?

I hope you can now see that this is what all the people you think are so lucky and blessed do to get to their desires. It's called strategic thinking, and anyone can do it if they try. Through strategic thinking, you can plan your life in your imagination, but you must live that plan to get to your desire.

What do I mean by living the plan to get to your desire? Not living a plan is where most people miss the boat in life. There are a couple of things that are involved in living the plan. We will break them down in the next few paragraphs and hopefully give you a path to follow in your life.

Using Your Imagination to Build the Why to Drive Your Desire

You must start in your imagination with the "why" for the plan to get to your desire. You should picture what you want to accomplish. Let's say you want to win an ultramarathon in your age-group. To most, that would seem like a crazy thought, but if this is what you want, you can accomplish it. You must have a strong enough passion that will carry you through the demanding work and necessary training. So how does it feel to win the ultramarathon? Use your imagination and feel what you would feel when you accomplish your desire. See yourself stepping onto the winner's box. Think about all the people back home who will be watching you take that winner's step. How does this feel?

Does the feeling you have from these questions give you the fire in your belly to back your why? You will need that fire. You can build your plan in your imagination, but without action, your plan is only a dream. Many people dream every day about what they want to be or what they want to accomplish, but they never commit to it and move forward. They are not prepared to put in the demanding work to take their plans from their imaginations and desires to working plans and then to successes. It's sad to think about how many wonderful things are stuck in people's minds and dreams that could change the world.

I ask you again, Is your passion behind your dream? Do you have the fire in your belly to carry it through?

If you can't answer yes to these questions, go back into your imagination and build a fire behind the desire. Keep going back and building a fire until it gets you off your butt and you move down the road to your desire. If not, then keep dreaming for your entertainment.

You can fulfill your desires. Many people such as Walt Disney, Henry Ford, and many others started with less than you, but they used these truths to get to their destinations. So why would you think God would not afford you the same luxuries in life? I promise it is not God, the universe, your boss, or anyone else stopping you. It's *you*!

AVOIDING THE SUCCESS PITFALLS
PRINCIPLES OF IMAGINATION

Captain Bon understood that there were at least two success pitfalls principles he had to be on the watch for when it came to the imagination. The first was imagination itself. Your imagination is one of the most powerful things your mind uses to propel you toward a goal and to hold you back from achieving it.

When the mind is imagining what will happen, you must be careful not to allow it to dream up all the things that can go wrong. The mind can see both the good and the bad in each possibility, and we must control the perspective it takes on. Your subconscious mind doesn't understand what's good or bad for you. However, it does understand what is painful or pleasurable to you. If you perceive something as pleasurable, the subconscious mind will aid you, but if it sees it as pain, it will avoid going down that road.

It is natural and even helpful to see the things that could go wrong. These images can alert us and prepare us for the challenges we may face, but they can also create fear, which may stop us from moving forward. Captain Bon understood that he had to question if he was looking at the negative images as warning lights or if they were holding him back from his desires.

If the images were holding him back because of fear, he had to find a way to change the fear into pleasure. He had to link more pain with not moving forward and taking a chance than with failing. Until the future became the past, his future wasn't in stone, and he could change the outcome.

Captain Bon also knew that this was what had held him back from taking the chance before. He had the perception that if he tried and failed, he would lose everything he had worked for in life and would be alone. His imagination had built up fears about what could go wrong, which were all negative. He hadn't used his imagination to see what he would feel if he succeeded. He never stepped out and tried to succeed.

But now he understood how others used their imaginations to propel them toward their dreams and desires. They used the fear of failure not as a roadblock but as a warning system to build a plan to get around the possible obstacles.

With this newfound perspective, Captain Bon could see the world and himself differently. The choice was his. His imagination could either serve him well or not. He realized that it was all a perceived reality and that it would be what he made of it in the end, whether it was a success or failure.

The second success pitfalls principle was not having an imagination at all or thinking it was foolish to imagine anything. Captain Bon felt that almost every person had an imagination, though there was no way to confirm this for sure. But he also felt that many had lost the key to using their imaginations. Some of these people thought that imagination was for children or artists and not for them. He had even heard people through his life say, "I have no imagination. I can't picture that." Bon couldn't understand not having an imagination. His imagination was vivid, as he could see things in his mind as clearly as watching a movie. Dreaming in his imagination was easy for him, though it had been used against him in the past at times.

Do others not have imaginations, or did they choose not to use them to help them achieve their desires in life? He concluded that it had been a choice. Both he and others had chosen not to use their imaginations to plan for success. Or worse, they had used it to keep themselves from trying.

The only images they could see in their imaginations were those of failure. They couldn't see past the failure. They couldn't imagine that failure could be an education, and so they were bound up with fear and chose not to consider their imaginations.

Captain Bon realized that his imagination would be one of the most important success principles but that he had to make sure at every step that he was using it to propel him forward and not to hold him back.

What Do We See about the Success Pitfalls Principles for Imagination?

We can see how our imaginations can be used against us and cause us to become paralyzed. The mind will always show you the possibility of failure. That's its job. Your mind is just trying to protect you, but you have the ultimate responsibility to use these images as warning signs and not as detours away from your desires. Changing the image of failure from one of paralyzing to warning is something anyone can do.

You can dig deeper into the image of failing to find the root cause and understand what your imagination is warning you may happen. Then you can use your imagination to learn how you will use this fear of failure to help you succeed. It's your choice about the actions you take after you use your imagination. You can choose to use the warnings to avoid danger, or you can allow them to paralyze you. It's that simple.

Sure, you will fail from time to time, and your imagination will have been right. Don't take it as an adventure-ending failure. Take it as a lesson. You will learn what doesn't help you get to your desire. If you take this approach and try one more time, you will eventually achieve your desire.

The second success pitfalls principle involves failing to understand that anyone can use their imaginations. Some of this comes from a belief that the person doesn't have an imagination or that imagination is for children and not useful in the real world. The idea that you can't use your imagination is just a fear of looking foolish or uneducated. Your imagination is where your genius lives. It's the part of you that creates, and like any other part of your body, it needs exercise to perform well. The more you use your imagination, the stronger it will become.

When people think they do not have imaginations, it's because they haven't used them in a long time. They have accepted what has come in their lives because they are fearful of dreaming and failing. They have associated more pain with the possibility of failure than they have associated pleasure with success. You must use pain and pleasure to drive you to your dreams and desires.

In the next chapter on your subconscious mind and beliefs, you will learn how to use pain and pleasure to help achieve your dreams, but you should now understand you can change the way you perceive pain and pleasure. This perception will help you associate pain with not moving toward your dreams and pleasure with heading toward your success. You will learn that you can overcome the fears of failure through replacing fears.

For now, understand that you do have an imagination and that you can use it to help you see and feel the achievement of your dreams and desires. However, you have to think about how you perceive the images you see in your imagination.

CHAPTER 8

SUBCONSCIOUS OR SUBJECTIVE MIND, BELIEFS, AND VALUES
THE UPGRADED ENGINE PACKAGE FOR YOUR BOAT

CAPTAIN BON HAD A STRONG will and a magnificent work ethic, but he knew that wouldn't be enough to sustain what was to come throughout his adventure. He knew all the willpower in the world couldn't do the work that his subconscious mind could do. After all, his subconscious mind controlled everything from his breathing to his habits. If he could train his subconscious mind to look for the small keys in life, he could succeed at anything.

How could he train his subconscious mind to do what he wanted? How could he train this major part of the mind that he had no real control over? He knew the answer to this question rested in changing his beliefs and values. He understood through years of studying how the mind worked that he believed his mind dictated what he perceived in life.

He also had come to realize that it took focus and deliberate practice to train the subconscious mind. He couldn't just tell his subconscious mind to change a belief or change what he valued in life. He would first have to prove to his mind that the belief or value had no true backing, and then he would get his subconscious mind to doubt the belief. If he was able to cause doubt on the belief, then he could insert his new belief. Once he'd inserted the new belief, he would have to develop backing for the new belief. He would have to cultivate the foundation that supported the new belief. Cultivating would take time. Captain Bon understood it wouldn't be an overnight change.

He knew it was possible to change beliefs that didn't serve him in his life and weren't helping him to realize his dream. He thought of all the examples in the world where people didn't just change their beliefs but changed others through changing their beliefs.

Consider one of the largest changes in belief we hold as concrete today. Many thought that the world was flat and that if you sailed too far, you would fall off the edge of the world and into oblivion. Then came a man named Christopher Columbus. Through his and other theories, he believed that the world wasn't flat and that he could find a water route to the Indies for trade. Now people thought Columbus was crazy and was going to get himself killed, but he was able to convince Queen Isabella of Spain to back his expedition to find the trade route.

Now we all know the after story. Columbus didn't find the West Indies; however, he did prove the world wasn't flat, and he did find the New World. You see, if you look at it from one point of view, Columbus failed to achieve his dream. Or did he? None of us know what his true dream was. It could have been to prove that the world wasn't flat. If that was the case, then he succeeded. He could have wanted to leave a legacy throughout time. If that was the case, then he was tremendously successful. Whatever his dream and desire was, one thing is for sure—he went after it.

Again, maybe Columbus failed in finding the Indies, but I think most of us would be happy to fail the way he did. You can find enormous success in failure. If nothing else, you will get an education on what not to do—that is, if you examine the failure with an open mind and take ownership of it.

Captain Bon thought about how Columbus had to have changed his belief that the world was not flat, for no sane person would sail to his death, knowing that he would die. Then Columbus convinced others to change their beliefs and sail with him. Again, if he couldn't change their beliefs, they wouldn't have sailed to their death. So how did Columbus change his belief and the beliefs of others? He found evidence that the belief had faults, and he tore down the old belief. He then replaced it with a new belief that he could sail to the Indies. He convinced others to change their belief through the same system and evidence. He also put a huge carrot in front of them. He promised them that they would become wealthy and leave a legacy through time for finding a shorter water route to the Indies for trade. The carrot of wealth and fame helped change their beliefs. Again, it comes back to pleasure and pain. In the case of the sailors Columbus recruited, the pleasure of wealth and fame outweighed the pain of possibly dying.

Captain Bon knew he could change his misguided belief that he would fail, and he set out to do it. He also knew he could help change others' beliefs that they, too, would fail to achieve their dreams by using what he had learned about beliefs. He and others would first find the legs that supported bad beliefs and cut away at them. They would have to understand how others had achieved the dream he was after. He would use them as models to support the new belief that he would succeed. He would then associate great pain with the old belief that failed him. The pain would help force him to change his belief. He would associate even greater pleasure with the belief that he could achieve his dream. Now he was forcing his subconscious mind to help change the belief. He knew that his subconscious mind would work to keep him out of pain and heading toward pleasure.

SO HOW DID CAPTAIN BON GAIN HIS SUBCONSCIOUS MIND'S HELP

What is our subconscious mind? What work does it take care of? Why do we need its help to get to our dreams and desires? It is the true control center, and many have said that it makes up 96 percent of your mind. It is the part of your brain that takes care of everything for your body without you having to tell it what to do constantly. It controls everything from the beating of your heart to the breath of air you just inhaled. It does all this work without any help from you or your conscious mind. It is also the true controller of your fate. While I do believe in free will, I also believe that without the aid of the subconscious mind, you can never get to your desire on the river of life.

Now the funny thing is that you cannot control your subconscious mind or tell it what to do. It is instinctive, and it has its programming that you have very little power over. And the only way to change or direct the subconscious mind into aiding you is through repetition, faith, and handing over your plans and desires. But again, it must be done with faith in yourself. If a plan is given to the subconscious mind once as a suggestion, it will ignore your desire. Let's be honest. It already has a lot of work to do to keep you alive.

There are many books, seminars, and teachers that show us the subconscious mind is the link between our finite minds and the ultimate wisdom of God or the universe. It is the doorway that you need to find the key to getting to your desires. But don't despair. We have the key to open the door and put you on the river headed to your desires.

You must understand that your subconscious mind truly controls your outcomes in life and that you have no control over the subconscious mind. Through this acceptance, you will come to understand the need for the system in the desired part of this book. Remember, you can gain the aid of the subconscious mind to upgrade your boat engine so that you can travel the river of life faster.

It will take time to gain the subconscious mind's help in your endeavors. Be patient with yourself and plan on failing from time to time. But at the same time, remember to evaluate and learn from your failures. If you learn from what went wrong, then it's not a failure. It's an educational experience in life.

Your subconscious mind is both friend and foe, ally and enemy! That's just a truth you will have to accept. There will be times when it comes to your aid like a large army to help you fight for your desires. However, there will be times when it arrives out of nowhere as the strongest enemy force you have ever faced. The funny thing is that most people do not realize this enemy is their mind working against them. They would rather blame someone, the world, or God for their failures in life when they need to look inward and examine their subconscious minds. Knowing that you need the aid of your subconscious mind and working to keep your desires in front of it daily will help you gain the subconscious mind's support in your travels down the river.

Self-Suggestion: The Onboard Programmable Navigation System

Our team of adventurers, led by Captain Bon, outfitted their boat with many extras to help make this trip easier. One of the extras was a programmable navigation system. This navigation system is very special in the way it operates. It was designed just for adventures like this one. It had many options to help the user navigate. It had GPS that worked in the most remote areas of the world, and it showed the maps in 3-D. The maps made it easier to recognize landmarks.

The one problem with the navigation system was it never lost anything programmed into it. The old programming could cause some confusion between the programmed maps and the GPS 3-D model. There was no way to get rid of the old information, so you had to look and make sure you were on the latest version of a map.

Though this could lead you astray if you weren't careful, it made the navigation system better in a way. If you were trying to understand how the area had changed, you could look at the old map. The reason this was helpful was that you could split the screen in three. One screen showed you the present GPS map. The middle screen could show you the newest printed map. You could also display the oldest map on the right screen. By comparing the three screens, you could tell how the terrain had changed over a given period.

Captain Bon and his team found this useful in this ever-changing landscape. They had learned how to quickly distinguish between the present and past maps. They helped when looking for fresh water along the river. Freshwater ponds had a way of drying up in this area, and if you just had the present map, the freshwater pond you had counted on being there may be nothing but dust now. But they have the option to look at where past freshwater pond locations were, allowing them to construct backup plans to get water.

You could also program areas in the navigation system you wanted to revisit or remember by just adding a pin to the location. The system also allowed them to add a few words to the pin to identify why they had pinned it. Maybe they wanted to flag a freshwater pond they could stop at on the return trip. It could have been an area that was abundant with fish they could catch, or it could just be a good place to make camp. Whatever it was, you could look back at it anytime and see why it was useful.

As you can see, this navigation system was very useful in the jungle. The team had come to rely on it, and it made the team's lives better once they learned how to use it to its full potential.

YOUR PROGRAMMABLE NAVIGATION SYSTEM

What's your programmable navigation system? What system is working now behind the scenes as you are reading? What system do you have in your mind that controls everything behind the scenes? It's your subconscious mind, and it's running 24-7. It's the largest part of your mind. About 90 to 96 percent of everything done by the mind comes from the subconscious. We only control 4 to 10 percent of our minds.

Now that you know these percentages, don't you think you need help from your subconscious mind? Of course you do!

Let's look at how you can access this powerful computer that you have. It will not be easy, and it will take deliberate practice. It's not an area you can tell one time to believe something and it accepts it. It's an area that you should train through repetition. However, once trained, it never loses information, belief, or habit. And there lies the problem with the subconscious mind.

Look at our onboard programmable navigation system. What is it? Where is it? Well, this system is the subconscious mind. Your subconscious mind is the part of your mind that is used to guide you unconsciously through life. Some call it your free will, and others call it your beliefs and values. All these are parts of the subconscious mind.

You see, you do program your subconscious mind either by accident or on purpose. Some of our programmings came through our life experiences and some through school and our teachers, our mentors, our parents, and our environment. You did not put all these programs into your subconscious, and you need to evaluate them to determine whether they support you or hold you back. Until you sit down and look into your beliefs and values, how will you know if they serve you or not? Think about it. Could you expect your navigation system to guide you if you did not turn it on, input where you wanted to go, and then hit start?

Let's try an exercise to see if we have the right programming for our desires. You will have to ask yourself questions about your beliefs and values to see if they are leading you to your desires or away from them. You may find some of these values seem to stop you rather than help you. All of us have these types of values and beliefs. If you look harder at these values, you will find your values most likely serve different parts of your life that are not 100 percent tied to your main desire. You should review these to make sure they are not limiting you in some way from reaching your desire.

Consider the following example:

Part of Life	Desire	The Belief Associated with Desire	Limiting or Propelling	Needed Belief
Finance	Become a millionaire.	If you are rich, you either inherited it or you took advantage of someone.	Limiting	God wants me to have my desire so I can help others.
Carrier	Write a book.	You must be a Rhodes scholar or have a master's degree to write a book.	Limiting	Anyone can put their thoughts in book form to help express themselves.

So how do you change your programming to the new propelling belief that will aid you in life? Well, we do this almost through the same system as we do with desire. We use the NLP techniques of anchoring to aid us.

Remember, you act according to your map of the world in your head, and your beliefs and values are the largest part of this map.

Your Beliefs and Values: The Warning Signs of the Rivers

Like most people in the world, Captain Bon struggled with his beliefs and the values they held in his life. He had lived most of his life with these beliefs. They had been instilled in him during his adolescence and teenage years, and he was taught to work hard and not to chase dreams. Dreams were for the rich and the insane. His parents and family meant well and only wanted the best for him, but they had never been successful, so they thought that it wasn't in the cards for Captain Bon. Now that Captain Bon understood how the mind worked, he felt that he could change what his future life held for him thus far. He felt that he could become successful. Señor Doubter raised his head often: but Captain Bon fought him off at every turn.

Captain Bon started to look at doubt and Señor Doubter differently. Whenever he had doubts, they signaled one of two things. It either meant that he hadn't completely replaced one of the old beliefs or that he still had a restraining belief to discover and change. As the doubt arose in his life, he would ask himself, "Where is this doubt coming from?" Instead of being worried or afraid as he had been before, he would analyze his doubts and fears. He would break them into their smallest parts to understand what the legs supporting them were.

Most of the time, he could get to the source quickly, but a few times it took a while. His beliefs had been built over many years, and some had very deep roots that had to be pulled out.

One of the hardest beliefs for him to change was that people would financially back him on this adventure. He had never approached anyone for financial support for something like this before. It was new to him and very much out of his field of comfort. He felt that they would see him as a beggar or crazy person and shoo him away. He also felt that the embarrassment would be a horrendously painful experience. The more he thought about being a beggar, the more he was ready to ditch the entire dream. Something about being a beggar went against his beliefs and values, but why did Bon feel this way?

Captain Bon spent days wrestling with this belief and the feeling of fear that was holding him back. He went through his mind, searching for the reason that he held this belief. He knew logically that many people in the world invested in these types of adventures. He also knew that it was possible that he could find financial support from companies that wanted to use his adventure for advertisement. So why did he feel as if he would be a beggar and not an explorer?

The deeper he dug, the deeper the hole went into his past. It was something from his childhood, but what was it? Captain Bon was almost to the point of giving up on finding the supporting legs to this belief when it came to him. Captain Bon remembered what his father was trying to accomplish with an invention he had developed. It was a tough time in Captain Bon's home because there wasn't much money coming in. Captain Bon's mother was against the idea at every turn; she would argue that Captain Bon's father should go back to his job at the refinery. Captain Bon's father tried hard to raise the capital to start the business, but he couldn't find backers. He remembered the conversations he had overheard between his father and mother during that time.

His mother would say, "David, you are running us into the poorhouse with this crazy dream. What makes you think you can start a business? What have you done in your life that makes you a businessman?" The argument went on for months, and it seemed to tear his mother and father apart. It also left the mental picture of his father's face when he gave up his dream and went back to the refinery job.

Captain Bon dug deeper into this memory to try to find out how he was associating working to find capital backing with being a beggar. As he went through his memories, the pain from what the family endured during this time came back to him in waves. He could remember the arguments, the nights with very little food to eat, the times at school when other children made fun of him for not having new clothes, and the Christmas during that time when there weren't any presents. That's when it hit him. He knew why he associated the feeling of asking for financial backing with being a beggar.

He had heard his father and mother arguing the day before Christmas that there would be no gifts for the children. His father was working hard, but the money he did make had to be used to pay the bills and put the little food they could afford on the table. He heard his mother in a fit of anger say to his father, "If you are going to be a beggar, go out and beg for gifts for our children, not this stupid dream of starting a business and becoming rich." That's where it came from—his mother's lips.

He now understood the supporting legs that he needed to cut out from under this belief. He could knock the legs out from under the belief. After all, his father wasn't a beggar. He was far from it. He was just a man who worked hard to provide for his family and had a dream. He realized his father gave up too early on his dream. His father hadn't prepared for success, and Captain Bon doubted he had even understood what it would have taken to succeed with his dream.

Nothing his father did was begging. He worked hard and tried to get backing the only way he knew how. His mother didn't mean what she said to his father. She loved the man and knew he was a hard worker. She was just protective of her family, and in her mind, that came from working at a job, not starting a business. She had never known anyone who had gone out and started a business, so she wasn't educated that the first few years were the hardest. Captain Bon's father wasn't educated on what it would take to get the business going and how long it would be before he could support his family. Had either one taken the time to educate themselves from the study of others who had started businesses, they would have been better prepared.

Being prepared was the difference between Captain Bon and his father. He knew the road that lay ahead of him. He knew what others had endured. He had spent time interviewing adventurers on how they had gotten backing and the dangers of the adventure itself. He had done his homework, and he was educated on what it would take to achieve his dream.

Now Captain Bon had what he needed to knock the legs out from under the belief that made him feel as if asking for financial backing was begging. He also had the evidence to support the new belief that asking for the backing would bring advantages to the companies and capital ventures that supported him. It wasn't begging if you had something to give back. It was an investment.

It wasn't like this was just like flipping a switch for Captain Bon. He would still have to work daily to reinforce the new belief and disprove the old one, but it wouldn't hold him back. He would push forward and remind himself daily why he valued the new belief and devalued the old one. He would use the avoidance of pain to get rid of the old belief as he used the pleasure of success to reinforce the new belief.

It didn't take Captain Bon very long before the old belief no longer held value, and his new belief was propelling him toward his dream. Looking back, Captain Bon was amazed by how a small memory from his childhood had given rise to such a strong belief that could and would hold him back. He knew there might be other disempowering beliefs that he would have to face in the future; however, he had changed his belief on this one, and that gave him the momentum to change the ones that were to come.

WHAT CAPTAIN BON UNDERSTOOD ABOUT BELIEFS AND VALUES

Captain Bon understood that these two areas of his life would make up eighty percent of what drove him. Eighty percent was the psychological part of his life and his mind. He could have all the tools, but he still needed to be motivated to gain his desires. He could have a perfect plan, but until he aligned his beliefs and values with that plan, he wouldn't succeed.

You see, the tools are only 20 percent of what you need and must know to succeed. These include school, education through life, your mentors, and other tools in the toolbox, but the psychology behind you will be the driving part of your life. You must always look to see if your beliefs and values are aligned with your desire. Look at your life, and then ask yourself, "Are these things aligning?" Here is an example. What if you desire to build a billion-dollar company, but your beliefs and values tell you that you can only work forty hours a week, which allows you to spend the rest of your time with your family? Well, then you have conflicts in your life, my friend. You must align your beliefs and values with your desires. You must analyze your beliefs and values and decide if these are true to life and will make you happy or if it is time to change your beliefs and values so that you can achieve your desire.

What are beliefs, and how do they warn us if we are doing right or wrong in our lives?

Your beliefs are nothing more than the thoughts you have given certainty to in your mind. These thoughts have gained support through experience, continued suggestions to your mind, or your surroundings. Your beliefs can either empower you or paralyze you. We can and do change our beliefs over time through different experiences in life. Think back to a belief you once held as the truth but now do not. We have all had these types of beliefs in life.

Again, one of the greatest beliefs the world once held was that the earth was flat. Because of this, many believed that if you sailed out too far in the Atlantic Ocean, you would fall off the world, but then along came a man named Christopher Columbus with the belief that he could sail to the West Indies and would not fall off the earth. Some of the people who sailed with Columbus did not believe in him or his plan, but they were being paid. Others believed, so they sailed with him. About halfway through the trip, most of the sailors started believing that they would never find land and would die. We can see from history that Columbus was right, but not about getting to the West Indies.

Let's look at some examples of beliefs that people hold in their lives. Through this, you will see both positive and negative beliefs. As you read them, think about how they can limit your life or propel it forward.

1. I will always be overweight. Everyone in my family is built the same as me.
2. I always find solutions to the challenges in life and business.
3. If you are rich, you had to have taken advantage of others and held them down. Or you must have ripped off people.
4. I do not have the education to become successful.
5. I work to live, not live to work.
6. If I do not make $100,000 a year and drive an awesome car, I will never find the person of my dreams.
7. When I go after anything in life, I find a way to succeed.

Can you see how your beliefs can propel you in life or hold you back? Look at these beliefs and look at how you can change those beliefs to serve you. Let's discuss one of these beliefs.

Consider the disempowering belief "I will always be overweight. Everyone in my family is built the same as me." Let's first look at how destructive this belief is. If this is what your mind thinks, how can you ever get in shape? Every time you try, your mind will say, "What's the use?" Do you think you can overcome your mind, the part of you that controls everything and does most of it without you giving it a second look? It's not going to happen.

But don't you know people who have lost weight and gotten into shape, even though their families haven't? Sure you do, and if not, turn on an episode of *The Biggest Loser*. Many of these people had those same beliefs when they started, but they changed the disempowering beliefs to get to where they wanted to be in life.

Okay, you may not become a super athlete or a gold medalist. You may not even get to your desired size and weight, but I bet you can get close if you change your belief. Will it be easy? No. Will it be a lot of demanding work? Yes, it will be a lot of work. Think of the possibilities that changing this one belief could bring. If you change this belief and lose weight, what will it do for your family? Maybe you can get them in the boat with you and add a few years to all their lives.

Your disempowering belief doesn't just affect you. It affects everyone around you. It can be passed to your children and maybe even their children. Is this the legacy you want to leave for the generations to come? Wouldn't you rather leave a legacy that shows your children that they can change their beliefs and succeed in their dreams?

You can change the legacy that you leave to your children and their children. The choice is up to you. Do you want to leave them with a legacy that they will always be overweight or with a legacy that they can change? But first, you must believe that you can change your beliefs and values.

SO HOW DO WE CHANGE OUR BELIEFS AND VALUES?

First, you need to think about your beliefs on happiness, love, money, and your abilities. Write them down and pick them apart. Analyze how they line up with your desires in life. Are they helping you gain your desires, or will they prevent you from getting them? If they help you get to your desires, then reinforce them by putting them into your action statement.

If your beliefs are in contradiction to the path to fulfilling your desire, then you must pick them apart and analyze why they do not line up with your path. This could be a warning sign that your desire, or at least your path to your desire, is not correct. Again, analyze why they are in contradiction to one another. Examine your belief and its supporting structure to see whether this is a truth or just something you created in your mind as a certainty through suggestion. You can see the negative belief in people who think they will always be overweight because of their family history. You will never see this negative belief in people that make fitness a priority. They hold a belief that despite their pasts and heritages, they can live healthy and energetic lifestyles that create their perfect bodies.

Let's go through the system of changing a belief by using the belief that you can't lose weight because of your family. First, let's look at the belief.

You say, "I will always be overweight. Everyone in my family is built the same as me."

What are the supporting legs?

1. I have been overweight my entire life.
2. When I have worked to lose weight, I have always gained it back and more.
3. My family has very little, if any, members who are not overweight.
4. I enjoy eating and lying around, and I do not like the pain of working out.
5. I don't have the time in my day to work out.
6. I travel for work and can't eat at the same times or can't find the proper food.

Okay, now we will look at each supporting leg for the belief and cut them from under the belief. This will be the process you will need to follow to change your belief. When you practice this in life, the steps can and will run consecutively. Okay, let's get back to cutting the legs out from supporting the belief.

Consider the first leg, "I have been overweight my entire life." Have you been overweight your entire life? Or have you been overweight for the time you can remember? Can you look back through pictures from your life and find at least one or two pictures of a time when you weren't overweight? I bet you can and will. When you find those pictures, put them on a picture board to remind you that you weren't always overweight.

Use the picture to build the new belief that you have been and can be in the shape you want to be.

Now think of the next supporting leg, "When I have worked to lose weight, I have always gained it back and more." This belief should first tell you that you can lose weight. This gives you the evidence to help cut down the first leg and the root of the belief. You see, you have lost weight before. Maybe you gained it back, but you lost it in the first place. Think about this for a second. There is a subcategory to this leg that needs to be explored. Why did you go backward? Why did you stop and go back when things were working in even the smallest way? This can be a couple of things, but for this exercise, we will say that you stopped thinking of losing weight as a priority, and it became a preference. So as a preference, you only worked out and ate correctly when it was convenient. You didn't keep your full focus on the dream, and you allowed your old habits to come back into play. Remember, habits never go away. You can get back to the habits that you built to lose weight. Both habits are in you, but you must choose which you will use and focus on it. Remember one other thing: if allowed, the mind will take the path of least resistance and work.

Now that we have worked on cutting away two of the legs, let's see whether we can cut away a few more. In cutting them away, we can find supporting legs for the new belief.

The next belief and the one that gives you the strongest excuse to retain your belief that you can't lose weight is as follows: "My family has very little, if any, members who are not overweight." In that statement, you find a key to destroying your belief. The way you look at it is the important part. You may believe that most of the family is overweight so you will be overweight, or you can say that a few members are not overweight and that you can be one of these members. If you change your value of this part of the belief, you can overcome it and change the belief to "I can get in shape and lose weight." It's that simple.

Most people will try to make it hard on themselves, and they never believe that changing a belief is this simple. But in reality, it is. It's all about our perspective of reality. Think about this for a second. Does everyone hold the same perspective as you? If you think most do and the belief is concrete, then find someone who doesn't. Nothing in this world is set in concrete, not even concrete. It is all your perspective, and if the belief is not serving you, change your perspective and change your belief to one that will serve you.

As for the rest of the supporting legs, you can easily cut them down, and I would like you to take time and figure out ways to cut them down yourself. There is no right or wrong answer. Just keep in mind that as you are cutting them down, you want to use the reason you cut them down as one of the legs for the new belief. Let's get started.

1. I enjoy eating and lying around, and I do not like the pain of working out.
2. I don't have the time in my day to work out.
3. I travel for work and can't eat at the same times or can't find the proper food.

Did you cut the legs out? Did you build legs for the new belief? If you have done the exercise, congratulations. You're on your way to changing your life. If you haven't, go back and do the work. You know you want your life to change, and you must understand how to change beliefs for that to happen.

How can we use our beliefs to help us gain our desires? After all, that's what we are here to understand. If beliefs are thoughts we hold in our minds with certainty, then what are values? A value is something you place importance on in your mind. This can be an object, feeling, or anything else that we hold dear in our lives. If you value a destructive belief, you will never change your life. You must devalue destructive or restricting beliefs. You have seen how you can do this by examining the belief, cutting out the legs, and building a new belief that will propel you through life.

I want you always to keep this thought in your mind: *My beliefs are my master, and I am the slave.* Your beliefs will dictate your actions in life. They will dictate the path you will take and the decisions you will or will not make along the river of life. The decisions will align with the beliefs you hold and the value you put on your beliefs. If you build supporting beliefs that align with your dreams, you will make the right decisions to get to your dreams. If you don't have alignment in your beliefs, values, and decisions, you will never move forward. You will spin in circles.

Many people never look at their lives this way. They will often say, "I can't decide." That's because you don't have alignment in the three areas. You need to align your dreams, beliefs, and decisions. One of the three needs to change. Look at the three areas again. Do you want your dream more than anything? You'd better. Now, look at your beliefs. Why are those out of line with your dream? What put them out of line? Can or will you change your beliefs?

You can change the belief. It's just a thought you hold that you have put a value on. Change your belief. You now know how to change the belief. You can change it, or you can give up your dream like most of the world does. For me, changing a belief that is holding me back is easier than giving up on a dream I have.

Think of it this way. Beliefs are the causes in your life, and your experience of life is the result. Are you getting the results you want in life? If not, it's most likely that your beliefs are causing you not to get your desires. Can you see how this is a big circle? It is a circle, and if there's a bad belief in that circle, you will not get the experience you are after in your life. Evaluate your experiences and work backward to find the belief that is holding you back. It's just that simple. Again, people want to make it harder than it is. Now I'm not saying it's not going to be challenging work to change the belief, especially if it is a belief you have held most of your life. Just as we go back to unhealthy habits, you may return to bad beliefs.

Tools to Change Beliefs

Two of the main tools to use to cement your new belief include affirmations and visualization. Let's look at these two tools and what they mean to us in changing our beliefs and supporting new ones. We will start with affirmations. If you look up the definition of *affirmation*, you will find it is defined as "the act of affirming, something affirmed, a positive declaration, an assertion."

Now think about the definitions. What we are saying is, you are taking a thought or belief and holding it as the truth. We are placing a high value on this belief. We are saying, "I believe this to be true and reject anything else." Everything that would conflict with the belief would be false to you.

Now can you see how you can build a new belief by using affirmations? If you repeat this belief with feelings, you are affirming it. When you affirm a belief repeatedly with emotions, you write that belief in your subconscious mind. Once you have done this, your subconscious mind judges your decisions by this belief. If the action or decision is in opposition to your belief, your subconscious mind will not let you proceed. No amount of willpower will change that.

Now if your decisions or actions align with your belief, you will move forward. The mind is taking the path of least resistance. It has been programmed through time to take the path of least resistance. And you're not going to change that forcefully. You will not change the path until you change the belief.

Now you may think, *I didn't program this belief into my subconscious mind*, and maybe you didn't purposely program it. But the belief was programmed from your environment. You didn't make a conscious choice. You allowed your mind to accept the belief through no choice.

Many of our beliefs form this way. They have come from our parents, friends, and the people we see as heroes. We never decided that this was our belief. We just accepted it as our belief. We accepted that it was correct without understanding whether it would support our dreams and desires in life. Most never even look deep enough to understand what their beliefs dictate in their lives. They make excuses and move forward with what life gives them.

After reading this book, you likely understand that you can change your beliefs and, in turn, change what you are getting from life. You know it's possible, so now it's time to use what you have learned to do just that.

Let's look at what we have learned about evaluating your beliefs and changing the beliefs that stand in your mind. As you work toward your dream, you need to evaluate what beliefs are not supporting your dream. Only you can decide what beliefs stand in your way. That is because you are the only person in the world who knows what belief is standing in your way. Once you have picked out the disempowering belief, start cutting out the supporting legs.

You can cut out all the supporting legs. You must find oppositional thoughts to the supporting legs. Once you have found the oppositional thoughts, you can build a new and empowering belief. Take the new empowering belief and build the supporting legs.

You can't stop here. You have to do deliberate practice through affirmations. Emotional affirmations bring your feelings that you pull from every part of your body and mind. Just as you created the feelings earlier of having your dreams, you need to create feelings that have supporting legs that you believe in totality.

Thoughts plus emotion creates conviction, and conviction creates the reality that your belief is true. Now with this truth and reality, you need to affirm it in your subconscious mind. This deliberate practice is just reviewing the new belief and its supporting beliefs until nothing else fights against it. This practice needs to be conscious. You must look at the feedback you are getting as you would with any other deliberate practice. And if things are not turning out as you need them to, change your approach. The change may be slight, such as the time of day you are practicing, rehearsing, and reviewing the new belief. Or it may be the way you are reviewing the belief.

If your review is silent, then start vocally practicing as if you are talking to an audience. Vocal reviews may sound crazy, but it's not. The mind will take anything we speak or write down on paper as reality. If you want to turn this new belief into reality, try writing it down and speaking it out loud daily. This practice will get you to change your belief.

Now let's go on to the visualization of your new belief. You need to use your imagination just as you have for so many parts of this system. You must breathe life into your new belief through your imagination and then visualize it into being. See a new belief and its supporting legs, see how it changes your life, then see how it aligns with your dream.

Keep refining this process of the visualization of your new belief. Look for more areas where the new belief ties to your dream. In doing this, you are doing deliberate practice, and as you already know, deliberate practice will get you to where you want to be sooner.

Again, it's a circle. If you look at the system to success in its entirety, you will find the intertwining work. Things are repeated and reused in each of the parts to come. Now go out and practice. Use your imagination for the visualization of the new belief. Do these things, and you will be well on your way to achieving your dream. You will be ahead of most of the world.

Captain Bon's Thoughts on the Success Pitfalls Principles for Beliefs

Captain Bon now understood that beliefs and values could factor into either the success pitfalls principle or the success principle. He would need to search himself for the beliefs that had been instilled in him about how people succeed and who gets to succeed and see if they served him or not.

He had already realized he had limiting beliefs about seeking financial backing, so what other beliefs did he have that would hold him back?

Through this searching, he found that he had let his parents and the rest of the world instill beliefs that weren't serving him. These beliefs had been slowly built up over a lifetime, and he had never challenged them. He just accepted that they were true and that he couldn't change them.

Now through educating himself on how the mind worked and the help of his mentor, Dennis Flemming, he knew that he could change the beliefs that didn't serve him. He had to change what he believed and gave value to if he was going to achieve his desires in life.

He did this by working with Dennis on a list of the questions that would reveal the beliefs that were holding him back. He would use the association of pain and pleasure to change his beliefs to ones that would propel him.

He now associated more pain with not going after his dream than he did with failure. He also used his imagination to build an image of the pleasure he would get when he did reach his desire. He could see himself in his imagination, reaching his destination and leaving a legacy as a great explorer. This image was as real in his mind. At times it felt as if it had already happened. This image gave him the drive to change the beliefs he once held about his ability to succeed.

Dennis and Captain Bon spent time reviewing his progress with the association of pain and pleasure. He used Dennis as a sounding board to assure he was walking the walk and not just talking the talk. They grew closer as they opened up to each other. Dennis became Bon's closest friend and confidant.

During the next three months, along with working on the plan and gathering resources, they worked together and dove into Captain Bon's beliefs. Some were as shallow as puddles of water on cement, and others were as deep as the Pacific Rim; however, together with Captain Bon's open-book personality, they started correcting the beliefs that didn't serve him. Now only time would tell if they had changed these negative beliefs and values, but from what the evidence suggested, things seemed to be changing.

Sitting and thinking over the past three months, Captain Bon realized that through changing what he associated with pain and pleasure in his mind, he was able to move past the fear of failure that had held him back for so many years. This newfound ability helped Captain Bon evolve. He now understood he had grown past the one thing in life that held most people back. He had gotten past the perception of fear that came with failure.

CHAPTER 9

PLANNING
THE DESTINATION OF YOUR RIVER TRIP

CAPTAIN BON KNEW HE NEEDED a plan for his adventure to Mount La Felicidad, but he wasn't sure where he should start. Where do you start with a plan as large as this one? There are so many moving parts to an adventure like this one. How could he plan for each one? What should come first?

Captain Bon finally decided that a plan was created in the mind as thought and then put on paper to point you in a certain direction. It was nothing more than a map, and you filled in the actions you would make along the way. If this was what a plan was, he could use his imagination to envision the adventure from beginning to end and write them down on paper. He would use his imagination to see the adventure. That was the answer. He knew it would take some time, but he had already seen most of it happen. After all, that was what had built a fire in his belly and gotten him this far.

Thinking more about the process of building his plan, he would write down what he had already seen in his imagination. Then he would spend time reviewing the plan in his imagination and examine whatever would come up. He knew he might not identify each part or everything he would need to be successful, but using his imagination, he could fill in many of the blanks.

The entire process still felt a little overwhelming to Captain Bon. There were so many details that needed to be captured and written down. Thinking of the plan in its entirety was too much for him. Then like a flash of lightning, it hit him. He knew what he had to do. He had to use *chunking*. He needed to break up the plan into smaller parts and see just the tiny parts in his imagination. Seeing all the stops on the map, he could dig deeper into each one. Then he could look back to see how each one tied to the part before and the part that would come after.

Each part of a plan is tied to others, but he understood he shouldn't forget how each part of the plan tied to the entire plan as well. Again, all the parts were intertwined. Using chunking would let him see each part, and then he could understand how they each tied to the plan in its entirety.

Using chunking would also allow him to explain the plan to people who would become part of his team. By subdividing the plan, each member could focus on their parts and improve it where they saw the need. Then they could bring the parts back together to improve the whole plan. Then he could subdivide his team so that they could learn and improve their parts. Next, he could bring all the team members together to examine the parts of the plan and understand how it all worked together.

Once he had the plan back together and done to the best of everyone's ability, he would give his plan to his mastermind group and the team to review it and give suggestions. After all, that was the purpose of a mastermind group and his team. They would find any areas where he may have missed some details and would give suggestions on the parts he had developed. Through the mastermind group, the plan would become the best it could be.

Captain Bon knew the plan wouldn't be perfect or all-inclusive, but it would give Captain Bon's team the best map to success that they could have. He knew even an imperfect plan was better than no plan at all. It would help prepare the adventure team for what they would face. It would give the logistics team details about how they would support the adventure team that was on the river, and it would outline the roots for a presentation to prospective financial backers.

The plan would do all this and more. It would tie the team together and help the team focus on the adventure. The united focus of the team would bring things to the plan that no one person could accomplish. That was the gift of having a mastermind team. The focus of a larger group would accomplish outstanding results.

CAPTAIN BON'S PROCESS FOR PLANNING

What is a plan anyway? It's simple. A *plan* is nothing more than a map of the actions you will take to get to your destination. Whether consciously or unconsciously, people use plans every day. You have a plan to get up in the morning, to get ready for work, to travel to work, and to do your work. You are creating plans every day. It's not that hard. All you must do is ask questions and write down your answers, and then you are on your way to creating a plan. The better the questions you ask, the better the plan you will build. And the more questions you ask, the more holes you will fill. Just remember to avoid getting in your way when you're asking questions. Too many people spend more time than necessary on the planning. No matter how much time they put into planning, real life will always put a fork in the river, and you will have to change direction during the trip.

Just concentrate on the basics of the plan. Yes, try to anticipate the rapids that may be on the river, but don't think that you have to answer every question or that you have to have an answer for every situation before you start your adventure. If you wait for the perfect plan, you may never get started. Or you may become disappointed when you must change the plan midstream. Plans are meant to be changed. Examine the results you are getting, and if the plan isn't getting you to your desired results, change your approach and plan as needed.

A plan is thought up in your imagination and put on paper. You can create your plan either partly or fully by yourself, but you should have others review it to gauge its success and soundness. A positive and knowledgeable person in the proper field should review your plan. It is not advised to have a family member review the plan at first. While family members may care about you, they may give bad advice in the name of protecting you from getting hurt or failing. Finding a person or persons to review your plan may seem hard, but as with everything else on the trip to your desire, you will need the help of others to reach the end destination. Having this person or other people review your plan can be the first step to building your team and achieving your desire.

Here are some steps you can use to create a practical plan to reach your desires in life. You can use these steps or devise your own system. Now while I advise that you tailor the system to your style, you should know that many of the wealthiest people in the world have successfully used the system outlined here.

1. Use your imagination to see the road to your desire.
2. Break the plan into small parts. Remember chunking and what it teaches us. The mind can handle smaller parts easier than larger, more complex plans.
3. Write down the path you see in your imagination. Be sure to include details and logistical parts that you will need to address.
4. Write and question. And then write more. But don't worry about capturing all the details. You will find the questions and answers while you are on the adventure.
5. You should partner with as many people as necessary to ensure the creation of a plan that will help you reach your desire. Remember, no one does anything alone in life. You will need help to reach your desire. Your mastermind group can be very helpful.
6. Before you organize and recruit the people to help you with your plan (or your plans), you first must decide what you will give them in return for their help. While some people will help a little at first without payment, they will not work indefinitely without a return on their investment of time and sweat.
7. Arrange to meet with the members of your team at least twice a week or more if possible. Meet until you have collectively developed your plan for fulfilling your desire.
8. Maintain harmony between the members of your team. You will need the vision, wisdom, and inspiration of other minds that cannot come out of an argument or an atmosphere that is not in harmony.
9. Create a system to monitor your progress and to determine if changes are needed.

As you and your team are developing your plan, remember that it will never be perfect. Nothing in life is ever perfect. You will not create the first perfect system on your first try out of the gate either. The best path for creating a plan is to ask questions about your destination of desire and to write down the answers. The questions could include the following:

1. What resources will be needed?
2. Who will I need to help me?
3. What skills am I missing that others will need to possess?
4. What dangers may be in my way?
5. If this was a movie, what steps would the character take?
6. Who is my competition?
7. What does my competition do better than me?

Think of yourself as Captain Bon—that is if you haven't already put yourself in his place in the story. Now, what do you think would be some of the questions you would need to ask?

I know the list is enormous, but give it a shot. Let's start slowly and name just a few of the larger questions that you will need to be answered. Now go ahead and list five questions:

1.
2.
3.
4.
5.

What were your answers? Did you even do the exercise? If you haven't done the exercise, go back and do the work. Sooner or later, you will have to do the work if you are serious about taking your dream on and not just leaving it on the shelf.

Now let's look at five possible questions that Captain Bon would need to address in the creation of his plan.

1. What supplies will we need?
2. What weather will we face, and what clothing will we need?
3. What are the best foods to bring with us?

4. What size of boat will we need, and what will it be able to carry?

5. What dangers will we face, and what do we need to protect ourselves?

These questions are just the start of your journey. I bet you came up with many more. But look at the questions we have here. How many more questions you can come up with from thinking about just these five? I bet you could create at least fifteen more. And that's the point. One question leads to another and then another. Be careful not to chase the questions too long and miss the journey. As we have talked about before, many people never embark on the journey because they want the plan to be perfect. It will never be perfect, but it can be good or even excellent.

With a good or excellent plan, you can reach your dream. The plan will become better as you go through your journey. When you look back at your plan, you will likely see the changes you had to make, and you will be glad that you didn't waste too much time digging deeper and deeper.

Planning is a double-edged sword. Taking too much time could cut the dream apart, and not enough time planning may stab it in the heart. You must decide how complicated your plan will be. Just don't miss the adventure while you are trying to plan it to perfection.

We have talked a lot about plans, planning, and questions that we should ask while we are developing these plans. Now we will look at the parts of the plan and what they are meant to represent. We are going to discuss the basics of the plan. You may choose to add additional parts, but I recommended you use at least these nine parts when developing your plan.

Parts of a Plan

1. Summary
2. Overview / activities to be delivered
3. Whys/objectives
4. Strategy / desired outcome
5. Financial
6. Staffing/resource requirements
7. Implementation/timelines
8. Process for monitoring progress

Summary

A summary is a thirty-thousand-foot view of the plan. It provides comprehensive details about what the plan will accomplish, how the team will go about the adventure, and what the financial needs and the return on the investment will be. The summary is used in business plans, but it should be included in all plans. It serves as the start of the dream.

The summary only needs to be a few pages at most, and it must hit mainly the high points. You are trying to give people an idea about what you are working to accomplish, how you will get there, and what it will take to make it happen. This may sound like a sales pitch, but we are all salespeople in life. Before anyone helps you, they need to know what's in it for them. This section will give them information that will pique their interest. This is the catchy line that will pull in potential team members.

Overview / Activities to Be Delivered

This section is designed to outline the objectives that the plan will fulfill. It can be laid out like a table of contents, though unlike a table of contents, it needs to explain what each section will deliver. There is no need to get very detailed in this section with your explanations. You only need to give the thirty-thousand-foot view of what each section will deliver.

Whys and Objectives

In this section of your plan, you will start with your why. You must address why this plan exists. What is the plan going to accomplish or provide to the world, your community, and you? This will depend on the dream you are working to achieve. It could be a simple plan about going on a vacation to Italy, or it could be as complicated as going to Mars. That doesn't matter. The complexity only affects the level of detail you will have to put into the plan.

In this portion of your plan, you will also state the objectives, the key deliverables the plan will produce, and a timeline in which they will be produced. Again, you want to put in as much detail as possible and include dates for when items will be delivered.

The dates will help to keep everyone moving toward a common goal in a designated timeline. The timeline is the most important part. If you want your subconscious mind to help you on this plan, it will need dates to remind you when you must finish things to achieve the goal.

Do your best to include realistic dates, but don't worry if you don't make the exact date. Just monitor your progress and adjust the dates. Now that doesn't mean you should procrastinate and push every date. If you do that, you will never accomplish the dream.

STRATEGY / DESIRED OUTCOME

Now we come to the heart of your plan. This is where you will list the logistical elements and the actions that you will take to achieve your dream and desires. This is also where you will define the desired outcome you want. In this part of your plan, you are creating a map of how you will get from the starting point to the realization of the dream. It is also the portion of your plan where you state the resources you will need and the stops along the way. I suggest that you begin with the outcome you want clearly defined and work backward to your starting point. But the choice is yours. If you want, you can start in the middle and go both ways. It doesn't matter. It's more about your preference.

Now don't get yourself caught up in thinking you will have every detail sorted out. It's not going to happen, but make sure you put in enough details so that you get from stop to stop. If it was a plan to go to the grocery store, you could use the following strategies:

1. Write a list of what you need to buy from the store.
2. Check the weather to determine what clothes to wear.
3. Dress your children to go to the store.
4. Talk to your children about the proper behavior in the cereal aisle. (Good luck with that one.)
5. Write a list of any other stops that you need to take before and after the grocery store.
6. Load the children in the car.

7. Map the route for the best use of time.
8. Consider the time you need to get home and cook dinner.

The plan is a simple plan; however, it has laid out all the details, and it has a timeline. That is what you are trying to accomplish when you create any plan. You'd even write out a bucket list for all your goals this way.

Again, this is where the rubber meets the road. It is one of the main actions you have to take to go from dreaming your desire to achieving it. Most people have more dreams and desires than anyone could accomplish in a lifetime, but they never commit them to paper or create a plan. If you do not put your dreams on paper, you will not move forward with them. You could still fail to achieve your dream even if you create a plan, but with every step you take, you increase your chances of achieving your dream. The universe is not about to give you anything just because you wished for it. You must put in the work and stay diligent in pursuing the dream.

FINANCIAL

The financial part of any plan is the one people usually hate the most. That is because most people in the world have no idea about the actual cost of anything. They don't take the time to educate themselves on what monetary resources they will need. To me, this is a tragedy. You should always create a budget for any adventure in life. Then you know what you will spend the money on and what controls you must put in place so that you don't overspend. And you can also look back and judge how well you controlled your monetary resource.

Most would say that I am anal about budgets and spending, and I would have to agree. I have seen too much personal heartbreak in both my life and others when people did not adhere to budgets. If you are a business owner or manager and do not adhere to budgets, you won't be doing business for long. This doesn't mean going without forever. It means going without for now. The business world mistakes "wants" for "needs". You have certain things to survey, whether in business or life. But comforts are not needs They are wants. Okay, that's enough of a soapbox speech for now. Let's get back to the financial portion of the plan.

Creating the financial part of your plan is a science, and you should approach it that way. You want to identify as much of the cost as you possibly can. What is the cost to start up? What will you have to buy? Who will you have to pay, and how much will you pay them? What's the cost of fuel? What's the cost of consumables such as food, paper, and so on? Do you need to rent a building? What's the cost? The list goes on and on, but you need to identify everything you possibly can and what the cost will be.

The next part of the financial plan details what you will make from the venture. In other words, you will outline what people will pay you for your dream. If it is a business, you will charge customers for your services or products. What will be the profit? If it is a vacation, what is the payback for your family in happiness and memories?

Everything has a cost and a reward side. It doesn't matter if there's no monetary return. There's a return, and you need to capture it. If you fail to capture what you will get out of the plan, you will not be motivated to move forward. And if it is a business, you will not motivate anyone to support you in the adventure.

Now, like most things, you may get this wrong. The more homework you do and the more questions you ask, the closer you will get to an accurate budget. So ask questions. Be that five-year-old kid again who is exploring the world and learning. Please don't let your pride get in the way of your education. You will not have all the answers. You may not have any answers. Ask questions and learn. The only person who looks foolish is the one who thinks or acts like they know everything.

STAFFING/RESOURCE REQUIREMENTS

In your staffing/resource portion, you will list the organization chart that will make up your plan. You will name everyone from the head person in charge down to the bottom manager. You could format this list so that it looks like an organizational chart, or it may look like a family tree. This will depend on how large of an adventure you are undertaking.

It isn't important that you list each position that will be part of the adventure. Most plans only show the key positions and include placeholders showing approximate amounts of other positions. Though you will not have to list every position, you will need a good placeholder for all the positions. This is important for the financial portion of the plan. After all, every position will cost you something. Remember, no one works for free.

Think through the logistics of your plan and determine how many people you will need to accomplish the plan. Someone needs to complete the work for each activity or duty in operation. As we have said before, it may be an operation of one person if you are going to the grocery store, but if you are starting a company, there will be many positions.

Let's look at an example of starting a small mom-and-pop restaurant. The restaurant will need a few key positions to operate. These would include

1. a manager,
2. a cook,
3. a waitress,
4. a second waitress,
5. a third part-time waitress, and
6. a busboy.

It would take six people to run a simple family restaurant, but that would only be true if the restaurant ran eight hours a day. If it were going to operate from breakfast to dinner, you would have to have additional resources with people working in the evenings. If this were the case, you would most likely need up to ten people working there.

While this is a mom-and-pop restaurant and many of the people who will work will become like family, no one works for free. Even if you only feed and clothe some of the employees, there is still a cost. Plus, we should use this portion of the plan to evaluate the responsibilities of each position on the adventure. This section could help you identify holes where responsibilities are not being covered. You wouldn't want to get on the river of life and find out you didn't define who would be responsible for navigating the river, would you?

In the second portion of this section, you will need to identify the material items you will need. Now when we typically speak of material items, we are talking about equipment and such. In our example of the mom-and-pop restaurant, you would need the following:

1. Stove

2. Microwave
3. Oven
4. Pots and pans
5. Tables and chairs
6. Silverware
7. Plates
8. Cooking utensils
9. Mops and brooms
10. Tablecloths
11. Food
12. Drinks

And the list goes on. You should list everything you will need when it comes to supplies and such. This list could be very lengthy, but it is your grocery list for essentials. Though just as with any grocery list, you will leave things off without realizing. As your mastermind group and team review the plan, however, you will get input about what you're missing. Remember, you don't have to create this plan alone. Bring in help and make it better.

IMPLEMENTATION/TIMELINES

As we move to the next part of planning, I would like to stop for a second and jump on that soapbox again. The reason that most people don't take action always comes down to this section. They either fail to set timelines and detail how they will implement each part of the plan, or they think it will just happen on its own. Even then, they still fail to set realistic timelines.

If you don't set realistic timelines, you will not get moving. Your dream will always start tomorrow, and tomorrow will never come. This is as true a statement as there will ever be. By setting dates, your subconscious mind will help you find the answers you need and will help keep you motivated. Without a timeline to deliver your dreams and desires, you will float on the river of life—that is, until you go over the waterfall and the game is over.

You must also make your timelines realistic. The mind will determine whether your timeline is realistic or not. Many people set a "hurry up" timeline thinking that if they give themselves and their mind this "must do" timeline, they will have their desires faster. That's not how it works, and you will not gain the help of your subconscious mind as a result. With this type of timeline, you will create an adversary of your subconscious mind. Your subconscious may or may not be at odds with you. It may try to help you solve the issues to get you to these dates, but when you blow by the deliverable dates consistently, your subconscious will start to see that you don't want this desire because you aren't realistic. At that point, it stops helping you and starts saving energy.

If that weren't problematic enough, your team would behave the same way as your subconscious. They will lose confidence in the adventure. They will lose confidence in you as a leader, and then they will go out and find a better cause or job. People must accomplish things to feel good about an adventure or plan. If you are consistently setting unrealistic deliverable dates, you will sap away their motivation. They will feel as if they are letting you or the team down by not meeting the dates. Now if you miss your timeline by a few dates, the attitudes of your team and subconscious mind will not suffer all that bad. But if you are missing these by months or years, you're in trouble. Both your subconscious mind and your team need realistic dates so that they can keep the wind in their sails for the next challenge.

Timelines are not hard to set, but you need to take time and think through the activities of your plan and understand how long each one will take you. Then set your timeline for each deliverable. Keep in mind that as you see the deadline coming up when you are working on your plan, you will need to adjust the dates. Adjusting the dates will create a sense of confidence in both your mind and your team. Don't just let the date pass by as most people do. Adjust it as soon as you see it needs to be adjusted. Then work hard to meet the new date.

As you think through your delivery dates, you will essentially be thinking through how you will implement the parts of your plan. These two areas go hand in hand in the real world. As you look at what needs to be done, write down how you will start each activity and who will be responsible for that part of the plan.

Now I am not suggesting you write down names. I never put names in my plans. I put positions because the names of the people often change, but the positions remain. The people you start the journey with most likely will not be the ones you finish the dream with.

Process for Monitoring Progress

In this portion of your plan, you will set out checks to verify the progress you are making and determine if any adjustments are needed. Just as you did in the timeline portion, you should set dates to review how your journey is progressing. These dates will depend on how involved your plan is.

If you have a plan that will only take a few weeks, such as a vacation, you may want to review your checks every other day. But if this is an adventure such as starting a business and will span a long period, you may want to review your progress once a month.

At the beginning of any plan, your review dates should happen more often than they appear toward the end of the plan. After all, plans have more of a chance of failing in the beginning. They haven't built up momentum, and they need all the attention you can give them. The more attention you pay to the progress you are making, the better chance you have of catching mistakes early on and correcting them.

You are also trying to create a habit. Your new plan must become a habit, and by reviewing your progress, you are focusing on the plan and creating a habit. As you progress down the river of your plan, you will check your progress more often. You may even check your plan daily. Many business leaders will check their plans on a daily cycle. They are not digging in for hours of their day, but they are looking over where they are on certain parts each day. In this way, they're connected to the plan and its progression every day. If they find they are not getting the results they expected in a certain portion, they work to adjust that part of the plan.

When you are doing these checks, don't just do them passively. Look at where you should be and where you are. Are you behind on certain deliverables? If so, what action in your approach do you need to change?

Many of us seem to have trouble changing our plans or approaches when necessary. We continue to go down the same roads, and we are surprised when we get the same outcomes. This is what Albert Einstein defined as insanity. The best method is to review your progress, and if it is not serving you, you can take a different approach.

You can consider a different approach by involving your mastermind group with the review. No one person has all the answers, so use the group. You must be open to constructive criticism to get the help you need.

You may be completely off the mark with the approach you are taking. If someone points this out, do not just ignore the point of view. Explore it. Take yourself out of the position of the parent and look at what the other person is saying about your plan. You can rise above your point of view and look down on the plan. If you do this, you will better see your approach or decisions compared to those of others. If you take yourself out of the position of the creator, you will be able to review each point of view objectively.

Too often we think of our plans as our creations and believe they are flawless, just as parents believe their children are flawless. Those are your emotions. Get past them and take off the rose-colored glasses. If you don't, you will most likely fail.

You see, there are two of *you* in your mind, as described in Ray Dalio's book *Principles*. You have the emotional you and the logical you. These two parts of your brain are at odds most of the time, though you're emotional you is the stronger of the two. Anything you believe with emotion will propel you. When these two aspects of yourself are fighting, the emotional you have that little something extra over the logical you.

You can override the emotional you with the logical you, but you must be aware that this is what is going on within your mind. Awareness will bring you to enlightenment. It will also help in bringing humility to your decisions and emotions.

So too, someone may disagree with our plan, approach, or beliefs, and we may take it as an attack. Logically, we know better, but part of our brain is telling us to fight. Don't feel like you are the only person this happens to. It happens to all of us. I'm sure it even happened to people like Gandhi.

This is your basic human nature. The animal part of your brain is called the amygdala. Each of us has this primal part of the brain, and our emotions control it. Many have called this our fight-or-flight part of the brain.

Though you can control this part of yourself with your logical brain, it takes practices to achieve this level of control. We have been given the ability by God and the universe to remove ourselves from any situation and look at it from a third point of view. We are the only animals that can do this. Your brain has evolved just for this reason, so use it.

When your plan or approach is being questioned, don't take it as an attack. Instead, ask yourself, "How do I know this is true? And how do I know I'm right?" If you ask this question, it will help you get away from the ownership that ties you to your plan and approach, and you will be able to see the other side. It also allows you to stay calm in a situation that your mind sees as an attack.

Once you are outside of yourself, look down at your approach and plan and review the plan being proposed too. See the differences between the two as if you were someone else. Ask the person who is proposing the opposing plan or viewpoint, "How do you know you're right?" From this objective point of view, look over all the answers given. You may not be completely wrong in your thinking, and they may not be completely right. But that doesn't matter. What matters is that you develop the best plan or approach you can.

Don't worry about failure. It will happen. No matter what plan you take, even if you mix elements of different versions, it could fail. Learn from the failure. If the plan wasn't yours and it fails, do not blame the other person. Learn from the failure and get on with life. You chose the path, so you have ownership. Stand up and own your failures. Fail well, learn, and then try again. Don't lose your momentum just because you failed.

We have all been taught through school and life that we are expected to be A students, and that is the path to success. That way of thinking will never get you to your dreams and desires. If you believe you must be the smartest or you must know everything, you will never get to your dreams. You may never get started because you are so afraid of failure.

Get past it and accomplish your dreams. Understand that you will fail and that you must learn from your failures and take an innovative approach. Life is just that simple.

Work to separate your logical you from your emotional you. Then you will build a stronger plan. Use your team and mastermind group to help you continually improve your plan, and then execute it. Be relentless in the pursuit of your dreams. Work to serve others as well as yourself. Build a great plan with help. If you do these things, you will be ahead of most of the people on this earth.

But it is up to you to decide about the life you will have. It will be demanding work, but demanding work can be fun and is very rewarding.

The next step is to follow the steps in the chapter on desire. These steps will not fail you in your journey if you do not fail to follow them throughout your life. But always remember, some of our desires are realized in as brief a time as twenty-four hours, while others could take a lifetime to fulfill.

THE SUCCESS PITFALLS PRINCIPLES OF FAILING TO PLAN AND OVERVIEW

As Captain Bon worked through his plan, he wondered why for so much of his life he had not done more planning. Why wasn't there a plan for everything he wanted in life? Sure, he had done some planning for his job or vacations, but these weren't the things that would help him fulfill his desires. And as for the planning at work, well, that was forced on him.

Why had he been content with going through life without a plan? He now knew most people in the world took what life gave them and never really thought much about it. It was the way they lived their day-to-day lives. It had become a vicious circle in Captain Bon's life, and he felt that it was the same for most people.

In the past, he would take what came and never created a plan to change it. As life threw him other things he didn't want to have, instead of planning to change the situation, he would take these and deal with what came.

But why wouldn't people plan to go after their desires? Why didn't he ever develop a plan to change his life? When he thought about all the things it would take to get to his desire it all felt overwhelming. It was more than his mind could comprehend altogether.

As Captain Bon thought more about chasing his desire to travel the river to Mount La Felicidad, he became scared because of the complexity of the undertaking. There were so many parts that he would need to handle.

How could he do it all? How could he create a plan to succeed, and how would he know everything that he needed to capture in the plan?

Fears clouded his mind, and he forgot his process for success. His mind was so clouded that he had forgotten everything he had learned. He had forgotten the system that he had worked so long to put together to help him. Fear of failure was all that he could see now.

It was simply too much to think about. Everything ran together into one blur. Captain Bon couldn't see how to create a plan. He became fearful that he would end up failing and being judged as worthless. This only strengthened his fears and gave strength to Señor Doubter. Señor Doubter was running rampant in Captain Bon's mind. It was because looking at the entire adventure was too much.

Captain Bon went to a quiet place and meditated to clear his mind. He needed to clear his mind of the fears that were clouding his vision. Captain Bon knew he could build his plan, but he needed his mind clear of the fears.

As Captain Bon meditated, he was able to release the anxieties and fears that were clouding his mind. With a clear mind, Captain Bon could see where he was going wrong. He was trying to figure out his plan by looking at it from start to finish. It was too much for anyone. What he needed to do was take it step-by-step. He needed to divide his plan into small chunks. Once he had it all broken apart, he could work with himself and others to develop each part.

Once all the parts of the plan were individually solved, he could then put it all back together as a complete plan. By chunking the plan, he could look at each part individually and then understand the full plan. He remembered now how he would succeed in creating the plan.

It was funny to Captain Bon that Franklin Roosevelt's inaugural speech came back to him at this moment. "There is nothing to fear but fear itself." Indeed, he had feared fear. He had allowed it to cloud his mind with doubt. He lacked self-confidence. He came back to himself and his principles. He had answers to each of the fears he faced in his system.

He had answered the principles that would help him develop his plan from chunking it into multiple parts and getting help from others in his mastermind group and team. The answers would come. He just had to be ready to see the answers. He had to clear away the fears and open himself to the principles of success.

Now with his mind clear, Captain Bon was ready to take on developing his plan. He knew that he would have to watch for the success pitfalls principles to arise again down the road, but he felt he could beat it by clearing his mind and breaking down whatever he was facing into its smallest parts.

He would then work on planning each part with help from others. If he followed this system, he could develop a plan to succeed in whatever he wanted in life. He didn't have to accept what life handed him. He could have whatever he desired. It just took a few simple steps and a clear mind.

CHAPTER 10

ORGANIZATION OF SPECIALIZED KNOWLEDGE
THE PROCESS OF ORGANIZING THE KNOWLEDGE TO TRAVEL THE RIVER

CAPTAIN BON HAD GATHERED MUCH of what he needed to succeed in the adventure. He had brought together the best supporting staff he could find. He had also gathered together the financial support with the help of Dennis and Fred Fisher, his main financial supporter.

Many people bought into his dream and wanted to be part of his adventure, but the main five were Dennis, Fred Fisher, Norris, Aaron, and Kelly. These were the main supporters Captain Bon needed to complete his adventure and his dream.

Each member brought different skills to the group, but these five brought passion and drive. They pushed Captain Bon to become the best leader he had ever been. They brought out the "want" in him, not only to accomplish his dream but to help others accomplish their dreams.

The trick now was how to stay out in front of them and keep everyone motivated. This is where Captain Bon's system would pull everyone together to work as one mind and one unit. Everyone had to be engaged. Everyone had to have input, and everyone needed to be valued for what they brought to the table.

No one's opinion would be valued less than any other. Captain Bon needed to create an environment that supported bringing out ideas without judgment. This environment would value ideas, not positions on the team. While it was Captain Bon's dream, he couldn't be the center point. The adventure had to be the center point if they wanted to make it a reality.

This was so important to Captain Bon, and it was part of his plan to achieve the adventure. He would push each member to bring their ideas to the table. Not sharing your ideas and thoughts would not be tolerated. Each person had to have input.

It couldn't be a judgmental environment, which could become the hardest part. Captain Bon knew that people would always feel they were being judged and would be reluctant to come forth. They would let their insecurities stand in the way of great ideas coming to the surface and helping the adventure.

Captain Bon knew he would have to gather each member's specialized knowledge and organize it into usable knowledge. Each member had experience in their area of expertise as well as knowledge in other areas that would help. Captain Bon's job was to bring together the specialized knowledge and direct it into an action plan. He was also in charge of bringing out each member's ideas and thoughts.

The organization of specialized knowledge was key to the success of the adventure. All ideas and thoughts on important decisions need consideration and need to be weighed for their possible flaws or improvements. Captain Bon knew that while experience provided the best information to pull from, it could also cloud a person's judgment. By triangulating all the ideas and thoughts presented on a decision, they could find the best plan.

He wanted to have all the ideas he could get so that he could have the best ideas to use for action. Captain Bon figured that if he could get everyone to pool together their thoughts and ideas, he could create a system to weigh each idea for benefits and possible shortcomings. He could triangulate all the ideas to find the best solution to any problem. It wouldn't just be his way. It would be the best idea or combination of ideas that would lead the way.

The triangulation of ideas wasn't a new concept. It had been used by many successful people in their adventures and important decisions.

Triangulating came for trigonometry and geometry, and it was a process of determining the location of a point by forming triangles from other known points. Captain Bon understood that he could take different ideas and decide what points they made and then find the best path forward. He would triangulate the path from the known points each idea had.

Triangulating would mean taking in all the ideas and thoughts on a given issue and looking at how they were the same and how they were different. Bon would prefer to have at least three competing ideas to triangulate the solution, but more would be even better.

He would have each team member give their suggestion a confidence number between one and ten and then assign a confidence number to each of the other ideas or thoughts on the same scale. The confidence numbers would be anonymous and only associated with the idea. This way, there wouldn't be any infighting among the team members. The object was to find the value in each solution, come to a consensus, and move forward. They wouldn't use this process on each decision, but they would with all decisions that were critical to the adventure.

He would then have each person look at the opposing ideas objectively and give a competitive debate about the pros and cons of the differences. The only rule was that the debate had to be positive.

By listening to input from everyone and triangulating the ideas to find a common path, he would organize the specialized knowledge needed to succeed. He knew everyone had their specialties within the organization. As individuals, they were smart, but as a group, they could be brilliant.

Captain Bon also knew that he had to foster an environment where it was okay to fail and that failing well would have to be the goal. Failing well meant that people could fail and keep their dignity intact. They wouldn't have to worry about being judged by the other team members when they were wrong.

They would only face judgment if they didn't learn from the failure. Captain Bon knew that failure was the greatest teacher. Even with the system he had designed to triangulate decisions and ideas, there would still be failures. Failures had to be built into the equation for future decisions. They would have to accept and learn from failures. Accepting failures and learning from them had to be a cornerstone of the system.

He taught each member that it was okay to fail if they learned, and he also taught them that the group would not tolerate judgment or resentment for failure. Hiding a failure wouldn't be tolerated either. When someone on the team failed, everyone on the team failed, and each member needed to learn from the failure. Through learning what went wrong, they could grow and become stronger.

Captain Bon felt that you had to take ownership of your failures and learn from them if you wanted to succeed. Then you had to pick yourself up and try an innovative approach. It didn't matter if you failed a thousand times. It wasn't a failure if you learned. It was an education. After all, he figured we were here to learn, grow, and contribute.

You see, the advantage to groups—whether it's a group of two or a group of twenty—was the experience that each person brought. A group that works together through harmony can become one very powerful mind. This mind could accomplish anything it desired, but again, they had to be in harmony.

Keeping harmony in a group could be the toughest part. How could a person keep everyone in harmony? Infighting or resentment would undermine the process. In turn, it would prevent the greatest ideas from coming to the top, and they needed great ideas so that the team could fully realize the adventure. Captain Bon understood that harmony was needed in any relationship if you wanted the relationship to thrive and not just survive.

Captain Bon thought of ways he could ensure harmony and prevent resentment and infighting. He would work with each person so that they felt they could voice their thoughts and opinions. He had built rapport with each of the members of his team, and he felt he could tell when they were holding back. He had built this rapport through truly caring for each team member.

He felt that the most important thing he could do as the leader was to build rapport with each team member through truly caring for each of them. He also felt the greatest lesson he could teach them was to care for one another and to build a relationship with each member that would withstand any disagreements or failures that were to come.

This wouldn't be an easy lesson to teach. Captain Bon figured the best way to teach caring and rapport was to serve as a living model of these traits. They had to be seen in each of Captain Bon's actions and decisions. He had to show that caring for each member was the single most important action of the adventure. After all, it was not just about the adventure. It was also about the journey and the people we work with on that journey. It was the interaction of the team that would bring happiness, not just the accomplishment of the dream.

But what if he couldn't tell if they were being forthcome? Also, would the method he had to weigh each team member's thoughts and suggestions work? This would be harder than he had imagined, but he knew it was important to the success of the team.

Captain Bon couldn't be totally sure that he could keep the infighting and resentment out. He only knew that by fostering an environment that valued ideas and truth above everything, he stood the best chance for success. He would monitor and change his approach if he had to. Much like everything else in his system, the success of his approach depended on another part.

WHAT HAVE WE LEARNED FROM CAPTAIN BON?

We have seen through Captain Bon's experience that the organization of specialized knowledge is imperative to the success of any adventure, but the gathering of that knowledge can often be difficult. In any organization, there is always competition and politics.

Captain Bon also knew he didn't want this type of organization. He didn't want the infighting that went with politics and office competition. It wasn't that competition was bad, but the competition between team members could easily go wrong and stall the team's advancement.

He needed harmony for the ideas of the team to advance and to come out when they were needed. A team with members in harmony with one another could accomplish wonderful things, but if they were at odds with one another, they wouldn't advance as quickly. Harmony is a balancing act, and one had to always be on the watch for attacks to harmony.

Each member could bring harmony or destroy the harmony of the group. It wasn't that they meant to destroy the harmony, but through the feeling of judgment, infighting, or resentment, they would inadvertently cause the loss of harmony.

If members thought they were always being judged and that they could be shown as inadequate, they wouldn't reveal their true thoughts. Even so, he also knew that creating an environment of full disclosure would also hinder the competition of ideas through constant debate.

So he devised a system where ideas could be anonymously suggested and assigned a value for confidence. He also added a component to the system where each member could anonymously weigh in on other ideas and thoughts with confidence numbers.

He would also allow members to debate one another's ideas anonymously. This would give each idea a full review and allow them all to consider competing thoughts.

We also learned from Captain Bon that failure is inevitable. We all fail, and as the old saying goes, "If you're not failing, you're not trying." The trick is to fail well and learn from the failure. Then you must pick yourself up, break down what happened, and determine why things didn't go as you had planned. Then take what you learned and change your approach as you try again.

Captain Bon teaches us that we never fail if we learn and try again. He also teaches us that we cannot tolerate hiding failures. Whether it's a failure of a single person or the team as a whole, the team must take ownership of the failure and learn from it. In learning from the failure and moving forward, the team will become stronger.

We must build rapport and a relationship with our members through caring. We must care about what is going on with each of our team members. We must care about what each team member wants to achieve. We must care about their ideas and thoughts, especially when they fail.

Captain Bon built rapport between himself and each of the team members. This rapport helped them whenever infighting arose. It stopped many of the political battles that could derail a team from their path to success.

WHAT IS THE ORGANIZATION OF SPECIALIZED KNOWLEDGE?

First, we need to understand what type of knowledge we are referring to. What is knowledge? How do you define it? How do others use this elusive thought we call knowledge? How do we use it? Is it what you learn in school or what you learn from life? Is it what your parents teach you as you are growing up or trivia as seen on game shows? Is it what you learn when you fail and do not get the result you want?

Many would consider all these types of knowledge—some of the general knowledge and some specific knowledge. We all hold both general and specific knowledge about subjects such as science, history, business, art, and many other subjects that we use throughout our lives.

So how do we use the vast knowledge we have or that we can gain from the world? Knowledge alone is not power. Nor will it get you what you desire. *To use knowledge to gain our desires in life, we have to organize the knowledge into a definite plan of action and direct it to a definite completion date.*

The way we organize the knowledge and use it is by first defining the decision that we need to make or the challenge that stands in our way. We need to define the decision or challenge clearly. Then we can break it down to its root.

Next, we need to gather as many thoughts and solutions to the challenge at hand. If possible, we should do this anonymously to prevent resentment or infighting from developing. We should have each member assign a confidence number to their suggestion or idea.

Then we can have each member review each of the suggestions and assign other confidence numbers. They should also write down their thoughts about the benefits and shortcomings of the suggestions. If possible, this also should be done anonymously.

The next step is to take the information gathered and to triangulate everything to find the best path forward. If the group has a strong relationship and rapport with one another, this system will work well without too much infighting, debating, or resentment being produced.

This system outlined here is but a small bit of information. It is also where our education system fails most of its students. It gives you the knowledge and doesn't tell you how to make it work for you to achieve your goal. Moreover, our education system rewards success and punishes failure. It fails, for the most part, to teach its students to work together to solve problems and instead pits each of the students against one another.

Many people think they must possess all the knowledge of the subject that involves their trip up the river of life. This is a huge mistake, and people tend to be this way because they have not been educated. You see, educated people know they cannot possibly hold all the information needed to succeed in life. But through the organization of others who hold greater knowledge in different areas, they will get to their desires with fewer failures.

My greatest successes in life and my most enjoyable journeys had come as a result of those times when I was *not* the smartest person on the team. These are also the same times when I have learned the most on any subject. My mind was open to listening, learning, and accepting the content offered by others. When you look at the most successful people who have traveled this world's river, you will find that this was one of their most successful traits.

So why do we feel that we must hold the most knowledge? It's likely because humans feel the need to be respected among their peers. They seem to believe that they are inferior to others if they show they are not experts. By doing this, they find others unwilling to work with them to achieve their desires.

Again, it goes back to the basics of seeking pleasure and avoiding pain. They believe that they should hide that they do not understand or know every aspect of a situation or endeavor. They believe they are better served not to ask questions that could educate them. This is just the opposite of the path they should take. If you understand the truth about looking at life as a young child, you will understand that you must ask all the questions you can. This does not show you are weak or uneducated. To the contrary, it shows you are secure in your abilities, educated on how to succeed, and trusting in others to help you achieve greatness.

People also fail at this point because they refuse to build rapport and respect with others, and thus, they do not receive the help they need. People feel that if they ask for help or knowledge from others who work for them, they will judge them. They are not judging you. They are most likely honored that you think of them as knowledgeable enough to help. But if you do not build rapport with them, they will never reveal the secrets of the universe to you. Or worse, they may point you in the wrong direction just for the fun of watching you fail. You see, unlike in the animal kingdom where animals don't harm other animals just for sport, humans are more than happy to watch someone fail.

The one truth I have learned to help remind me that I must build rapport with others to succeed comes from John Maxwell. Maxwell teaches that "people do not care what you know until they know you care." If you take this statement to heart, you will easily understand the importance of building rapport.

Let's evaluate this saying now. We have learned that no one will help you unless that person is getting something in return. For most, it's not about their pay or the benefits that they could gain. It's about having people who care about them. It's about being valued for what they bring to the team or organization. Too often leaders fail to show their people that they care about them as individuals.

We are all busy, but it takes a very small part of your day to show people you care. How long does it take to ask someone, "How's your family doing?" Or "What do you want to achieve?" These questions will only take a little bit of your time. Maybe it'll take an hour at the most as you listen and understand the person. But what you are giving them is invaluable. You are giving your time, and the other person will understand how valuable your time is. Time is our greatest value in life, and when we give it to others, we are giving the greatest gift we can give. This shows the person that we care, and thus, the person will care for us.

You may think, *How do we build rapport or show others we care to attain their help?* Well, the first thing to note is that we should not just build rapport to get what we want. That's not caring. Nor is it going to get you very far in life. You see, people can identify if you are not sincere, and others are watching your actions at every moment. If you are not doing it from your heart, people will realize what your true intentions are and will refuse to help you gain your desires. Furthermore, people want to know what's in it for them, so you have to offer them a return for their efforts.

No one does anything for free. You can lie to yourself and say, "This person did this out of the goodness of his or her heart and wants nothing in return," but that is the biggest lie there is in the world. We all have alternative motives. It may just be the feelings we get when we do something, but we get pleasure or avoid pain in the end.

Many times, we act more out of our need to feel loved or respected. But even those great people like Mother Teresa had a reason to do the seemingly unselfish giving she was known for in her life. She didn't do it for fame or money. She did it because of the feeling she had experienced many years earlier toward the less fortunate. When she tried to help a poor dying woman get medical aid to ease her pain, Mother Teresa realized that not everyone was treated with dignity in the last minutes of their lives. She vowed to help the less fortunate retain some dignity during their last days on this earth. Now, this is as unselfish as you can get in life, but she still did it to receive something. In short, she felt fulfilled by helping the less fortunate.

One way to build rapport and respect with a person is to mirror and model the specific individual. Now I'm not talking about becoming a clone of that person. I'm talking about mirroring his or her voice tempo, volume, and facial expressions. We do this naturally with people we have a rapport with already. It is built into us by our creator at birth. We just never realized that we could do this on demand to create rapport with people we have just met.

However, as you are working on your mirroring, you need to practice pacing. While mirroring and matching will create rapport and respect when done correctly, some may think you are mocking their actions, and then they will close out from their inner circle as a result. Just think about what your feelings would be toward someone you felt was making fun of you through mocking your habits. You would be hurt and avoid the person in the future, wouldn't you?

Some of the less conspicuous ways to model and mirror a person to establish rapport include slowly copying posture, facial expressions, voice volume, and expressing interest in a subject people are discussing. Use the person's name during the conversation to show respect. People truly love hearing their names said out loud.

During the conversation, repeat back key points of the conversation to ensure you fully understand what the other person intended you to understand. This will help you build rapport with the other person. In any communication, you are responsible for 100 percent of understanding— both yours and your audience's.

The Success Pitfalls Principles That Destroy the Organization of Knowledge

Captain Bon had watched many groups and organizations starve for knowledge. It wasn't that these groups didn't have the availability of knowledge or that they lacked it within their organizations. It was that there was no harmony within these groups, and consequently, the knowledge couldn't be organized.

There was dissent within the groups that came from the members seeking popularity and power instead of seeking what was good for the organization. The leaders of the groups couldn't bring their members together to drive the organization to a higher level.

Captain Bon felt that some of these leaders did this to create competition within their groups and find the strongest leaders. But when these people's animal natures came out, it became a game of kill or be killed. The organization was torn apart by this infighting.

In the end, this competition didn't create stronger leaders, which was what the leaders had hoped. It created infighting and the withholding of knowledge. This also created cliques within the organizations. Thus, cliques did not share knowledge with the other cliques, and the overall knowledge couldn't be organized to create a stronger entity.

Captain Bon wanted to protect against this success pitfalls principle more than most. He knew that infighting could cause the failure of his adventure faster than any other mistake. If members of his mastermind group or team fought, they wouldn't work together and share their thoughts and ideas openly.

If this happened, how could he create the best plans? Though competition is important, it had to be the right competition. It had to be an internal competition with oneself. It could drive you to do better than you had done before. The competition with oneself could drive the person to become better through the help of others. Each person would then share knowledge, and the organization would grow as a result.

Captain Bon's organization would grow strong through the sharing of knowledge with one another. They would challenge one another's thoughts and ideas so that the group and plan would become stronger. They would also openly question the plans and ideas to get at their strengths and weaknesses. This way, the team could debate and triangulate their thoughts and ideas to find the best path forward.

In this way, they could organize specialized knowledge and use it to develop the organization and the adventure. This organization of knowledge is a must if one wants to realize his or her adventure.

Two other success pitfalls principles that are also against the organization of specialized knowledge are a know-it-all attitude and closed-mindedness. Though these two are normally the same, there are times when they do work independently.

A know-it-all attitude is displayed by people who feel they can't be taught or explained anything. They feel that they must have all the answers to be respected and to have power. Respect and power are their ultimate drivers, and to be seen wanting for knowledge is their downfall. Thus, they fail to take advice from others, and consequently, they lose specialized knowledge.

Closed-minded people won't allow for the organization of specialized knowledge either. As you can with the know-it-alls, closed-minded people do not take advice from others. They often don't listen for the same reasons as the know-it-all people, but they are also closed off completely from the advice of others and do not seek out specialized knowledge.

It is not that they think they know everything. It's more that the person thinks he or she must find the answers themselves without the help of others. While know-it-all types have people around them but don't use their input, closed-minded people do not surround themselves with the thought or suggestions of others at all.

With all this in mind, Captain Bon decided to create a "rules of engagement" pledge that he would share with his team. He also decided that he would explain the why behind the rules of engagement.

Thinking over what the pledge would be, he came to the following pledge of partnership:

"Pledge of Engagement"

I pledge my allegiance and forthcoming to this team. My part to play will advance the team as a whole and not just one person or group. I pledge that I will be openly honest and open-minded to others while not causing hurt to my fellow members. I will remember that I will make mistakes and that I do not retain all the necessary knowledge, and I know others will do the same. I understand that we are all in this adventure together and that the success of one is the success of all. So too, the failure of one is the failure of all. Together under God, we do make this pledge to each partner.

In developing this pledge, Captain Bon understood what he would be asking from his teammates, and much like the instructions given by flight attendants on a plane, they would need to recite the pledge at each meeting. This way, it would become a part of each member.

Through reciting the pledge of engagement, each member would be reminded of how they would treat other members. Through the reciting, they couldn't with good conscious act wrongly to the other members.

Captain Bon knew that some individuals wouldn't take the pledge to heart and live by it, but he felt that he would be able to find these individuals quickly and remove them from the adventure. No one would be above the pledge, not even Captain Bon.

Through explaining the pledge to his partners, he found that they understood the reason before he ever explained it. Most of the members had seen these same three success pitfalls principles within organizations and had firsthand experience of their destructive powers.

When he thought back over about introducing the pledge, Captain Bon was amazed at how it was accepted. It brought a feeling of accomplishment that he had taken the time to pick the right partners for his adventure. He knew this through the way they accepted the pledge as well as the way they interacted with one another. Together they would defend against the success pitfalls principles that could destroy the adventure.

CHAPTER 11

YOUR THINK TANK OR MASTERMIND GROUP
THE PEOPLE ON THE RIVER TRIP WITH YOU

CAPTAIN BON WAS FINALLY ON his way to the river of life, traveling to Mount La Felicidad. He hadn't gotten to this place in his adventure alone. It took a team of people. This team consisted of the advisers Captain Bon had gathered as his mastermind group, his logistical team that worked behind the scenes, and the two adventurers on the river with him.

It all started with the mastermind group that Captain Bon had put together. This was a group of five advisers he had asked to join a group that he had originally called a think tank. He developed it to help him with his plan to reach Mount La Felicidad, but he knew they wouldn't help unless there was something in it for them.

Therefore, he called it a think tank. He told each member that they could come together to help one another solve the problems that stood in the way of reaching their desires and dreams in life. As a team, they could solve most any problem that stood in their way. If they didn't know an answer within the group, they could ask one of the associates of the six members.

One member could have access to ten others with the needed information, and a group of six meant that they had six times that access. So now they would have access to sixty advisers or more to help them succeed.

Captain Bon was wise enough to know that he had first to give than receive. During the first few meetings, he explained that each member should bring before the group the challenges or decisions that they needed to make in their adventure. Captain Bon restrained himself from bringing up his need for them to review his plan until after six meetings.

He used the first six meetings to help the other members find solutions to their challenges. He also spent the time building rapport with the other five members. He did this through caring about their needs before he brought his up for them to solve. He showed true caring for each member by asking about their families and life goals. He spent time listening and advising where he could.

He practiced mirroring their actions and took in their beliefs to understand each person's perspective. This helped him establish the much-needed rapport through caring. In caring enough to understand why they looked at things the way they did, he understood what life had taught each of them. Understanding the why behind their desires and dreams helped Captain Bon help them.

Through the meetings, Captain Bon introduced the other five members to his system for organizing specialized knowledge and weighing the suggestions and ideas through assigning confidence numbers. He also worked with them to stay in harmony with one another as they worked to solve their challenges. He explained that through harmony, caring, and rapport, they could accomplish anything they set their minds to. But if they allowed infighting or resentment to sneak in, they would surely fail.

Once Captain Bon felt that he had built rapport with the other five members, he asked if they would review his plan and advise him. He knew he had captured most of the key points; however, the plan needed work, and he didn't have all the knowledge necessary to succeed. He needed the advice of the mastermind group, but more than advice, he needed their support.

This adventure would be a great undertaking for anyone, and no one could do it alone. The team needed support in so many ways, but none more than the support to continue when times were hard. They needed the motivation to go on when everything was going wrong. They needed reminders that they had succeeded in the past and could succeed again and that the tough time was nothing more than the winter season of an adventure. Things seem cold and dead in the winter. But then the spring comes, and the plan can grow.

PUT YOURSELF IN CAPTAIN BON'S PLACE

You are now Captain Bon, and you're on your way to the river in your adventure. You can choose two people who will accompany you on this adventure. You must choose who will be the best to help you during the journey. These two people will hold the specific knowledge of things like navigating, finding food, setting up camp, and other things that are needed to survive and get to your destination. It's not that you do not possess some of these skills; however, their skills are sharper in some of these areas than yours, and they also complement your skills.

These partners can also help you figure out the areas that none of you have experience in. By working together closely, your minds will meld together. You will know what the others know, and your minds will become one powerful mind. The power you all have together will be immeasurable. Let's look at what you can do together.

The three of you are in the boat on the river, and the water has become rough. There are many rocks on each side of the boat, and the water is churning. The boat is being pushed side to side, and you are in danger of smashing into a large rock and sinking at any moment. Your equipment in the boat is starting to move side to side and needs to be secured. You don't want to lose the equipment after all. If you lose this equipment deep in the jungle, you will not make it out. You will be lost here, and you will not have completed your adventure.

It is up to the three of you to navigate through these dangers to a safe and calm area. Together your partners work to stabilize the equipment by the two of them working together, all while you steer the boat as best as you can. Once your two partners are done securing the equipment, they go to either side of the front of the boat and advise you of the dangers ahead. They yell out instructions and advisories. You hear, "Rock on the left side. You need to steer right." The second adventurer says, "Not too far right. We have large rock a hundred feet off the right side. Prepare to shift back left."

These advisories help you to navigate the dangerous water and keep you from damaging the boat beyond repair. As the three of you work together, it becomes seamless. You know your next move from the instructions. Your partners learn how to explain better what is coming and the course that you need to take. Together the three of you are one mind. Though it would not appear that way to an outsider, the three of you feel it. The three of you have a keen sense of unity. Your joint achievements will become more than what one person could ever have done alone.

WHAT HAVE YOU LEARNED FROM CAPTAIN BON AND YOUR OWN EXPERIENCE?

After hearing these two stories, can you see why a mastermind group is so important? Maybe you think, *Can't I just reach my desire on my own?* Well, if you believe that any successful person made it to the top all alone, think again. You may not see who helped these people, but they had helpers. We all need a support team and not just a group of yes-men. We need those who will stand up and tell you what you need to hear, no matter how hard it is to say.

We also cannot stand in our way. We must listen to those close to us and grow from what they have to offer. Henry Ford once said (during a lawsuit to prove he was not an educated man) that he could press a button on his desk at any moment and summon any number of experts in any field he needed information in and receive the knowledge to advance his pursuit.

Now that was a man who understood how to gain true knowledge. Ford's dependence on great minds and his open-minded attitude to not get in his way is what led him to become one of the most successful and most powerful men of his time. None of us have the answers to all the questions, and we should never rely just on our knowledge. There are too many variables in any venture in life, and we all need advisers.

So how do we know if we have the right advisors? Well, we need to ask ourselves the following questions:

1. What are they after, or why do they want to help me get to my desire?
2. How will my mastermind group get to their desires in life by helping me?

3. Does my team tell me the truth or just what I want to hear?
4. Are they the experts in the field of my desires?
5. Do these individuals or does this team work in harmony? Or do they fight?
6. When working with this mastermind group, do our minds meld together to create solutions?
7. Do the people in the mastermind group bring together the necessary accumulated experience to reach our desires?

If we do not ask these questions, we only set ourselves up to fail. While it is important to have a team, it is even more important to have a team that works in harmony toward the same goals. If a team is not in harmony, the members will only pull in different directions. As most know, not only will this not get you to your desire, but it will also create great pain in the lives of your team members and you.

You will find that sometimes you will make excuses for your team or say, "They are the best I can find. They are really good people." But these are just weak excuses and will not get you the mastermind group you need.

Each team needs why people as well as how people. The why people put out the vision and mission. The how people create the systems that will take you to the desired destination. If you want to learn more about why people and how people, I advise you to read Simon Sinek's book *Start with Why*. It's not just a great read, but it may give excellent information to you on this subject.

No adventure will work without both groups. You will see why people who fail because they can't complete what has to be done to get through the rough waters or even finish the simple things that would make the voyage easier and more fun. They are too busy thinking of the reasons to do what they are trying to do, and they miss all the logistics that are needed to get to the destination. These are the *visionaries* of the group.

The same holds for how people. They are excellent at creating processes and procedures for what must be done. They are typically also good at creating auditing procedures to check that things are getting done. But they can't create the grand dreams that change the world or make a difference in people's lives. It's not that they don't see the vision or take it as their own. It's that they are more comfortable in creating the logistics and plans to get to the vision and aren't concerned with the *why*. They are focused on the *how*.

A notable example of this kind of team was Bill Gates and Paul Allen when they created Microsoft. Bill Gates was the why person. He wanted to change the world through software. Now I'm not saying Paul Allen didn't want to change the world or that he didn't share Gates's vision. But he was the how person. Bill Gates is the better known and recognized person, but Bill Gates couldn't have succeeded the way he did without Paul Allen. Similarly, Paul Allen couldn't have created the why that would push him to create what Microsoft would become.

Okay, that's enough about examples of mastermind groups. How about we look at how it works or how it should work? You have a vision of a company, venture, or some worthwhile adventure you want to take. You have taken your vision and put it down on paper.

Then you find others you feel would want to take this adventure with you—people who will get behind your vision and help make it better. It could involve one person or a team of ten. That is up to you, and it depends on the size of the adventure you are undertaking.

Now it's time to get the mastermind group together and share as a group how you can accomplish this vision. You will likely hold multiple meetings. The first meeting will be the most difficult. The team must learn to work together. They must learn what each person contributes and how they think. But over time, each meeting will become more productive and flow with ideas or solutions to the problems you face on the adventure. Some of these meetings will be planned, and others will happen at the spur of the moment. Don't be set fast in how or where you meet. Be set fast in that you meet and share your minds and thoughts. You will find even a conference call will work. It's about getting together to brainstorm. You will get more out of a brainstorming session with a team than you will be beating your head against the problem. This comes from having different perspectives and different life experiences to pull from.

Most people think choosing like-minded people for their mastermind group or team is the way to go, but it isn't. You want people who have different perspectives than you, partners who have different life experiences to bring to the table. If everyone in your group thinks the same or goes along with whatever the leaders think, you will never get the most out of the group. You need people who will challenge you and the rest of the group. With these challenges, the brain starts thinking. It digs deeper than it has before and finds the solutions it is looking for to solve the problem or challenge.

There are many theories on how this happens. Some say that everything you need to know is in you, but until you stretch your mind and resources, you will not find them. Others say that it comes from minds working together as one, that our minds will blend and become one powerful mind to access the universe's knowledge. Then others say it comes from God or some other heavenly form. Whatever theory you believe, know that it works. You will get more accomplished and solved through your mastermind group than you will alone. After all, two minds are better than one. If two are better than one, how much better will three or four be?

Now you have your vision, and you have your mastermind group. How do you get to the starting point? What do you do to get this boat in the water and begin the adventure? Well, the easiest way to start is to meet with your mastermind group and begin brainstorming about how you can take your vision and make it a reality. What things will you need to get there? What are some of the problems you think you will face along the way? How can you avoid these problems in the first place, or how can you get around them? Remember that the more time you put into planning, the better prepared you will be when the issues arise. And they will arise.

These sessions are a training ground for you and your team. It gives you the time to practice and to explore the options. If done often, it becomes deliberate. And the more it is done, the more comfortable everyone becomes with the process and with one another. Each person learns the others' strengths and weaknesses, their areas of expertise, and the areas they know little about. Each member also learns more about the others' domains, and from there, they can help them expand through questions. It has been widely acknowledged that through teaching a subject, we learn more about the subject.

THE SUCCESS PITFALLS PRINCIPLE THAT DESTROYS THE MASTERMIND GROUP

Like most in the world, Captain Bon felt for years that people who had been successful in their adventures and attained their dreams were somehow special. They had somehow come by the knowledge and could make decisions that the rest of the world couldn't. He wasn't sure whether they had God-given talents or they had learned skills in a school or from their families, but somehow they could do what very few others could do.

Henry Ford or Bill Gates, for instance, were larger than life and seemed to possess something he didn't have. Captain Bon studied their lives and successes to see what was different in them from most people, and what Captain Bon found amazed him and set him down the road to his success principles.

While these people were smart in one way or another, they weren't any more intelligent than most people. Some didn't even have very much education at all, but they did have something others didn't have. They could inspire and listen to other people. They could put together teams that accomplished more than anyone else. And while they were the sparks that lit the fires of their adventures, they weren't necessarily the heavy lifters. They relied on their teams to advise them and help them accomplish their dreams.

The way they did this was by choosing their teams wisely and working to keep them in harmony. When the team members weren't in harmony, the leaders worked hard to take away the barriers that caused the disharmony. If they found that an individual team member was causing the disharmony, the leaders would work with that member to return the harmony to the group. If they couldn't change the team member who was causing the disharmony, the leaders would break their connection with that individual.

The harmony of the group was the main objective to keep the growth of knowledge in the organization. This knowledge was organized and used to grow the team. It wasn't that there weren't debates and arguments, but these were conducted with mutual respect. Furthermore, the greater good of the team and its vision was more important than any one team member.

Respecting each member and putting the vision and mission first kept the harmony intact. Each member received payment in one way or another for their work, but it wasn't at the cost of any other member.

Teams such as this could be seen in any organization or team that was accomplishing things that others thought were impossible. The size of the teams didn't matter. Some teams had only two members in the beginning and grew over time as the adventure grew. Each of these teams grew through harmony and knowledge. As they grew, they attracted other members with the specialized knowledge that they needed to meet the challenges they often encountered.

Through the organization of this specialized knowledge, the team was able to grow. Organizing the specialized knowledge meant that with the introduction of new knowledge, each member could learn and challenge what had been held before as a belief. Through these challenges to beliefs, the team could find whether the belief was serving them or not. They could challenge each belief to help one another get past the beliefs that hold them back.

They did this by examining the supporting legs of the beliefs and figuring out where the person had gained the belief. Through logically examining the supporting legs, the members could break down the belief and figure out how to change the belief.

By having harmony, the group could approach any issue or challenge within their adventure or personal life without the fear of judgment. Without the fear of judgment, the members were free to open and share what they believed.

Captain Bon worried he couldn't keep the team in harmony. He knew that fears drove people internally, and then they wouldn't share what needed to be solved. The fear of judgment was the strongest success pitfall that could destroy a mastermind group. So how do you stop this fear? How do you keep the team members fearless? It had to come from caring. This support showed each member that their growth and the growth of the team were the main objectives.

Captain Bon thought hard about caring. When people knew that they had the support and that others cared about them and their dreams, they could get past their fears, which often paralyzed them. Captain Bon knew these fears were normal. After all, they included the fear of judgment, the fear of the unknown, and the fear of being alone. But if caring relationships with other people were present, anyone could get past these fears.

Captain Bon felt that the only way he could keep his mastermind group in harmony was through caring. While building his mastermind group, he would have to make sure that each member truly cared about one another and their dreams. He had to make sure that every member helped the others grow and achieve their dreams.

CHAPTER 12

BEGINNING YOUR
JOURNEY TO SUCCESS
CAPTAIN BON BEGINS THE
JOURNEY WITH SIX STROKES

WHILE THINKING ABOUT THE ADVENTURE ahead and all the things that he would need to accomplish before ever stepping foot on the boat at the mouth of the river to Mount La Felicidad, Captain Bon thought about what he had already accomplished. There had been so many steps of his journey that he had already taken, but they mostly involved six of the ten parts within his system for success.

These six points included

1. dreams, desires, and decisions;
2. imagination;
3. subconscious or subjective mind, beliefs, and values;
4. planning;
5. your think tank or mastermind group; and
6. organization of specialized knowledge.

Looking back over the last four months of his life, he could see how he was using his system daily and how he was taking steps toward acquiring his dream through the use of the system. Though he had made small progress on the remaining four principles of the system, he hadn't made as much progress as he had with the first six principles.

He had a dream and desire, and he had made a true decision to change his life and not just accept what life gave him. Through using his imagination, he had started to put together the plan to acquire his dream of exploring the rivers and jungle to Mount La Felicidad. This wasn't just a dream in his mind anymore. It was becoming a reality.

Step by step and relationship by relationship, he was building his adventure. He had gained a mentor in Dennis Flemming, who was helping him refine his system and holding him accountable so that he grew and achieved his desire. Together they were starting the task of setting Captain Bon's path to a great new future and life.

Dennis also helps in recruiting a mastermind group to advise Bon on his plan and the possible shortcomings that may lay in his way to success. But more than being a group of advisers, they, too, became mentors to Captain Bon just as he became a mentor to them. Through their time together, they became personal friends who would be there in his darkest hour.

A feeling of warmth covered Captain Bon as he thought through the relationships he had developed over a short time. Many of the mastermind group members, like Dennis, had come to mean so much to Captain Bon. He wasn't sure what he had been like before he began this adventure, which had led him to these great friends and teachers, but he knew he wasn't half the person he was now.

Captain Bon suspected that the feelings he had were the same anyone would have when they developed true friendships, but he couldn't be sure. He spoke with Dennis about the feelings of love, compassion, and camaraderie he now had to see if Dennis had experienced the same feelings.

Unsurprisingly, it was the same for Dennis as it was for him. Because Dennis had been on the journey to success longer than Captain Bon and had built more relationships, his experiences were even deeper. He told Captain Bon, "Once you go down the path of helping others and you achieve dreams, nothing else can take you as high."

Thinking over what Dennis had said to him, Captain Bon wondered why more people didn't take this path in life and gain these rewards. Of course, it came down to pain and pleasure. Others felt the pain of putting themselves out there and being judged, but they didn't understand the pleasure they would receive from building relationships and helping others. The pain for them was just greater than the pleasure, and that was because no one had educated them about how it felt to help others succeed.

Sharp pain and heartbreak for these people came over Captain Bon. It was as if they had suffered a great injustice, and they weren't even aware. Why wouldn't everyone want this warm feeling that came from building relationships with no other reason than helping other people? Well, there was another reason, and that was the feeling of accomplishment you received from helping others.

Captain Bon felt that part of his duty was to help educate others on the feelings they would get from helping. As he thought about his new goal, he giggled. It was funny to him how in life, when you made a small direction change, you ended up in a different area.

Before all this, he was content to take what life gave him and enjoy what came, but now as he designed his life, he got to choose what would come and what he would enjoy. This made all the hard work look easy and the goals accomplishable. He thought, *It's funny how a small change of perspective can change your life.*

THE JOURNEY THUS FAR

Reviewing the past four months to see the progress he had made toward accomplishing his dream, Captain Bon was surprised by all the checks of completion he had next to his deliverables. He had accomplished a lot more than he thought he would, and he was ahead of many of the delivery dates he had set just four months ago.

Now he reviewed his plan weekly to see where he was, but he hadn't looked at the entire completion of steps for his system. Looking at everything others and he had accomplished brought a warm feeling of pride into his heart. He felt that his voyage of a thousand steps had begun. He felt he was well on his way to completion.

He understood that he still had a long way to go, including the actual adventure up the river to Mount La Felicidad, but he was already more than 30 percent through the entire adventure, and he had finished more than 50 percent of the planning and gathering of resources. He had done so by taking steps every day. Now looking back at his actions, it was inspiring to see how far he had come.

Looking over his timeline and checklist again, he went through each of the steps he had taken in chronological order according to his principles of success. He had to rearrange a few of his achievements to review them in the order the system dictated, but it wasn't because he had skipped a step. He had just worked on some of the steps consecutively.

Now that he had them in order, he could look for areas he needed to work on and improve or areas that were complete and could be left alone—that is, unless there was a change in the plan. If, for some reason, he had to go back and change a portion of the plan, he could use what he had already completed for a starting point.

A smile came across his face as he looked at the first item on the list— dreams, desires, and decisions. He had defined his dream of traveling the river to Mount La Felicidad and the desire to be remembered as a great explorer in the history books.

He had made a true decision and cut off all other options when he decided that he would design his life and achieve his dream. Working as a designer, engineer, and CEO of his life, he had taken control and was quickly moving to accomplish his dream. All the new parts of him were helping out and kept him accountable so that he could achieve his dream.

How funny it was that a simple decision could change the direction of a person's life. He was no longer the man who just wandered through life. He was now a man on a mission who was headed toward his dream. What a change this had made in Captain Bon. His confidence was growing with each victory, and his education was growing with each failure.

Sure, he had learned a lot through the books he studied, but compared to what he had learned over the past few months, his previous education seemed minimal.

Now looking over the second part of the system, he could see how he had used his imagination. Through his imagination, he had changed his dream into a plan of action and was well on the way to seeing the plan come to fruition.

His imagination had shown him what he would feel when he accomplished his adventure, and it had given him the confidence he needed to push through the barriers that were in his mind. His imagination was now helping get his subconscious mind on board with the plan. Through his imagination, he had found the beliefs that had been holding him back all these years, and with the help of NLP, he was able to replace the barrier beliefs with ones that served him.

Captain Bon realized this process of programming his subconscious mind would be a life journey, but he also knew he had figured out the key to changing disabling beliefs. He needed to change what he was associating with pain and pleasure. Pain would now be found in not accomplishing his dreams and not in the fears of failure that had once held him back.

These actions took him to the meat and potatoes of his system, which was planning. Using his imagination and the help of Dennis, he created the outline of his plan to accomplish his dream. He started from the end of the journey and worked backward to the point of gathering a mastermind group. In his plan, he wrote down every step he could think of that he would need. It included things such as creating a mastermind group, recruiting the right team for the adventure, acquiring funding to support the resources needed, and even determining how he would explain his system to everyone.

Trying not to leave out a single detail took time, and it also took questions. Every time Bon felt he was complete with a branch of the plan, he would go back and ask more questions. The more he dug in with questions, the more he seemed to find more questions to ask. It was almost like a never-ending branch.

On one of these exercises, Captain Bon realized he was wasting too much time with the small details. It wasn't that he didn't need to find the answers. Rather it was that he needed to find them through more experienced and knowledgeable people than himself. He could spend eternity trying to figure out the answers, but that wouldn't get him to the adventure. It would only give him a lifetime of planning, and that wasn't the point.

This realization brought him to the decision that it was time to put together his mastermind group and get their thoughts and advice on the plan. It also helped him realize that it was time to start finding the people he would partner with to accomplish his dream.

With the help of his mentor, Dennis, he had recruited people to join the mastermind group. To his delight, it wasn't as hard to find these people as he thought it would be. The people he approached were honored to be part of a think tank, and all but one (Jimmy) had already done something like this adventure before. Two of the members (Aaron and Kelly) turned out to have a dream that was similar to Captain Bon's, and they joined the team that would take the adventure with him.

The adventure was coming together with the formation of his mastermind group, not to mention the two members wanting to take the adventure with Captain Bon. The more Captain Bon looked over his progress, the more he felt that he could achieve his dream.

Now it was time for the mastermind group to review his plan and help add to it. With sweaty hands and a fast heartbeat, Captain Bon went into the weekly meeting and asked the group to help him review his plan. He knew he had the support of Aaron and Kelly, as he had approached them when he discovered that they, too, had dreams of taking an adventure of discovery. He felt that his dream would be something they would want to be part of.

Though he had shared some of his dreams with Aaron and Kelly, he hadn't shared his plan with them yet. He felt he needed to introduce the plan to the entire mastermind group rather than sharing the plan with any member before the others. It was more about keeping harmony within the group than anything else.

He didn't want any member to feel that he was hijacking the group just for his purpose, even though that was why he had originally started the group. But through respect for the other members, he had to follow this path.

When the meeting first started, the other members spent time catching up with one another. After about half an hour of pleasantries, they moved into what the group would address this week.

At that point, Captain Bon knew it was now or never. He knew if he didn't speak up at this time, he would lose his courage to ask for help in the future. This was the pivotal point for the life or death of his dream. It was the point that would decide if he dared to truly take this adventure. If he stalled, Captain Bon knew Señor Doubter would jump on him and use every trick in the book to put the fear of failure deep in his heart.

Inhaling deeply, he spoke up to the group. "I have a plan that I would like to put before the group to review and pick apart." He just blurted out the words before he realized he had just taken the next step in his plan and his life.

Jimmy was the first to speak up and ask what information Bon had to offer the team. He could sense Bon's anxiety, and he wanted to help his friend. He knew that this must have been the reason behind Captain Bon starting the mastermind group in the first place, and since he had been patient for so many weeks and had worked to put others first, he wanted the review of Captain Bon's plan to have all their attention.

Taking the lead back from Jimmy with his heart beating 190 beats per minute, he spoke to the group and introduced his plan in full. The members were happy to accept Bon's plan and were eager to read what Captain Bon had come up with. Captain Bon had been so supportive of everyone else in the group, so they were receptive. Plus, they could hear the passion he presented his plan with.

They knew it would be a very detailed plan because it was coming from Captain Bon, but once they were deep into reviewing the plan, they were surprised by the attention to detail he had put into his plan. They agreed to take the next week to review the plan and come back with any suggestions they may have in the following week's meeting.

After the meeting, Aaron and Kelly stayed over and discussed Captain Bon's adventure. They were shocked that he had put in so much time into his plan without the help of anyone else, but they had already spotted some issues with the resources part of the plan and wanted to jump in early to help him fix these issues.

They also thought he needed more backing than he had in his plan. Aaron figured Captain Bon would need about two times the capital he had planned, but they realized they were missing something that could change that amount. Bon could feel the goose bumps coming out on his skin. It didn't matter where he was in the plan. His dream was moving each day, and soon, he would take a huge leap forward with the help of his mastermind group.

The week that followed soon became a fog in Bon's memory, but at that time, it was one of the best weeks of his life. He spent a couple of hours a day with Aaron and Kelly reviewing the plan and their suggestions. Aaron had created a list of potential investors, while Kelly had come up with her plan to help fund the adventure through a sponsored donation site. Each of the three was excited about taking on this adventure, and they were putting their hearts into it now.

By the time of next week's meeting, they had answered many of the questions about Captain Bon's original plan, but they were looking forward to what the other members had discovered may be missing.

The meeting started pretty much as normal with the same old courtesies and greetings, but everyone seemed to be in a hurry to start the meeting today. Now it was understandable that Aaron, Kelly, and Captain Bon were excited to hear the others' thoughts, but it seemed that every member of the group felt the same way.

Once everyone was settled and the hellos and questions between the members about one another's week were out the way, Dennis stood up and brought the meeting to order with an unusual urgency. Clearing his throat, he said, "We have an excellent opportunity in front of us to make our founding member's dream a reality. Not often will we be able to give to another in such a way as we can now give to Bon. He has put in front of us a magnificent and well-thought-out plan to explore an area that most would not even consider exploring. In this plan, we can work with one another to learn many new skills both in business and life. I have read through his plan as I am sure all of you have, and short of concerns about acquiring financial backing, I feel it is as solid a plan as I have ever read. So to get started, I would ask that we go around the room and bring out our concerns and work through them toward solutions as a group. I would also ask that each member keep notes and turn them to Bon at the end of the meeting."

With that, the members started sharing their concerns and working through them to the best solutions. They brought up many points, but to Captain Bon's surprise, they didn't have as many as he had feared. Most involved the financial backing of the adventure, but that was expected. In this area, Captain Bon had very little experience compared to others in the group, but he had a great starting place already. Within an hour, the team had come up with more than ten solutions to acquiring the needed financing, and most were things that he could easily do.

The meeting lasted longer than any other had in the past, but time went fast for all the members. Dennis had to mention that it was getting late and that they had to end this session. Dennis knew that the members were excited and could have gone all night, but he felt that it was better to offer a special meeting in two days instead of burning everyone out. This would also allow them to reflect on the solutions that had been presented and the addition of these points to the plan. The group all happily agreed and set a special meeting two days later.

With his head spinning from the meeting, Bon took all the notes from each member and graciously thanked them for their help and input. With the notes in hand, he headed toward the door only to be stopped by Dennis before he could leave. Dennis asked him how he felt and how excited he was. Bon said, "I am higher right now than I have been in my life."

Dennis understood his friend's feelings; however, he worried that once Bon sat down to compile the notes, he would get overwhelmed and that doubt would set in. To stave off the possibility of doubt entering his mind, he hatched a plan of his own. Slowly rubbing his chin and putting on his mentor face, he said, "As your mentor, I want you to put these notes in your folder and not look at them till tomorrow evening. Aaron, Kelly, and I will come over after work and review them together with you. For tonight I want you to go home and enjoy these feelings with Theresa and share with her how you are feeling."

Captain Bon didn't understand his mentor's reasoning, but he knew he should follow his instructions. He said, "I will do it, but it's not going to be easy." Then Dennis laughed and said, "The best things in life are seldom easy." The friends parted, and with his head spinning from excitement, Bon headed home to Theresa.

The time Bon spent with Theresa was the best they had had in a while. He brought flowers home to her, and when she asked, "What are these for?" he just replied, "Because they are almost as beautiful as you and I am happy to be alive." Though he didn't comment more about the flowers, they did speak about the meeting. She could see from his excitement when he arrived home that he was chomping at the bit to tell her about it, and as always, she enjoyed hearing about his progress on his adventure. He spent the next few hours recapping the entire meeting for her.

Time seemed to pass the next day slowly, but Captain Bon had to prepare at work for his next trip up the Mississippi River, so he kept himself busy with the details—that is, until five in the evening. Then he rushed home to prepare for his guests and their meeting.

Aaron was the first to arrive, and he spent a few exciting minutes asking Bon questions about his thoughts of their adventure. He was looking forward to the adventure as much as Captain Bon. As they were talking, a knock at the door came. It was Dennis and Kelly, and they seemed in especially great spirits. Bon invited them in and explained that Aaron was already in the office, waiting on them.

The four of them sat down and reviewed the notes from the meeting, and together, they adjusted Bon's original plan with the additions they had. It only took them an hour and a half before they came to the end of the notes. Aaron and Dennis joked that it would have gone faster had Bon allowed Kelly to handle the computer input. Kelly just laughed and said, "Well, Bon did his best, but we may want to do a proper check for spelling and grammar."

With a hearty laugh, the group agreed that Kelly would take care of the notes next time. With that, they spent the next hour reviewing the details one more time before deciding they had a strong enough plan to move to the next stages of the adventure. That next stage would be recruiting the logistics team. They would seek volunteers as much as they could, but they knew that the logistics manager would be a full-time position and that they would have to pay a salary for that position.

Captain Bon said that he knew the right man for the job and that he believed the man would work for a lower wage than normal. He had worked with Norris in the navy and knew he was as strong a logistics manager as one could ask for. In the past ten years, Norris had started his own company of logistic managers, and now he was the CEO. He had spoken to Norris about helping him, and Norris seemed very interested. He even joked that he would do it for a reduced rate if he could do it in his spare time. At least Bon thought it was a joke.

Before adjourning for the night, the four of them agreed that Bon should invite Norris to the mastermind meeting the next day. If he could make it, he would have a better understanding of what he would need for logistics planning.

The next morning, Bon contacted his old friend Norris again to see if he would attend the mastermind meeting at six o'clock tonight. At first, Norris joked with his friend about the short notice, but then after listening to Bon squirm a bit, he giggled and said he would be there.

That evening meeting was a bustle of the business, and the entire group was now engulfed with the adventure at hand. They went through the plan step-by-step and explained their additional thoughts as they came to the different sections.

After the meeting, Norris had a strange look on his face as Bon approached him. It wasn't a disappointed or doubtful look, but he looked as if he were peering into a faraway land as he bit his bottom lip. Bon wasn't sure of his friend's expression, but he figured this was as good a time as ever to see if he could help.

With a deep breath, Bon asked, "So Norris, what do you think of all this?"

Norris took a minute to respond as he was gathering his thoughts. "Bon, we have known each other for a long time, and this seems to be not just out of your box but out of your universe. It is a well-thought-out plan. As for a success rate, I put you at about 90 percent. But again, much of this lies on your shoulders, and it is not something I have seen in you before. I hope you don't take offense at my statement."

Captain Bon wanted to rebut Norris's comments outright, but he thought better of himself. As he thought of his friend's comment, he knew it was true, or at least at one time it would have been true. With a deep breath and a long exhale, Bon replied, "You are correct in your statement, Norris, and I would have been the first to agree just a few months ago. But something in me has changed, and that change would not allow me to quit or fail. I will succeed as long as I give it my all."

Norris again took his time to respond, but Bon could see his friend's expression changing in front of his eyes. Once his expression finished its transformation, he replied, "Bon, I can see a difference in you. It's in the way you speak and hold yourself, but I wanted to hear your response, and now I have my answer. I feel you will succeed in this adventure, and I want to play a part in that success. I have some spare time and would love to be part of the team. I know I can bring great value to your adventure, and I think I can learn a thing or two along the way."

Bon wasn't sure what to say, but he said, "Thank you. What will all this cost us?"

To the question of cost, Norris laughed and said, "More than you can afford so I will do it for the experience and expenses, of course."

TWO RIVERS OF THE MIND

Bon couldn't believe his luck. He had hoped to gain Norris as the logistics manager, but he could have never expected that Norris would do it for free. That was more than he could have dreamed.

With the conversation finished, each of the members said their goodbyes and agreed to return to their scheduled weekly meeting time. They also agreed that they would continue helping Bon with planning his adventure.

CHAPTER 13

PERSISTENCE AND DETERMINATION
THE FUEL FOR YOUR RIVER TRIP

CAPTAIN BON HAD SPENT MUCH of his life floating down the river of life. This didn't take much persistence or determination, but now he had a dream and desire that had to be fulfilled. This changed the way he viewed persistence and determination. He hadn't given either much thought throughout his life. He now could see how and why he hadn't succeeded. He hadn't been persistent in chasing his dreams or in planning, and he hadn't been persistent in finding the help he would need to accomplish his dreams.

Now that had all changed. Captain Bon had built a fire in his belly to go after his dream. He had witnessed completing the adventure in his imagination. He knew it was as possible as anything else in life. This fire ignited something in him—a determination that he would reach his dream. Maybe he wouldn't succeed on the first or second try, but eventually, he would have his desire.

The determination that was in him now created persistence. He could step out of his comfort zone and create a plan. The same persistence had helped him seek out his mastermind group. His dream was now a plan, and the plan was becoming a reality.

As he worked his system to success, he gained a greater belief in himself. Though he knew hard days would come and he would have to remember days like this when he felt invincible. Those thoughts would keep him determined to complete his adventure and realize his dream.

But what about his team? How could he build the same persistence and determination in them? This was a question he knew he would have to answer. He had to find some satisfactory compensation for helping him reach his dream of navigating the river to Mount La Felicidad. But what would it be, and was it fair to leverage their payback? This was just another question to answer.

He would always first consider if what he asked them to do would benefit them. Knowing he would have to carefully analyze every situation as to mitigate any dangers they would face. But was it fair to use their reasons for taking this adventure against them?

He would have to consult others about this question because he was torn on what the right answer was. It would be okay for them to use the leverage on themselves, but he wasn't sure it was okay for him to use it, especially if the adventure put them in a life-threatening situation.

No, he couldn't use leverage if it would put someone's life at risk. That would have to be their decision. Captain Bon was sure about that. He could endanger his own life, but not the lives of his crew. He wouldn't be able to live with himself if he had used leverage on them and they had died.

Captain Bon had made up his mind on how he would use his persistence and determination. He understood that persistence and determination were tied to leverage. He also understood that leverage had to be used for good and not in an abusive way. You shouldn't use leverage to force anyone to do something that was not in their best interest.

He always asked himself, "Will this benefit all the people involved? Will this take advantage of someone or hurt them?" By asking these questions, you could decide if the leverage should be used to produce persistence and determination.

Captain Bon understood that leaders throughout time had used leverage to manipulate people into doing their bidding, and it wasn't always something the individual wanted. The greatest example that came to mind was Adolf Hitler.

Many people argued about Hitler's leadership and how he was a monster. Captain Bon and many others argued that in the purest sense of the word *leader*, Hitler was one of the greatest leaders of all times. He had been able to command an entire nation of people to commit atrocities that they would have never done before.

Hitler used leverage and fear to build persistence and determination for his cause. Many had so much persistence and determination that they carried out his plan to their deaths. They had no lack of persistence and determination, though it was misguided and not used for the greater good of the world.

But how would he keep himself persistent and determined through the completion of his goal and the achievement of the dream? Captain Bon knew that persistence and determination for anything in life could make anything the flavor of the day. Many dreams have both attributes at the beginning of an adventure, but people often abandon them when times get hard or a different dream creeps up. So how does anyone stay persistent and determined throughout the adventure?

It would have to come from daily, weekly, and monthly reminders of the why behind the dream. This would come from different areas. Captain Bon would have reminders on his phone calendar, his computer, and pictures in his office. This way, he had reminders that checked his progress and gave his imagination support. He knew this would be important to keep the fire built under his persistence and determination.

Persistence and determination are both parts of a funny circle. They both needed reminders of the dream to keep them alive. You need persistence and determination to keep the dream alive. It was a circle that would take work. Though Captain Bon understood the circle, he also understood you could break it if you weren't careful. Just like dropping a fine glass, if you dropped the why for a second from your mind, you could break your persistence and determination. Here is where the reminders would help him so that he didn't drop the glass on the floor and shatter his dream.

WHAT HAVE WE LEARNED ABOUT PERSISTENCE AND DETERMINATION FROM CAPTAIN BON?

Captain Bon looked back over his life at how he had thought of persistence and determination before, and now he understood why he hadn't used them productively to gain his dreams and desires. They hadn't been something he had focused on. He understood that to keep his persistence and determination alive, they needed support in the form of reminders.

Persistence and determination were living things, energy to be used to gain one's dreams and desires. But if they weren't fed a healthy diet of reminders, they would die out. Captain Bon had to keep these reminders in front of his mind. This way, they would engage his subconscious mind, which would, in turn, help him. His subconscious mind would be the trigger that would keep his persistence and determination going when his conscious mind was thinking of other things that had nothing to do with the dream.

Captain Bon also understood that the system he was using was a circle and that persistence and determination were parts of the circle. Every part of the system depended on another part, and they all tied together to help you turn a dream in your imagination into a reality in life. Each part had its role to play in delivering the desire, but they depended on other parts too.

The system wouldn't work without persistence and determination, but persistence and determination wouldn't work without imagination and a plan. Each part needed the other parts, and persistence and determination was the glue that tied them together.

Captain Bon also understood that he would have to help the others on the adventure with him to build their persistence and determination so that they could complete the adventure with him. He also understood that he only wanted to apply leverage ethically. He couldn't build persistence and determination blindly in others. It had to be done for their good and not his. He understood that by applying the leverage involving what they would receive from the adventure, he could be taking advantage of these people, and that wouldn't be ethical.

SO HOW DO YOU DEVELOP PERSISTENCE AND DETERMINATION?

What is persistence? What is determination? Aren't they the same thing? Well, yes and no. Both are attributes that push us forward in life and get us to our destination. Persistence is staying with action and seeing it through. Determination is an attribute that may or may not take you to a result. They often work in conjunction with each other, and both find their basis in your willpower.

Some people will tell you willpower doesn't exist and we work off of instinct. While science has tried hard to prove or disprove willpower, a scientist has not been able to determine the truth either way. But if you look at the animal kingdom, you will find that humans are the only species that has the power to create or destroy. This is where we find the willpower. We have the will to create a world through love instead of destroying it through hate. We can *will* ourselves to become educated and not just take what's given to us. We can cite more examples to prove the case that the *will* exists. But as with everything in life, what you truly believe is up to you.

Let's get back to persistence and determination. We can now look at how persistence and determination work and how each will get us to our destination. The first test is to follow the steps in the "Desire" section and use persistence and determination to find your desire.

Does persistence come easy to you, or do you have to work hard to remain persistent in your journey? For most of us, we would answer yes to the second question. As humans, many things compete for our attention, and often, our persistence and determination is watered down.

But it's not like the first desire was bad or would not have enriched our lives. It's that we did not have a good plan or we didn't make our desire a truly burning desire. Or maybe it was that we did not have strongly defined reasons for why we wanted or needed the desire. Too often it is that we struggle with the journey to our desire, and instead of finding the strength in ourselves, we give up and make up some excuses.

For example, consider the people who need to lose weight and make a New Year's resolution to go to the gym and exercise more and eat better. During the first month, they get a gym membership, go to the health store, and buy every weight loss product they can afford. They then go to the local grocery store and buy fruits, vegetables, and lean meats. And after thirty days, what do they have? Well, for 96 percent of them, they have yearly gym memberships that they never use. They have a bunch of bottles of pills that will end up in the garbage, and they didn't like any of the healthy food. These people would have been better off donating that money to the hungry of the world.

So why did they fail in the journey to their destination? Well, they failed for one of many reasons. The most likely reasons they failed include

1. a weak desire,
2. a short backing to drive them to the desire,
3. inadequate reasons for the desire,
4. failure to get themselves into an emotional peak when thinking of their desire,
5. failure to create a plan,
6. failure to review their plan and the reasons for the journey each day,
7. failure to adjust the plan when it's not working,
8. remembering that failure is nothing but an opportunity to learn,
9. failure to try just one more time,
10. a weak or missing mastermind group, and
11. a lack of persistence and determination.

If you follow through the previous outlined actions, how can you hope to succeed in any journey to any desire? To get to the results and desires you want, you will need to apply persistence and determination. Wealthy lives will come to those who practice persistence and determination, and poor lives will come to those who do not practice these two attributes. The choice is yours to make. You may not get to your desire on the first shot. The truth is that the odds are against you during your first journey. You typically do not possess the necessary knowledge the first time out. But if you have surrounded yourself with a good mastermind group, you greatly improve your chances. And you will find at least one person in your mastermind group who will help you with persistence and determination.

We all need help both internally and externally to keep our persistence and determination alive. We can build reminders within ourselves and in our environment. We can do this through our phones, computers, and even recordings of our voices telling us why we want to go after our dreams. We can meditate, which will help remind us, and we can create picture reminders that show us the rewards of achieving our dreams. All these reminders will keep your dreams and desires in front of your subconscious mind.

Though this is the strongest way to help keep your persistence and determination alive, it's not the only way you can do so. You also do it through accountability (leverage from another person). This leverage can be as useful as any other form of internal leverage you use and possibly more powerful.

There are some people that respond better to external leverage from others, than they do from their own internal leverage. Many believe that leverage has to do with the feeling of acceptance by peers or the need to be a success in others' perspectives. If you look at how the external leverage works, it comes back to your internal leverage.

Many others and I truly believe you cannot make anyone do anything they truly do not want to do. There are too many examples throughout history where the greatest leverage that could be applied externally to a person didn't work. You can look at the Christians in Roman times who were nailed to crosses or fed to lions because of their beliefs. Now if the threat of death doesn't change you, nothing will. But then it comes back to your beliefs and values. External leverage will only work if it lines up with your beliefs and values. It must be something you ultimately want anyway.

When it is in line with your beliefs and values, it acts as an accountability action. It motivates your persistence and determination. It doesn't make you act, but it helps feed the fire of the persistence and determination you already have within you.

You can also develop accountability partnerships within your mastermind group, with your team, or with someone outside who has a vested interest in your success. These people can check with you from time to time to review your progress. You may do the same for these people in return and help them with their dreams and desires. Thus, both of you have a reason to help each other.

This accountability relationship shouldn't be taken as an attack. It should be used to serve as a reminder of the why and to check one's progress. The why acts as fuel for your persistence and determination. These sessions need not come every day. They can come once a month, or better yet, you can meet a few days before a milestone within your plan. It's a wakeup call to your subconscious mind.

Remember, your subconscious is working behind the scenes to help you or to stop you. With these accountability time outs and internal reminders, you are telling your subconscious mind that this is something you must complete and that its help is needed. You are training the subconscious mind to be an ally when you are not concentrating on your desire with your conscious mind. You are asking it to help you find a way to achieve your dream and desire.

By doing this, you are feeding the circle of the system. If fed through these reminders, it will build your persistence and determination. This, in turn, will see you through the tough times that will come.

Some things to remember about persistence are as follows:

1. There is no substitute for persistence. It's an insurance policy against failure.
2. Persistence will bring the knowledge that there are no failures, only learning opportunities.
3. Persistence is the courage to *fight on*!

As Thomas Edison always said, "The surest way to succeed is to try just one more time." This is a quote that cannot be repeated enough. If we ever really want to succeed, we need to try just one more time and have the faith that we can achieve anything we set our minds out to accomplish.

SUCCESS PITFALLS PRINCIPLES THAT DESTROY DETERMINATION AND PERSISTENCE

Captain Bon knew the success pitfalls principles that destroy determination and persistence as well as anyone. He had lived with them most of his life and could write books on what they were and how they had stopped people from succeeding. He identified that there were at least two success pitfalls principles that destroyed determination and persistence, and they were hesitation and self-sabotage.

Looking at hesitation first, Captain Bon focused on why he or anyone had hesitated so many times in life. It came from their beliefs about fear of failure. They would hesitate when faced with the fear that they could fail. It was easier to stay in the lives that the world gave them. It was just easy to float along the river of life and not challenge life or himself, so he hesitated and let the opportunity pass by.

Hesitation was a killer of dreams and desires. This was the truth Captain Bon had faced, and now he was finding a path past it. He realized that he could spend his life hesitating and let his dreams and desire disappear into oblivion. Or he could challenge life and his beliefs for the chance to achieve his dreams. It hadn't been a choice in his mind before, but now it would be.

Anytime he felt that he was hesitating, he would kick himself in the butt and get moving. Captain Bon realized that the cure for hesitation was movement. It didn't have to be a huge leap. It only needed to be a step forward. Movement cured the success pitfalls of hesitation.

When Captain Bon found himself in the state of hesitation, he would look for something that he needed to work on to reach his dream. It could be something as simple as going over the load list, reviewing the progress the team had made, or working within his imagination to figure out what could happen along the way. It didn't matter what he did if it was something that dealt with the adventure and helped it get one step farther down the river.

By working on the adventure, he was building his persistence and determination as he combated hesitation. Captain Bon knew that once he started any activity involving the adventure, it would pull him in, and then his determination and persistence would push him forward.

As Captain Bon thought about hesitation, he considered the second success pitfalls principle that kills persistence and determination, and that was self-sabotage. Captain Bon was thinking about self-sabotage, he realized that this success pitfalls principle affected both successful and unsuccessful people. It wasn't just something that kept people from becoming successful, but it also caused people to lose their way when they were successful.

But why would anyone sabotage their success? That was a question Captain Bon had to answer to prevent it from happening to him. For people who were trying to become successful, they sometimes felt they weren't worthy or didn't have that "something" in them that was needed to succeed.

Many times, when these people were on the road to their dreams, they felt scared of the unknown and either did things that would cause their failure or did nothing on purpose to stop them from succeeding. This would seem like the acts of an irrational person, but so many rational people acted this way.

Through his research of the many people trying to achieve the same adventure to Mount La Felicidad, he found that they had gone off track for no apparent reason. When speaking to the members of this adventure, he learned that it seemed to be a case of self-sabotage. Now he couldn't be 100 percent sure that this was the case because most people never openly admitted to self-sabotage, but all the signs were there.

Captain Bon thought about the signs of self-sabotage. He wanted to look for any indicators that people could use to warn them that they were afflicted by this success pitfalls principle. He found that when people began to self-sabotage, their personalities seemed to change. They became either distant or annoyed with anything that involved their adventure. Their relationships with others who were helping them grew more distant, and they kept to themselves more. Captain Bon felt this was because they were afraid to share what was going on inside of themselves.

He knew from his own experience that he and others felt that they couldn't share their fears of failure with the people around them. This fear often led to acts that would cause self-sabotage. Captain Bon had felt this before when he first dreamed of embarking on the adventure to Mount La Felicidad. He wouldn't get much past researching what others had done to make the adventure, then his action would derail him and lead him back to a life of mediocrity.

Though he also knew that, he hadn't found the other supporting parts to identify self-sabotage. He needed to use his success principles. They would help keep him on track. But were these other principles enough to stop self-sabotage? Could he use his imagination to see the dream and its realization when he found he was in a state of self-sabotage? Or maybe that wouldn't be enough to fight off the fears that often took a person down this road of destruction.

Captain Bon felt that using the system would indeed stop him from self-sabotaging his dream. It would force him to focus on the fears that caused self-sabotage and give him ways to combat the inner enemy. Through imagination, he could see his dream happening. Through his mastermind group, he had trusted partners to share his fears with. These individuals faced the same fears, and through the harmony of the group, he could share his fears without the added fear of being judged. The mastermind group would help keep him positive as they helped solve the problems that gave rise to the fears. And because he had a plan in writing and continually improved that plan, he could reassure himself that he could realize the dream.

As Captain Bon thought over the system, he could see many parts that would help prevent him from self-sabotaging his dream, but he had to use the principles if he hoped to stop this destructive behavior. He also had to trust in his mastermind group and team to help along the way.

Captain Bon felt there was another root cause of self-sabotage that caused people to fail once they had attained success. This root cause was boredom. He realized that while many people were successful, they hadn't yet realized the true dreams they were after and had become bored with their lives. It wasn't that they weren't achieving things, but those things weren't enough to keep their attention. These people self-sabotaged the success they had realized for no apparent reason except out of boredom.

To Captain Bon, this was a ridiculous reason to derail your dream. Though he hadn't ever experienced this in his life, he had heard from others who had. It seemed that they weren't getting the rewards or satisfaction out of their success. As Captain Bon thought over why this was the case, he realized that they hadn't identified what they wanted. They hadn't identified the why behind the dream. Their whys were more about the physical world (such as money) or about what they thought the realization of their dreams would bring (such as happiness).

Though both whys would keep many people on track and engaged, it wouldn't nearly be enough to keep them from boredom. Captain Bon realized that money made some things easier, but it also brought its own set of challenges. If one were not prepared for these challenges, a person would become discontent with just the money. He also realized that happiness couldn't be found in just the achievement of a dream. Happiness came from the journey to the dream. Once the dream was realized, that happiness would quickly go away.

To keep from becoming bored with the dream and adventure, it had to keep growing. Once the initial dream was realized, it had to grow into a bigger dream. And that dream was tied to some even bigger dreams. This way, the person would always be working toward a goal and not become bored.

Captain Bon now could see the connection between people who had set out to achieve their dreams and had become successful through many different adventures. These people had never stopped dreaming. As they realized the achievement of certain dreams, they were already working on other dreams they wanted to achieve. They continued to push themselves to become better and to grow. They hadn't settled for attaining one dream or desire. In this way, they could prevent boredom and self-sabotage. As they continuously strived to reach new heights, they warded off the success pitfalls principles that killed persistence and determination through sheer momentum.

CHAPTER 14

LEVERAGE AND STRETCHING YOURSELF

THE ENGINE THAT MOVES YOU THROUGH THE RIVERS

CAPTAIN BON FELT THAT HE was at the end of what he could do. He didn't have the needed knowledge or experience to go further. He was frustrated that all the efforts he had put forward weren't paying off and that he may be at the brink of failure because he hadn't had the time to gain the experience he thought he needed. This could be a negative turning point, and he realized that if he didn't do something, his dream would drift away from him.

Just at that moment, he received a call from Aaron from his mastermind group. He was calling in to see how things were going with acquiring financial backing for the plan. Aaron wasn't just a member of Captain Bon's mastermind group. He would also be one of the two other adventurers who would be on the river with Captain Bon.

Aaron had become a close friend of Captain Bon in a brief period. He truly believed in Captain Bon and his plan. Aaron had found in Captain Bon's system what he had been missing in his own life. Now he could achieve his dreams. Though he had achieved many of his dreams already, he didn't have a system such as Captain Bon's to repeat the success anytime he wanted to.

Furthermore, Aaron had seen something in Captain Bon that he wanted for himself—the relentless determination to achieve his dream. The passion he had built from his imagination was new to Aaron, and he marveled at how Captain Bon could use his mind to propel him forward to his desire.

Aaron asked Captain Bon, "What's up today, Bon? How's is it going with the financial backers?"

Captain Bon's response didn't sound like him in Aaron's mind. He seemed down and not his normal positive self. Though his response was generally positive, Aaron could sense something in his friend's voice that told him Bon wasn't completely honest with him.

Aaron probed a little deeper in a gentle but straightforward way. Aaron said, "Okay, Bon, that sounds good, but I don't feel like I am getting the entire story here. Something is off in your voice, and I can hear it. So what's up?"

Captain Bon took in a deep breath and decided to come clean with his friend. "Aaron, I am at an impasse. I don't have the knowledge or experience to get the financial backing. I keep getting turned away before I can even get a meeting in front of the right people. This is so frustrating to me. I feel like I am at the point that this may never happen."

Aaron took a second before responding. He knew what to say, but he had to find the words that would resonate with Captain Bon. He felt as if he had only one shot at getting Captain Bon to understand what he was doing wrong. It came to Aaron how to deliver the lesson so that his friend would get it. With that, Aaron let out a loud laugh, one that was larger than Captain Bon had ever heard from him. It took Captain Bob by surprise.

Captain Bon asked, "Aaron, what are you laughing at?"

"I'm laughing at you!"

"I know that, but why?"

Aaron took a second to contain himself and said, "Bon, you are the man who has inspired so many of us to chase our dreams. You have no formal training, and yet you have put together a system for success. And in my opinion, it is spot on and the best system I have ever seen. Now this great man I have come to respect sits here and tells me he has forgotten how to use his system? Come on. You are just caught in the moment. You have stretched yourself through leverage further than anyone I have ever seen."

Captain Bon thought about what his friend was saying to him and then let out his laugh. "Aaron, you are right. I think I just got caught up in my self-pity and forgot what I know to do."

Aaron said, "So what's the next step, Captain?"

Captain Bon responded, "It's time to stretch myself a little further and try one more time."

Captain Bon needed the wake-up call. He had stretched himself in the past, and it hadn't killed him. It had educated him and made him stronger. He realized it was just time for a little more stretching. With this, Captain Bon talked with his friend more on the possible paths to gaining financial support from outside sources.

They discussed how others they knew could call in favors to get the meetings with potential financial backers. They also discussed how the mastermind group could help them prepare the best presentation to deliver. They talked for about an hour and agreed to get together the next day to put everything in motion.

As Captain Bon reflected on the conversation, he realized his friend meant the laugh as a wake-up call. It wasn't something that just happened. Aaron meant it to happen. Aaron understood that laughing at Captain Bon would bring him back from his depressed state. It was like a slap in the face to bring him into the here and now. That slap was exactly what Captain Bon needed to get his persistence and determination back.

He knew he could stretch himself a little further to succeed. He knew he could use leverage on himself to motivate his subconscious mind into helping, and it had worked. He now had a host of ideas about how to approach investors. He also had thoughts on who could help him get the meetings set up.

It was funny to him how he had been at the edge of an abyss just minutes before Aaron had called, but now he had solutions to what was holding him back. And the solutions weren't that hard. He just needed to stretch himself a little more.

What Is Stretching and Leveraging Yourself?

So how do we stretch ourselves? Is yoga involved? Will it take some crazy contraption that looks like it came from the Middle Ages? Or is it just doing a little more to get things done?

Well, the answer is just doing a little more and doing the things that are out of our comfort zone. You see, to grow at anything, you must take the first step. Many times, this is a step of faith over a great canyon, but it must be taken if we are to grow.

Have you ever wondered why some people are so successful but others with more raw talent, education, and experience are not? It comes down to a simple answer. They took the first step of faith and stretched themselves and their abilities to grow. By stretching, they grew, and this growth helped them get to their desires in life.

Stretching yourself in life is much like weight lifting to build your muscles. It will hurt, and you will not see instant results. (Some of the results may not come for five to ten years.) You also have a greater chance of failure than others around you. But without stretching yourself, you will never move forward down the river of life. No one can or will do it for you. The first step is all yours.

As humans, we do not like being alone in anything. Through years of evaluation, we have developed the need for others' help, approval, and support. This is hardwired into our brains through the generations that came before us. But as we discovered and discussed before, we can use our minds to rewrite the programming of our brains. By doing this, we can create the self-confidence to take the first step in any journey down the river to our desires.

Now I am not saying go out and try to jump the Grand Canyon with a rocket car. Not just yet! First, you should do your homework, create your plan, gather your mastermind group, and work toward your desire. This will get you across the canyon and to your desire, or at least it will give you the best chance of making it across. Sometimes we do fail, but if we live life with the understanding that "failure is just a chance to learn," the failure will not kill us.

Then stretch yourself just out of your comfort zone daily till you get to your dream. As we have said before, stretching is not comfortable, but it is required if you want a better life. You could lie back and take it easy, but then you will never have the dreams you want.

Stretching ourselves requires getting leverage. You must build the passion and determination in your mind for the why of your desire/dream. It has to become a fire in your belly that the world can't and will not be put out.

Then you can develop the leverage you need through the image in your mind to force yourself to stretch. It will not be comfortable. It will be work, but in the end, you will have the dream and desire you wanted. Plus, as an added advantage, you will be a more resourceful person. You will be a more knowledgeable person because you stretched yourself outside of your comfort zone.

Now, like everything else in this system, be cautious not to stretch yourself too far. The mind learns from stretching a little and succeeding. But if you try to stretch way beyond your capabilities or the capabilities of your team, you will teach yourself a much different lesson if you fail.

If you are trying to do something that is completely out of your realm or your team's realm of expertise and you fail, you run the risk of teaching your mind that stretching is not a good practice. So tread with caution on how far you stretch.

Again, think about people who start working out for the first time. You have two groups—one that understands their limits of working out and pushes a little further each day to become stronger and a second group that goes into a gym and tries to work out for hours, thinking they can *will* their bodies into doing it.

The first group grows their muscles each day, and in a month or two, they can see great gains. The second group hurt themselves and never return to the gym. Each group had a good plan and wanted similar goals, but the second group created greater pain than pleasure from the experience and ultimately failed.

You can and will have to stretch your abilities to grow in life. That is just one of the laws of the universe. You just must understand your limits and push just beyond them. This is what most people refer to when they speak of continuous improvement. It's going that step further each time to gain more bandwidth. Just think of it as gaining a little more ground each day. You're not trying to complete a marathon the first day out, but over time, the marathon will come to you.

If you evaluate your abilities honestly, you will see your limit. Then look at what is just past your limit and push to achieve it. It's not that difficult of a concept if you look at it through a few steps. Think of it as chunking for education. No one can speak a foreign language right away, but after stretching themselves daily to learn unfamiliar words and expressions, they can speak that language in just a year or so. It's all about not over- or underpacing yourself. It takes discipline and determination.

Now I know some of you are having trouble connecting the dots from learning a language or working out to achieving a dream; however, the dots are not miles apart, and there is a way to stretch yourself between the dots. Our next section will help you with the system for stretching and leveraging.

WAYS TO GET LEVERAGE ON YOURSELF

1. The best way to get this leverage is to write out a list detailing why your life will be better if you go down this branch of the river of life. You will also want to consider the path your life will take on the river if you do not take this branch. By comparing both results, you will be able to see the quality of life you will be living in the future.
2. Next, you will need to write down what you will have to give to get to your desire (and what you are willing to pay to walk this path).
3. Whose help will you need, and what will they get in return for helping you? Who will help you stay accountable?
4. Review your plan with your team while looking for the boulders or rapids that could cause problems.
5. Set a date for when you will arrive at your destination.
6. Evaluate the areas you or your team need to stretch in. Do this by finding where you are presently and where you need to get to.
7. Set a plan to stretch continuously to meet the new needs. Remember, this should be small stretches at a time.
8. Begin stretching.

9. Evaluate your progress and learning. Adjust your approach if you are not getting the results you want.

10. Again, review your plan daily to keep it in front of your subconscious mind (to gain its help and support on the trip). The more often you think and plan, the more it will become an instinctive path for your mind, and just as you do not have to tell your body to breath (the subconscious does this for you), you will not have to tell your mind to work toward your desire.

If you will follow these ten items and repeat them, you will learn and grow. It's not an arduous process, but you have to practice it. In the beginning, it may feel inadequate, but in time, it will become like riding a bike. The results will depend on the time you put into the practice.

Also, as a reminder, this practice should be deliberate practice. You want to get feedback and evaluate your progress. You are looking for what is working and what isn't working. Then adjust the approach you are taking for the things that are not working.

This system works better with two or more people involved, but it can be done alone. The thing you must remember is, the feedback has to be brutally honest. If you are alone, that can be challenging. I'm not saying being brutally honest in a group is easy. It's just easier than being brutally honest with yourself.

We all have blinders on when it comes to ourselves, and we can also be our worst critics. We speak to ourselves in an unpleasant tone when we feel we should be able to do something and can't. The advice or opinion is not normally constructive when it comes from within. You need to guard against your self-destruction. Being hard on yourself is okay, but being ruthless is not.

You are here to leverage yourself and to stretch. It's all about growth, not destruction. You can and will make it to your dreams if you follow the system. But you want to make it to the dream better than you are today, not torn to pieces.

IN COMES FRED FISHER

Kelly called Captain Bon early in the evening to share some exciting news. With an unusual fluster in her voice, she started the conversation by saying, "What are your plans tomorrow night?" This was outside of Kelly's normal demeanor, and Bon could sense that whatever it was, she needed the next night; it was important.

"Well, good day to you too, Kelly! To answer your question, I have no particular plans for tomorrow night."

"Good. I have someone I want you to meet with. The gentleman's name is Fred Fisher, and he is an old friend from high school. I think he can help us with more financial backing."

Kelly had become the one person most responsible for acquiring backing for the adventure. She had taken on the role without anyone even asking her. It was something she seemed to enjoy doing, and she pushed the others and Bon when it came to approaching people and companies to fund the adventure.

She had already succeeded in securing a large outfitting chain as one of their backers. It took a few meetings to get the outfitter on board with supplying the needed camping and boating equipment, but through all ten meetings, Kelly was resourceful and unstoppable. She never gave up or gave in. Even after the first meeting when the VP of marketing for the outfitter said that he didn't think this was a good promotion for their stores, she stayed after him and eventually convinced him that this was just what his brand needed.

During the countless meetings, Captain Bon was ready more than once to give up on the outfitter, but Kelly would always say to him, "We have them right where we want them. We need to change the path of attack a little."

With that, he would laugh and say, "Okay, Kelly, how do we go at them this time?" In the end, Kelly convinced the VP to support them by studying the demographics of the people who shopped at the outfitter's stores. She visited five of their stores in the state multiple times to research who was shopping there, what they were buying, and why they were buying the items. Through interviewing both the outfitter's employees and customers, she had learned that they were shopping at the outfitter out of last-minute needs. For larger items, the customers were shopping online and not in the store. She had also learned that this was hurting the brick-and-mortar stores, but as a company, the outfitter was still doing well through their online store.

Her research grew into a plan to have events at the store with Captain Bon and his adventurers to promote both the adventure and the outfitter. This plan would brush some dust off the outfitter's image as a stale store and help turn it into the store to outfit your adventure. She created signs and pamphlets as well as online advertisements that the store could use on their social media pages.

At the next meeting with the VP and others, she unveiled her marketing plan, and it was an instant hit. Though the company agreed that they would not give the team cash for the adventure, they would give whatever outfitting equipment they needed. This in itself would be 50 percent of the cost of the adventure.

But they still needed capital to cover the other costs. That was why Kelly had set up the present meeting.

At six o'clock, Bon met Kelly and Fred at Baronne's on the River for dinner. Kelly had given Bon some background information on Fred. He was a board member for a private equity group and an investment banker. He had graduated from Penn State before joining the US Marines as an officer. He had been wounded in battle in Iraq during the war by an explosion and had lost both his legs just above the knees. But this hasn't slowed him down. He still competed in business and life. He was married and had two daughters who were everything to him. Though most times he walked with prosthetic legs and canes, he did still sometimes use a wheelchair. Kelly mentioned this information so that Bon wasn't surprised when he met Fred.

She also said, "Don't feel sorry for him. He is still a fierce competitor. He competes in wheelchair races and basketball. Though he has gone through a tragedy, he hasn't let it stop his life, and he hates any sign of pity."

With that information, Bon prepared for the meeting and what to say to Fred to gain his support.

Once at the restaurant, the three sat down and went through the normal dance of getting to know one another. It began with Fred asking,

"Why would someone as old as you want to risk your life for an adventure like this?"

Bon laughed and said, "Well, I am older than you, but I'm not ready for the rocking chair just yet."

Laughing himself, Fred said, "Well, that's good to hear, but are you ready for the challenges that lie on the river? Are you physically ready? Because you don't look like it to me."

Bon tried to speak, but Fred interrupted and said, "Hear me out." He continued, "There is no doubt you are mentally prepared for the adventure you are about to take. If not, you wouldn't have been able to convince Kelly and others like her to join you. But this adventure will be physical as well as mental, and anyone who backs you or puts their faith in you has to have no doubts you can endure the physical aspect of this adventure."

To this statement, Bon took a minute to think and then replied to Fred, "I am not in the best shape of my life, but I can and will get there before we step onto the river. This is my dream and my greatest desire. I will not let anything stand in my way. I can understand your concern. I am older than both Kelly and Aaron and not close to the physical condition they are in, but with help from them, I can get where I need to be. I will not die or give up on this journey. You can count on that."

Taken aback and understanding now why Kelly believed in Bon so much, Fred wasn't sure how to answer. He thought of going all in from the sheer passion that Bon had shown. It was more than the confidence in his voice that was so convincing. It was the fire in his eyes. Fred had seen that same fire before in himself after he was wounded in Iraq. He wasn't going to let anyone or anything stand in his way after his injury, and he was sure Bon wouldn't allow anything to stand in his way either. With that, Fred thought of a plan that would determine if Bon was all in.

Sitting back in his chair and taking a sip of water, Fred said, "Okay, I will make you a deal. Over the next month, I want you to start getting into the shape that you will need to be in. You will need help to create a lifestyle that will promote an active and physically fit body to complete this journey. If in the next thirty days I see you are committed completely, I will back you in this adventure."

Bon didn't hesitate. He took Fred up on his challenge. Fred said, "Okay, let's hear your plan for this adventure."

With that, Kelly and Bon explained the complete plan to Fred over dinner.

THE SUCCESS PITFALLS PRINCIPLES OF STRETCHING AND LEVERAGING ONESELF

As Captain Bon was going through and determining ways to stretch his abilities and the leverage he would need to apply, he thought of what would stop him from stretching and growing. He understood that stretching meant leaving his comfort zone and doing things he had never attempted before. With this would come the fear of failure.

Captain Bon understood that he wouldn't fail if he tried again. You have only learned how not to do something when you have failed, but the fear was still there. It seemed that the fear of failing and being labeled as a failure was always present in humans. He didn't know anyone who didn't have this fear, but he knew some people who were able to get past the fear. They did it by creating a bigger fear of not pushing forward. They also created an image in their minds that showed the rewards they would receive for succeeding. This image created determination, which, in turn, created persistence.

Could he get past the fear? Had he created a real enough image of what it would feel like when he achieved his dream and desire to master the river and make it to Mount La Felicidad? These were questions he would face multiple times along the adventure, but he realized that he couldn't allow fear to hold him hostage. He would have to take the leap and grow his wings on the way down.

To Captain Bon, leaping and growing his wings on the way down meant that he wouldn't know how to do everything that would need to be done but that he would learn how to do it along the way or find people to do it for him. He knew fears would bring uncertainty to his life, but he could find resources within himself or others to achieve the adventure and reach his dreams.

He understood fears were part of life, and everyone had them, but they didn't have to kill your dreams. You could fight past the fears through persistence, but fear could kill persistence and determination. You had to work on getting past the fears daily. You must face the fears every day and determine how they are standing in your way and what you will do about it each day.

This is where persistence comes into play. You must look each day at what fears you are facing. By not hiding the fears from yourself and your team, you can get past them. By sharing the fears with your team, you are opening yourself up and being vulnerable. You are getting help to get past the fears. And getting past the fears is the main goal here.

Captain Bon knew that by sharing his fears with his mastermind group and team, he could receive help to get past the fears. He also knew that if he was courageous for just a few minutes and shared his fears, it would open the door for others to share their fears and to receive support to get past their fears. This was the core of his system after all. It was about people helping others get past their fears and reach their desires. By doing this, they could beat the success pitfalls principle of fear of failure.

Captain Bon also felt that another success pitfalls principle that killed persistence and determination was laziness. He felt that he had been lazy about chasing his dreams earlier in his life. He hadn't put in the effort to receive the desires he wanted in life. He had always felt that it would cost more time than he had to give. All he could see was the amount of work he was doing today to survive. In his mind, taking on his dreams would mean he had to work an additional forty to fifty hours a week.

This was a misconception he held until the day when he couldn't live the way he had been living. The pain was just too great to continue down the road he had been traveling. His life had to change, and it would no matter what amount of work he had to do.

When he reached this point in his life, he wasn't sure how much time he would have to put in to achieve his dream, but he knew the price would be worth the reward. He had a fire in himself now, and he kept building it bigger and bigger. Through his imagination, he could see how he would feel when he achieved the dream. He knew whatever price he had to pay, it would be worth it.

As Captain Bon started going after his adventure, he found that the cost of time wasn't as much as he thought it would be. It wasn't forty or fifty hours more work a week. It was between ten to twenty hours and he knew he could afford the time to accomplish his dream. It wasn't like his job that paid his bills. There wasn't anyone standing over him and deciding the hours he would have to put in. There wasn't anyone saying, "You must be here from 8:00 a.m. to 5:00 p.m. to get the rewards."

The cost of time was up to him. The schedule was mostly up to him. Now there were times when he had specific time schedules because of others who were helping him or educating him, but even that was somewhat flexible.

Some weeks Captain Bon put in only five hours, but he was five hours closer to his dream after that. Other weeks he put in forty hours and got even closer to reaching the dream. The one thing Captain Bon did find through this flexible schedule was that it built his determination.

In the beginning, it was Captain Bon's *willpower* that drove him to put in the hours, but as he received the rewards for the time he put in, his determination grew. The more time he put in, the more rewards he received. He felt the rewards he received from the time he invested in achieving his dream were greater than the money he received for his day-to-day job. Though it wasn't yet paying his bills—and he needed his day job—he was receiving greater happiness from chasing his dream.

It was funny to Captain Bon that the time he put in mattered more to him on a personal level than his day job ever had. It was also funny to him that the more time he put in, the more his determination grew. It was like throwing gasoline on a fire. And the fire was now in his belly and pushing him closer to the achievement of his dreams and desires.

Captain Bon was happy that he had decided that he couldn't live how he had been living and was surprised that it didn't take as much of his time as he thought it would. It wasn't twice as much time. It took barely 25 percent of what he had feared it would take. Captain Bon realized he had wasted so many years of being lazy because he was afraid of the time planning and preparing would cost him. He was upset that he hadn't tried before, but that was the past. He couldn't change the past. He could only build the future.

He was building his future now, and he was being rewarded tenfold for the time he was putting in.

Captain Bon felt that many people wasted their lives because they were lazy. But laziness wasn't an external enemy. It was an internal enemy. It was an internal enemy that only the person could fight. It was the one enemy that no one could help you fight. Captain Bon knew some people claimed they could help others fight this enemy, though he knew that no one beats laziness with outside help. It was all internal, and he had found that anyone could beat this enemy through persistence and determination. But again, you have to take the leap and grow your wings on the way down.

CHAPTER 15

RELATIONSHIPS WITH
PEOPLE, BODY, AND SPIRIT
THREE ADDITIONAL PARTS NEEDED
TO SURVIVE THE RIVER

CAPTAIN BON'S PLAN WAS WORKING well, and things were progressing better than he thought they would. He was pleasantly surprised that not as many difficulties had come his way. He now even had a potential financial backer, but there was a catch. He now had to get into a better physical shape. Plus, there was more.

While thinking over what was missing, he happened to see Theresa's Bible sitting on the end table. He was missing the rest of the triangle. The triangle was mind, body, and spirit.

He had worked hard on his mind and getting it into the shape it needed to be in. Through getting his mind fit, he also raised his spirit. He had meditated more and spent time building the spiritual Captain Bon, but the spirit still needed work, and the body definitely needed a lot of attention. He would need help to build his body and spirit as he continued building his mind. He would need to develop relationships with others to attain his triangle.

Captain Bon had gained weight over the years, and he had allowed his endurance to dwindle. He knew the mind couldn't survive without the body, and neither could make it without the spirit. He needed to find a way to build his body and spirit the way he had built his mind. But how could he devote time to more training and meditation? Where would he find the time?

Between his full-time job and the activities needed to keep his adventure going, there wasn't much time left in a day. He had already stolen too much time from his family to put toward his dream. It wouldn't be fair to his wife, Theresa, to spend even more time away. She had been so supportive, and she wanted him to reach his dream almost as much as he wanted. So where could he find the time he needed to achieve all three parts of the pyramid?

Thinking about how to create more time, Captain Bon came back to his system. He would need advisers and experts who had accomplished this before. He had a few people in his mastermind group and on his team who seemed to be able to find the time to keep their families, careers, dreams, health, and spirit. These advisers could help him develop a plan to manage his time more efficiently to have it all. He would have to ask for help with these people, and he would need to build a different type of relationship with these advisers.

He now needed a physical relationship with these advisers. This would take a different type of trust from the advisers. Though they had built strong alliances within the realm of the mind, he would now be asking them to share a relationship in the body and spirit. He knew it wouldn't be as hard as when he first asked them to be part of his mastermind group or team, but this time, he would be invading personal parts of their lives. They would have to get even closer. He would do it by building deeper relationships with them.

Captain Bon was sure each of these people had faced what he was presently facing, namely a lack of time. Was it a lack of time or misuse of the time he had? Before he even asked for help, he thought of things he could give up.

Again, it was back to the system for success. Anything you want in life has a price, and you must pay the price to achieve your dreams and desires. You must envision having it, and you must feel it with emotion. Captain Bon knew he could do it; however, it would take one special supporter, and he needed to talk to her first.

The person that Captain Bon needed as his main supporter was his wife. He needed her help and support to meet this desire. Captain Bon wanted this plan for both his wife and he. He wanted them to share in growing spiritually and getting in shape so that they could share a long and prosperous life. He also wanted the relationship they had when they were younger. It wasn't that they had a strained relationship, but any relationship could and should grow stronger.

Captain Bon felt he could realize the adventure even if he had to do it alone, but this adventure would be more rewarding if he could share it with Theresa. If they did it together, they would grow as a team. The demanding work on both their spirits and their bodies would bring them closer than ever. This would also allow them to spend more time together. This was something they had both missed since Captain Bon had started planning his adventure. Through the hard workouts and spiritual time together, they would grow closer and stronger as a team.

After talking to Theresa, he was surprised to find that she, too, felt she needed to build her spirit and body. She had already started a plan to get in shape and was hoping to find a partner to work out with her. She loved the idea of that partner being Bon. She had wanted all along to ask him to be her partner, but she hadn't wanted to add to the workload he already had on his shoulders.

She also believed that through building their bodies and spirits together, they would build a relationship that was stronger than they ever had before. They could have a relationship that most in the world dreamed of having.

For her, hearing that Bon wanted to share this adventure of building their spirits and bodies together was a dream come true. She knew how busy he had been and how hard he had been working on getting his adventure going. She felt that his adventure needed to be number one in his life at this time. She wanted to see all his arduous work pay off. After all, he had been such a supportive and giving husband throughout their lives. Now it was time for him to have his desires.

As they talked, she told Bon about the plan she had developed and the why she had for completing her plan. Unlike most people's plans, her plan for health and spirit was a lifelong one.

She didn't want to reach her sixties and later years and not be able to enjoy her retirement. She had a bucket list, and she wanted to explore the world. She needed to be in good health to take on these adventures later in life, and she wanted Captain Bon to be in shape to enjoy the adventures with her.

She also knew that for Captain Bon to survive and thrive on his adventure, he needed to get back into shape. When they were younger— and until about ten years ago—both of them had been in great shape. When they were in their twenties and they first met, they were all about working out and staying in shape.

Over the years, life had beaten them down, and they had had to give some things up—or so they thought. But most people allow their health to go because they think they will be able to recoup it later in life. The sad thing was that they now realized that they had allowed their health and spirit to get away from them and that it would be hard to get those back. But it wasn't impossible. Together, Theresa and Captain Bon would work with others who had found ways to make time to work on their health and spirit while keeping their other dreams alive and moving forward.

Theresa and Captain Bon spent time with Aaron and Kelly to learn how they held down full-time jobs, worked with Captain Bon on the adventure, and worked out daily. What Aaron and Kelly taught them was nothing they didn't already know. It was about making healthy and spiritual habits a priority in your life. When you failed to work out or spend time meditating, you just had to look at why you failed, learn from the reason, and take a different approach.

They also reminded Captain Bon that to be healthy and to build his spiritual self was no different than starting a business or even exploring a foreign land. You had to use the same system for each of these desires, and Captain Bon already had the system to make it happen.

The relationship that Captain Bon and Theresa were now building with Aaron and Kelly made them close friends and confidants. The four of them grew closer with the training and lessons. Each of the four now had relationships that were built through struggling together.

Through the struggles, they opened themselves up to fears they had held in for years and shared these with one another. Each had fears of judgment, and none of them had allowed many as close as they had become to one another.

Captain Bon, Theresa, Aaron, and Kelly spent the next two days discussing their whys and realizing the physical and spiritual health they all wanted. They wrote down the things they discussed and imagined having. They also wrote down their short- and long-term goals for both their health and spirituality.

From there, the four of them developed plans outlining the days and times they would work out and the meals they would prepare. They divided the workouts into cardio and weight training. They would work out for a half hour in the morning with weights and a half hour in the evening with some cardio exercise. They also decided that after six weeks, they would change up their exercise program so that their bodies wouldn't get used to the workout and stop growing stronger. They would do this program together for six days a week.

As for their spiritual sides, they decided that they would spend ten minutes meditating after their morning workouts and thirty minutes after the evening workouts. On Sundays, the day when they didn't work out at all, they would attend church in the morning. After lunch, they would spend an hour reading and discussing a verse from the Bible. This would give the four of them some spiritual and educational value. Then after dinner on Sundays, they would do a thirty-minute walking meditation.

The four now had their plan and began working it. Of course, each member had to give up time watching television and sitting on the couch, but they were spending time together, getting healthy, and building their spiritual selves. They felt the sacrifice of what they were giving up paled in comparison to what they were now receiving.

Just four weeks into their plan to get healthier and build their spiritual selves, they felt better than they had in years. Captain Bon and Theresa had lost weight and had a glow about them that people constantly commented about. The compliments only fed their reasons for working out. They hit the gym harder now than they had when they were younger.

And now it was time for Kelly and Bon to meet with Fred again.

Review Meeting with Fred

Kelly set up a dinner meeting for the end of the week with Fred, and the three of them met at five o'clock at Mason's Diner. Bon was already there when Fred and Kelly showed up. He had a feeling that he couldn't shake all week. It was like he was covered in ants and was dancing around to get them off.

Though outwardly, he didn't show his anxiety, he was full of knots inside. After all, the fate of his adventure relied on Fred feeling he was committed.

As Fred came up, he was surprised to see the progress Bon had made in just thirty days, but would it last? Pulling up to the table, he commented on how great Bon looked. With that, Bon said, "I'm feeling better than I look. I feel ten years younger. Thanks for the challenge."

Fred laughed and replied, "Don't mention it." But Fred had been keeping tabs on Bon's progress through Kelly. He trusted Kelly, and if she said Bon was committed, then he believed this guy was committed. And the proof was the man sitting in front of him.

Fred also could sense the spiritual change in Captain Bon. Kelly had told him of the spiritual growth that the four of them had added into their plan of physical training, and he could see that both his friend and Bon had grown spiritually. To Fred, this was a bonus. He hadn't mentioned the spiritual strength they would need, but given his fights to regain his life after losing his legs, he knew they would need God's help as well. He was happily surprised that they had found that path on their own.

Fred thought for a second and then said, "Bon, you have proven to me you are up for any challenge and are willing to go beyond what is required to achieve your dream. I will be happy to back you in your adventure. Now we will exchange financial support for you and your team's help in the promotion of our brands. This will require your time for interviews and speaking functions both before and after the adventure, but you will have our help. Is this agreeable to you?"

"I will happily agree to this plan with you, Fred, but I cannot speak for the others. However, I don't see it being a problem."

Just then Kelly spoke up in a joking manner, "Hey, wait, Fred. If you want this beautiful face in your advertisement, it's going to cost you a little more, but I'm sure we can work it out."

Laughing as hard as he had probably ever laughed in his life, Fred said, "I wouldn't have expected anything less from you, Kelly."

Giggling, she just responded, "You know me! But in all seriousness, I don't see your request being a problem, and I will work with the others to get them comfortable with being stars."

"Well, that sure is mighty nice of you, Kelly!"

With that, the three finished their conversation about financial backing, contracts, and the type of advertising Fred had in mind.

BACK TO THE TRAINING

The group's cardio walks soon became jogging, and before the first six weeks were up, they could jog a 5K without stopping. Their attitudes also changed. They weren't as on edge as they had been before, and they laughed a lot more. Pushing themselves seemed to agree with them.

It wasn't easy, but they knew it was worth the work. Each member could feel it in their minds, bodies, and spirits. They were rebuilding themselves and their relationship. They had been given a bonus as a result of exercising and meditating. They had become closer as husband and wife.

At the six-week mark, when it was time to evaluate their progress and see what changes in the approach they needed, they discovered that the system had rewarded them. Their approach was working. They were now in better shape than they had been in years, and they were closer to God than they'd ever been in their lives.

Now they knew they had to change their workout routine so that their bodies would keep growing, but they didn't want to change the approach. They decided they would push more toward cardio for the next six weeks. They wanted to enter a 5K charity run, and that would take a little more endurance than they presently had.

All in all, their plan stayed the same, and they were more dedicated to it and to one another than before. Captain Bon realized that his system had once again worked and that if they focused on the system and their reasons, they could be winners in the game of health and spirit.

Through the relationship they had built with Aaron and Kelly over the weeks, Captain Bon and Theresa now had friendships they hadn't had before. Aaron and Kelly had become their closest friends and supporters. They now had a bond that could beat any fear that could come up. Aaron and Kelly also had something they hadn't had before. While they were both stronger in body and spirit, in the beginning, they hadn't had the kind of relationship with others that they now had with Captain Bon and Theresa. They now had a friendship built through struggles with body and spirit. These relationships were like metal that had been heated to become stronger. Their friendship had been heated and now was as strong as any metal on earth.

What Have We Learned from Captain Bon?

We can see through Captain Bon that there is more to a successful life than just money and fame. To be successful in our lives, we need companionship, health, and spirit. Failing to have these three parts only diminishes the lives we could lead.

By sharing our desires and dreams with the people we care about, we can go further than we can alone. It's not always about getting to the destination or dream. It's about the journey and the people we share it with. We can share many good times when we take on demanding work with people we care about. We can build relationships stronger as we build ourselves.

Captain Bon and Theresa realized that both were missing something in their lives. Many of us realize this but can't or will not identify it. Relationships with others, health, and spirituality are three things in our lives that we seem to throw away easily. This may be because these three areas take more focus and are harder to make progress in.

Health

Getting in shape and building your body takes a lot of dedication and pain. We are lazy by nature. This comes from the mind working to find a way to store energy and food for a later date. The mind has been programmed over thousands of years to preserve energy. Choosing to exercise and burn energy goes against its programming, and consequently, the mind will fight you. You can fight back and reprogram your mind so that it understands that this exercise is necessary, but it takes focus and determination.

You may not see results quickly, and this is another reason people fail when it comes to building healthy bodies. With the right exercise program and healthy eating habits, you will get there. Your body and mind will resist you, and your urges will tempt you; however, you must follow your plan and stay focused.

Health should be a lifelong plan. Many of us stray away for one reason or another, but the benefits of staying healthy outweighs the work ten to one. Healthy people feel better about themselves. Plus, they are happier, and they have fresh minds.

Always remember that your mind is part of your body and that it can't survive without your body. Work your body as you work your mind. You will see the benefits.

SPIRITUALITY

Spirituality is something everyone needs to decide for themselves. Some people are not spiritual at all, and they still succeeded in gaining their dreams and desires. That's a proven fact. But if you compare them to spiritual people who have attained their dreams and desires, you will find that spiritual people are happier than the nonspiritual individuals.

Spirituality is whatever you want it to be. I'm not here to tell you to believe in a religion or doctrine. I have seen spiritual people in every religion on this earth. They found what spirituality meant to them, and they embraced it. Then they grew in it by studying and reflecting.

Spirituality doesn't rely on your religion. It is a sense of connection with someone or something greater than you. Even if you believe in evolution, you must see that there is a greater power at work than just you. Look around you at all the moving parts and how they come together. You can call it the big bang, the universe, Muhammad, Buddha, or God. It is a connection to what surrounds us in this world. It is a spiritual power that connects you to your surroundings.

Though many would debate the fact that spirituality can help you achieve your desires, let's look at the science behind it. Think of it in this sense. If you embrace spirituality, you are focusing on someone or something higher than you that can help you in your daily life. It is someone or something that you can talk to or pray to for help.

When you are talking to or praying to this spiritual entity, you are focusing on the challenge you are facing. Your mind is seeking an answer to a problem. With this focus and deliberate practice of spirituality, your mind will help you find the answer.

Now it most likely will not come as a flash of light that solves the problem. If it does, please write to me at CJBourg@olcresources.com and tell me what it was like. But it will come in clues that can tell you what you are looking for and then how to find the answer. All of us can find solutions to the challenges we face. But we sometimes get caught up in the problem and not the solution.

Bringing spirituality into your life and using it to give thanks and to seek answers will help you solve your challenges. It will give you time to meditate with a clear and unworried mind. You need to clear away your worries to get out of your way.

There have been many books that speak of the idea of giving your desires and challenges to God or the universe. Many say your desires will come to you if you give them up to a higher power. This isn't completely correct. You must act, and you have to work. The spirituality will help bring things to you that you need, but not without you doing your part.

You also must be on the lookout for the answer. Your spirituality may already have put the answer in front of you, but you're missing it. There is an old joke that I think of when I can't seem to find the answer. The joke goes like this: A man was at his home during a terrible rainstorm, and the water was rising. The water had reached the top step of his house when a rescue truck came to his door. The rescuer said, "Get in, and we will take you to safety." The man said to the rescuer, "I have faith in God, and he will save me." The rescuer left the man after a few more attempts to get him to leave.

The next day the water had risen to the bottom of the second floor of the man's house. He was sitting next to an open window on the second floor and praying to God to help him when a rescue boat showed up. The rescuer said to the man, "Get in the boat with us, and we will take you to safety." The man replied to the rescuer, "I have faith in God, and he will save me." The rescuer argued with the man and explained that the water was still rising and that he would possibly drown. Again, the man said, "God will save me. I have faith."

On the third day, the water had almost completely covered the man's home. He was sitting on a portion of the roof that was still out of the water when a helicopter rescue unit arrived. The rescue team lowered a rescuer from the helicopter to the man on the roof. The rescuer pleaded with the man to come with him, but the man once again said, "I have faith in God, and he will save me." Seeing that he couldn't convince the man to leave, the rescuer left him to save others in need.

That night the man drowned and went to heaven. He was really upset and asked to have a word with God. Once in front of God, the man said, "God, I have believed in you my entire life. I have placed all my faith in you, and when I needed you, you left me. Why?"

God replied to the man, "My son, I did not forsake you. I sent a truck, a boat, and a helicopter."

You see, all of us can miss what the spirit sends to us. This is an old joke, but it points out an important lesson. When you ask for something, look for it. It may not come in the package you are expecting, but it's there. Too often we believe the answer must be a certain way or that it must come in the way we want it. Answers are not always what we want them to be, but we can use them to save ourselves. And sometimes we can use them to save us from ourselves.

RELATIONSHIPS WITH OTHERS

Connections with others are part of the reason we are here on earth. No one can do anything without the help of others. Building relationships with others can give us self-confidence and happiness. It is built through caring for others and them caring for us. As we build our relationships and open ourselves to others, we become exposed to our fears, namely the fear of being judged.

Though we are open to the fears of judgment, we are also building the alliances that will combat the fears. Through caring relationships, we have people who care about our well-being. They care that we are happy. They care that we reach our dreams and desires, just as we care about them. Through this mutual caring, each party becomes stronger.

There are many types of relationships—business, personal, health, and spiritual. These four relationships are often intertwined. When we can intertwine all four parts of life with people in our lives, we build relationships that can stand any struggles or fears. These relationships are forged through the struggles faced in life. All four parts of our lives improve from the support of our relationships, and we gain success in all parts of our lives then.

Building these type of relationships takes opening up to others. You must allow people into your life and also allow them to see your fears as you see their fears. Building these relationships is work. You must put the other people's needs ahead of your own. Only by caring for them first will you get caring in return. You must give before you receive.

The rewards for caring about others are more than can be written in these pages. Truly caring that someone is happy and successful will give you more satisfaction than you can imagine. Of course, it will be demanding work and require self-sacrifice. You must forget what you want and need, and you must care that these other people are getting the support they need.

Most parents know this kind of care. This is how most parents care for their children. They don't often see the return on investment for their caring until the children are grown and have matured, but they get the children's love. That unconditional love from children is one of the greatest rewards in life.

When we build relationships with other people the way we build relationships with our children, we get as much or more in return. These are the relationships you should work to build with others, but not for the rewards you will get. You should do so because you care for that person the way you care for your children.

People do things that we do not like or that hurt us, but we need to remember why we built relationships in the first place. You may not be able to forgive the act that offended you, but you can forgive the person. We are more than willing to do so for our children, so why wouldn't we do the same for close friends we have built relationships with?

Go out and build the relationships that will enrich others' lives as well as your own. Then you will be even wealthier than the richest people in the world.

DEVELOPING YOUR PLAN

Now it's time to move forward and use the system you have learned to create a plan to meet your desired health and spiritual lifestyle as you build relationships with others.

1. Remember dreams, desires, and decisions. It's time to create the dreams and desires you want for health and spirituality. What is your desire, and what are the reasons behind the lifestyle you want? Make a true decision either way and move forward.
2. Imagination is your next step. Imagine what you will look like when you reach your desired lifestyle. What will your body look like? What compliments will you get? How will you feel about yourself? What will your spiritual relationship be? How will you use your spirituality to help you with your dreams and desires?
3. What is your subconscious mind saying about you getting into shape or about spirituality? What are your beliefs and values? Are any of your beliefs and values holding you back? How did you come by these beliefs and values? Is it time to reevaluate your beliefs? Maybe it's time to build new beliefs.
4. Now we move on to building the plan to get the health and spirituality that you desire. You will build your plan and again see if it conflicts with your beliefs and values.
5. It's time to gather knowledge to help make your plan bulletproof. You will have to organize the specialized knowledge on creating a healthier lifestyle and a spiritual one. You can find this information by looking on the internet, reading books, asking friends, or consulting experts. Seek out the knowledge that you need to build your road map and organize it so that you can use it all.
6. Now you need your mastermind group. The members of this group will help keep you going when times get hard. The group will give you feedback on the results you are getting. They will

give you suggestions about exercises or the spiritual lessons you need to learn. Just as with any other adventure you are working on, you need advisers to help you stay on course so that you can accomplish your desires. Your mastermind group could include your spouse, a trainer, and a group of people who work out with you or raise your spiritual adventure. There are many people out there who can help you. You only need to ask.

7.   You must care first about the people you are working out with before they will care about you. Work to help them before you ask them to help you.

8.   Now put what you learned into persistence and determination to keep moving and gaining on your dream. Remember, persistence and determination are about using willpower to help you create habits and also to get your subconscious mind to help you achieve your dream. Use the relationships you have built to help others with their persistence and determination, and they will help you with yours.

9.   You will have to leverage and stretch yourself during any adventure in life, but you'll need to do so even more with relationships, health, and spirituality. You must leverage your present-day self to do what is needed to get to your future self. Stretching yourself is a must when it comes to spiritual growth. There is a lot to learn about being spiritual and healthy. You will need to learn new things, things that may not come easy and may also conflict with the person you were before. You must decide for yourself what your future will look like. This will take more stretching than you are used to, but it will help you grow internally. This is true for growth in relationships, health, and spirituality.

10. Have faith in yourself and develop your self-confidence. Even if you can't do one push-up today, you will be doing twenty in a month, maybe more. Have faith in yourself that you can build your spiritual self and find a peace that you haven't had before. When you hit a hard spot in your physical or spiritual journey, have the self-confidence that you will get past it, and in a brief time, look back on it as a small challenge. With relationships, you must have the self-confidence that you can open up without being

hurt. You must put your faith in the other people and believe that they have your best interest at heart. There is always a chance of getting hurt, but with self-confidence and faith in others, we can build relationships that serve us for a lifetime.

Now you are on your way to the new physical and spiritual you. Things will seem like they are not changing, but when you have been on your journey just a few months, you will see how far you have come. Keep pushing and know you are getting better.

When setbacks come—and they will come—go back to the system and do your checks. Is the setback coming from your plan, your leverage, or your self-confidence? Find the root cause and change your approach. Then try just one more time. Well, you know it's not one more time by now, but for now, try just one more time.

SUCCESS PITFALLS PRINCIPLES THAT HARM YOUR RELATIONSHIPS WITH PEOPLE, YOUR BODY, AND YOUR SPIRIT

Captain Bon knew all too well the success pitfalls principles can hurt relationships with people, your body, and your spirit. He had lived his life fighting these success pitfalls principles at one time or another. They attacked daily and required persistence and determination to combat. They also required building relationships through caring for others as well as yourself.

SUCCESS PITFALLS PRINCIPLES THAT HURT RELATIONSHIP WITH OTHERS

It started with building relationships. Captain Bon was, by nature, an introvert and had to push himself to be an extrovert. It didn't come naturally to put himself out in front of people. He was more comfortable watching from the sideline or hiding in the shadows when he could.

Now to achieve his dreams and desires, he needed to be an extrovert. Many people would be watching his every move and action. It would also require him to take center stage to secure the required backing he needed to embark on the adventure to Mount La Felicidad.

He would have to build relationships with advisers, team members, and supporters. Captain Bon knew he could do this through caring first for these people before asking for their help. He would have to show them the rewards they could and would attain by building a relationship with him.

Captain Bon was a caring person and would be genuine when it came to caring for these people, but he would still need to get out of his shell and open to others. This was one way to beat the success pitfalls principle that killed relationships. He would show them that he cared for their happiness, dreams, and desires before asking for their help. He would also open himself up and expose his fears so that they would not fear opening up to him.

Captain Bon understood that being an introvert by nature could kill his efforts to build relationships, but what did other people face that would stop them from building relationships? Why would people go through life and not try to build relationships that would support them? He knew it all came down to fears, but some of these fears came from people's attitudes toward others.

Another one of the success pitfalls principles Captain Bon found that killed true relationships were using people. He had found some people built relationships to get what they needed without caring what the other person would benefit from the relationship. While looking into this, he noticed that this was why many people changed jobs. The relationships they had with their employers were too one-sided.

Yes, they were paid for their work, but they were not part of the family. The company wasn't bad, but more likely, a manager didn't consider that humans needed to contribute and be part of something greater. The employees were just a gear in the machine.

Then the manager probably didn't make an effort to engage the employees and understand what they needed from the company other than monetary compensation. Each person wanted to feel that they were serving a greater purpose. Whether it's two people working together or a thousand at a company, they all need to feel that what they do for the team brings value that no one else brings.

Now Captain Bon knew you could have relationships with others as social friends and never build real relationships with them, but that wasn't the relationship he was considering. Social relationships rarely grow into relationships where you share hopes and dreams. They have less substance than the relationships needed to achieve your dreams and desires. Captain Bon realized that those were the types of relationships most people had with their managers at work. It wasn't that the employees wanted this type of relationship. The manager wanted this type of relationship.

To build relationships that take someone to their dreams and desires, Captain Bon understood each partner in the relationship had to feel important and had to be able to contribute. By listening and being heard, each member felt needed and respected for what they contributed to the group. These were the relationships that would grow each of the members.

Captain Bon resolved that he would always ask himself first, "How will the other person benefit from this relationship?" By seeking first how others would benefit, he could start with caring as his first action. By caring that the other person would receive something before he did, Captain Bon could build the relationships that would benefit him as well.

HEALTHY LIFESTYLE SUCCESS PITFALLS PRINCIPLES

Captain Bon knew that poor health could kill success. These success pitfalls principles involving health are almost too many to list, but Captain Bon worked on a list that he could use to raise his awareness as he worked to regain his health. Here is the list Captain Bon came up with. He had to watch out for

1. unhealthy eating through poor planning or impulsive eating;
2. laziness and not pushing himself to get off the sofa and start moving;
3. not enough time to work out because of poor scheduling;
4. pain, pain, and more pain (as exercise would make his muscles sore);
5. lack of motivation because he didn't have a strong enough why;
6. lack of accountability either because he did not have someone to help keep him accountable or he did not set his accountability;

7. putting everything before his health by thinking that there would always be time to regain it;

8. fear of judgment from others when he compared their abilities and health levels to his present condition; and

9. not making getting in shape a lifelong journey and allowing it to become just a passing phase.

Captain Bon knew other things killed one's path to a healthy life, but these were the main success pitfalls principles that had killed his healthy living. He needed to watch out for these nine success pitfalls principles and battle them each day if he wanted to lead a healthy life.

To live a healthy life, Captain Bon needed to make it a daily habit. His plan had to address what he would do in the morning when he woke up, how he would plan his meals each day, and what he would do to motivate himself when he just wanted to sit on the couch and watch TV.

This plan needed to take into account the fact that he wouldn't always be in a controlled environment and that there would be times when it would be difficult to control his time and urges. His plan had to address these real concerns.

He felt that the daily healthy habits had to be simple. If he made them too complicated, he wouldn't continue when the time was short. Captain Bon and Theresa's plan at home was stringent, but they needed to build a simpler version for the days that didn't adhere to this plan.

As he thought about a healthy life, it came down to moving and the choices he made when he sat down to eat. It was a simple formula that he could track on his phone. He needed only to count the calories he took in against the calories he burned from his daily activities. The calories he ate had to be one third less than the calories he burned. Now, this wasn't a foolproof plan. The calories he consumed couldn't be just from junk food or the like. No, he needed to avoid indulging in sugary foods when he wasn't working out in the gym or doing long walks/runs. He also needed to be conscious of the portions he consumed, limiting them to smaller portions at any one sitting.

He knew that no matter how busy he was, he could always make time for a short walk/run workout. Even if this required him to get out of bed a half hour earlier than normal, he could make time for some exercise. He could also do things like walk up the stairs instead of taking the elevator or park farther away from buildings than he normally did. This way, he could get a few more steps in.

These simple plans would keep him on track to a healthier lifestyle. It was all about the choices he made throughout his day and the why behind those choices. After all, anyone can make the time to live a healthy lifestyle. It just had to be one of their priorities.

SPIRITUAL SUCCESS PITFALLS PRINCIPLES

Captain Bon thought to himself, *What are the success pitfalls principles that would harm or kill spirituality?* Captain Bon turned his view inward to determine why he hadn't been as spiritual as he could have been to find the success pitfalls principles.

During his adolescence, he had a strong spiritual connection, but as he had grown older, it had faded and was now almost nonexistent. As he looked over his life, he realized there was a time when he was closer to God than others, but why was that? Was it just that his faith was shaken by things in his life, or was it something else?

As he thought over his relationship with God, he realized it was somewhat of a one-sided relationship. He was there, but he felt God wasn't there. Now it wasn't that God had walked away from him, was it? As he evaluated the differences of his relationship with God as a man compared to when he was a child, he found that he hadn't made the time as a man for God as he had when he was a child.

As a child, he had been involved more with learning about God from teachers and peers, but as a man on his own, he hadn't tried to learn more about God. Now, like most in tough times, he looked to God for the answers, but like any other relationship, how could he expect answers when he hadn't built the relationship with God?

Like most people, Captain Bon started making excuses for his actions. He would say, "When I was a child, I had more time. And my parents made me go to religious studies when I was a child." These were all excuses. The truth was that he hadn't made time for his spiritual growth. He hadn't seen the benefit in spiritual growth as he had seen in growing his mind, but through the growth of his knowledge, he found he needed spiritual growth.

Through learning about meditation, Captain Bon found that being spiritual was more than a religious belief. It was a connection to a higher power and the world around him. As he spent time meditating and clearing his mind of the day-to-day garbage, it opened him to hear God's voice in his life.

He couldn't be sure if it was the voice of God or the voice of his childhood self, but it spoke to him of the things he had learned from the Bible as a child. This voice gave him both peace and knowledge. He realized that others had faced trials and tribulations in their lives and had still found peace in God.

It didn't matter to Captain Bon if he was hearing God's voice or not. The peace he received gave him the strength inside to realize that he could prevail in his adventure. This was the peace he had searched for throughout his life.

As Captain Bon examined the why behind the peace, he realized he had found the success pitfalls principles that harmed his spirituality. Captain Bon could see three success pitfalls principles that had harmed and almost killed his spirituality. They included a failure to seek the knowledge of God, a failure to make God a partner in his life, and a failure to clear his mind of the daily drudgery to hear God's voice.

These three success pitfalls principles were easy to find once Captain Bon looked for them, but that was the key to spirituality. You had to seek it out, and you had to be prepared to hear and take in the knowledge. It couldn't be on your terms. You had to clear your mind and listen for the words that would give you inner peace.

Through meditation, Captain Bon was able to hear the words that gave him peace. These words weren't a voice shouting in the room. It whispered words he had read from the Bible. They were the stories of the believers who had come before him.

Captain Bon finally understood how true believers in any religion or faith found peace. It was through a connection with something higher than oneself. It was the knowledge that there was a force above us that worked to help and teach us.

Captain Bon also realized that to grow in his spirituality, he had to research and understand others that had been spiritually strong not just in his religion but in all religions. He read books on Gandhi, Buddha, Mother Teresa, and many others. He found that these people had a profound sense of caring for others and that much of their spirituality came from trying to help others. He also found that they gathered strength through their faith. Now all three had different faiths, but all three believed there was a higher presence working in this world.

Through studying others who had been successful through their spirituality, Captain Bon knew he had to build his spirituality through daily meditation and reading. Captain Bon was a Christian, so he read his Bible and meditated on what he had read. But he didn't focus only on the words or actions of the people in the stories. He meditated on the faith they had and the strength it gave them to persevere.

As Captain Bon immersed himself in daily reading and meditation, he found he could fight off the success pitfalls principles that harmed spirituality. He was now focused on his spirituality, and with that focus, his spirit grew.

The more Captain Bon focused, the less he was led astray by the success pitfalls principles. Captain Bon knew that people's energy went to where they focused, but he hadn't before understood that people could focus on many things at once. They could focus on being four-dimensional. They could develop all parts of themselves if they had plans to do so and if they followed those plans.

Captain Bon had come to find that these were his success principles. They outlined a plan to develop himself into a four-dimensional person. Through practicing his success principles daily and avoiding the success pitfalls principles, he could grow his mind, body, spirit, and relationships. Through the growth of these four areas of life, he would succeed in achieving his dreams and desires.

Achieving his dreams and desires wasn't about what he was born with or what education level he had achieved. It was about developing the four parts of his life. He realized that most people only developed one or two parts of their lives. They were missing parts that would help them succeed. He now knew that the journey that would create happiness in his life would be the one that helped him develop all four dimensions of himself.

To develop the four dimensions of himself, Captain Bon would need to be healthy, be spiritual, and develop relationships with others. Then he could use his success principles as a plan to go after and achieve his dreams and desires in life while he developed his mind.

CHAPTER 16

FAITH IN YOURSELF AND
SELF-CONFIDENCE
BELIEF IN THE MAP OF THE RIVER

CAPTAIN BON REFLECTED ON A conversation he had had with Aaron and how he had allowed the faith in himself to diminish in the face of hardship. He had forgotten his system because he was focusing only on the problems. He wasn't looking for the solution or what his attempts thus far had taught him. He was wallowing in self-pity.

Aaron helped Captain Bon realize that he was missing a crucial part of his system to success. He needed a checklist to restore his self-confidence that he could achieve the dream and desire he was after. He had a checklist for every other part of the system, but not a strong checklist for self-confidence.

How could he have missed such an important part as faith in himself? He thought about the question and came up with a few reasonable answers. He had assumed that each victory, no matter how small, would build his self-confidence, and they did. But he hadn't built in reminders of these victories.

When the tough times came, he doubted himself. He didn't have reminders that showed he had faced adversity before, stretched himself, and succeeded. He now understood he needed these reminders. Though

Aaron was his reminder this time, he may not be there the next time, and he needed reminders of past victories to help support his self-confidence.

But what would be the best type of reminders he could build? As he thought about it, he felt that reminders in pictures brought the greatest emotion. He knew that during the tough times, he would need more than his logical side to say, "You have accomplished hard challenges before, and you can do it again." That would help, but it wouldn't bring as much emotion to his mind as pictures would. He could use pictures from different challenges he had faced and succeeded at. If he didn't have a picture of the event, he could take a picture of himself thinking about the accomplishment and a picture of what it had brought him and put them together. Whatever it took to remind him of the accomplishment would work.

He could put the picture on a board and take a picture of the board with his phone. This way, he would have the picture board in his office as a reminder and also a photo on his phone for when he was away from the office. He also thought about other ways he could set up reminders.

One thing he came up with was to take the picture he had taken of the picture board and set a calendar reminder to review it once a month. He knew he probably wouldn't need the reminder at the time it popped up, but it would create a review for his subconscious mind. Every little reminder would help keep his faith in himself and his self-confidence up throughout time.

Reflecting more on self-confidence, Captain Bon wondered what it really was and why sometimes he was full of it and empty at other times. Self-confidence to him was self-assurance. It was the action of assuring yourself that you could accomplish something and that you had the power within yourself to take the necessary action.

After all, self-assurance was just a state of mind, and he knew how to train his mind to do his bidding. He did not always get it right on the first try, but he could build the assurance in his mind over time that he was positive about. It may take a few different approaches, but he would push forward with persistence and determination.

Thinking about the state of mind a person would have to be in to develop self-assurance and build self-confidence, Captain Bon knew it would be much like changing a belief. It would take putting himself in a positive state of mind, seeing his past success in his imagination, and tying it to his future success.

He could also use the reminders to help him build the assurance that would support his self-confidence. But he wasn't sure he understood how self-assurance developed into self-confidence. What was the connection?

If all he or anyone needed was just assurance, why could they be self-confident whenever they wanted or always retain the inner confidence that they needed to take on anything? Thinking more about it, he realized it was due to experiencing past failures and not trying again with different approaches. The failure had left a ghost of doubt in his subconscious mind. It was funny that he had to work so hard at building self-confidence, but a ghost from the past could destroy the assurance he had in himself.

With this realization, Captain Bon understood that failure wouldn't stop him now. He would try a different approach. No matter how many different approaches he had to take, he would find a way to succeed at the things in life that mattered enough to him to go after. He would push through the struggles to find the pot of gold at the end of the rainbow.

With the new realization he now had, he needed those different reminders of past successes to help him keep his self-confidence.

WHAT HAVE WE LEARNED FROM CAPTAIN BON ABOUT SELF-CONFIDENCE?

We see through Captain Bon's experience that anyone could face self-confidence issues. Even well-trained people or teachers could lose their way and their self-confidence. We all need a plan to remind ourselves that we have succeeded in the past and can succeed again.

This plan had to provide reminders of past accomplishments and the path back to self-confidence. The plan could include pictures, boards, calendar reminders, and even pictures in Captain Bon's phones that pop up from time to time as appointments to remind his subconscious mind of his past successes. This way, his subconscious mind would aid him in maintaining his self-confidence.

We can also use team members or mastermind groups to help us with the reminders of past accomplishments. When working with teams, we learn from Captain Bon that each member can and will help one another with their self-assurance to keep their self-confidence high. To receive support, one must first give support. No one will help without something in it for them. For most, this support isn't tied to a financial reward but to feeling good that they helped and returned support.

We learned that self-confidence is the self-assurance that we have accomplished dreams and desires before and that we can do so again. We can build the assurance we need anytime we want to. Self-assurance is nothing more than a state of mind. It is your mind, and you can assure it anytime you choose to; however, you have to make a choice to put yourself into a positive state of mind and realize that you have succeeded in the past and can do so again.

Many people's issues are not with self-confidence or the ability to build it in themselves. They have issues putting themselves in the state of mind to build the assurance to support self-confidence. People don't understand that their state of mind is dependent only on their decisions and choices.

We all choose our states of mind. Your state of mind isn't dependent on exterior sources or people. It's dependent on you, putting yourself into a positive state of mind. You can do this and reassure yourself that you have whatever it takes to succeed whenever you want to. Here is a system of putting yourself into a positive state of mind and building self-assurance and self-confidence:

1. First, clear your mind of the problems facing you and of the world around. The state of mind you are after is similar to meditation.
2. Second, think back over the things you have accomplished and pick one win that was challenging when you took it on.
3. Think and feel the emotions you had when you achieved the win.
4. Look in your imagination and figure out how you accomplished the win.
5. Feel the process you used for the win.
6. Associate the feeling of accomplishing the win you had with the present challenge you have.
7. Go after the new challenge with the assurance that you can win as you have others in the past.

8. Anytime you are not feeling confident in yourself, return to these simple steps.
9. Remember one last thing: you only fail if you quit.

I know this system sounds simple, and you may doubt it will work; however, if you put your emotions in the right perspective, you will find the confidence through self-assurance that you need to push on to your success.

WHAT IS SELF-CONFIDENCE AND FAITH IN YOURSELF?

Faith is what gives life, power, and action to all thoughts and desires. Faith is required to achieve anything in life. Without faith, you could not operate in this world. What if you did not have faith that the sun would come up again? What fear would that bring into your life? What if you didn't have faith that your body would remember to breathe? Now that would scare you, wouldn't it? However, we have faith that these things and more will happen. So why don't we have faith in ourselves and the fact that we will succeed in whatever we put our minds to?

Extreme sports stars have faith in themselves that allows them and drives them to believe they can climb mountains, skydive, do backflips on a motorcycle, and jump bicycles to unthinkable heights. Many people believe they don't have that kind of faith or that they cannot develop it.

There is a quote by Robert Collier that is worth reminding yourself of daily. "All power is from within and is therefore under our control."

Faith is nothing more than a state of mind. As we spoke earlier about the techniques of NLP, you can create any state of mind you want and use your anchors to help you program your subconscious mind through self-suggestion with feelings.

With faith and self-suggestion, we can achieve our desires. This is where many people fail in life. They have plans. They have reviewed these plans strategically in their imagination. They have found the right partners, and they are on their way to their desires. Then they let self-doubt into their minds through a lack of faith, and they abandon their desires. This is the greatest tragedy in life.

You see, instead of imagining themselves as successful, they imagine failing and not being loved or respected. Most people stopped well short of their abilities. In their minds, they have painted this fast-moving movie about failing, and they get scared. They are so full of fear that they cannot move forward. Then all they can see are the failures ahead. So they feel defeated and abandon the trip. The bottom line is that they quit on themselves.

You need to understand that the only time you fail is when you quit. The rest is just a result and a learning opportunity. Think about this explanation. You did not fail if you did not get the outcome you wanted. You (should have) learned how not to accomplish what you want. Now you need only change your approach to the challenge.

There's a famous story about Thomas Edison's 9,999th try at creating the light bulb. He caused an explosion that almost seriously hurt his friend and himself. Edison then started writing notes in his journal about the experiment and started thinking about what he had learned and what he would try next. His friend asked if he was crazy. He told Edison in a very angry voice, "This is the 9,999th failure, and this one almost killed us." Edison replied to him in a calm and firm voice, "I have not failed. I have found the 9,999th way not to invent the light bulb. But I have found a way to create an explosion, and that may be useful in the future." Now that is the picture of a man of true faith and self-confidence.

THE THREE PARTS OF SELF-CONFIDENCE

1. Self-awareness is understanding your good and bad traits and learning from your mistakes to avoid repeating them.
2. Self-acceptance is accepting your shortcomings and working to improve them. This means you understand there may be some personal traits that you cannot change.
3. Self-assurance is building assurance within yourself about your ability to succeed through the successes of the past.

You can build the same self-confidence as Edison through the steps we looked at earlier. This will help you reassure yourself that you have succeeded before and will again. All you must do is try one more time and use each failure as a learning experience.

It's hard for us to look at failure as educational because our formal education through school and upbringing teaches us that only people who succeed get rewards. The people who went through school and could memorize subject information made As and were treated as special compared to the students who couldn't memorize things as well and didn't get such good grades.

But real life is different from school. You will learn ten times more from a failure than a success if you take ownership of the failure, evaluate what went wrong, and take a different approach. If you find it in yourself to do these things when you fail, you will build your self-assurance and keep your self-confidence intact.

It's that easy. Now I know there are people that the world has beat down to the point of giving up. It's hard to say they should try again, but they should. Success may be one try away, but they will never know it if they don't try one more time.

You only have one life to live. Why would you give up on yourself and not attain what you desire in life?

THE SUCCESS PITFALLS PRINCIPLES THAT DESTROY SELF-CONFIDENCE AND FAITH IN YOURSELF

Looking over what causes people to lose their self-confidence and faith, Captain Bon found three success pitfalls principles that affect people. Unlike most of the success pitfalls principles, these three seemed to follow one another rather than work separately. The three success pitfalls principles are fear of the unknown, doubt in yourself, and loss of self-confidence.

To Captain Bon, it seemed people first became fearful of what they didn't know about something. This caused them to doubt their capabilities, which caused them to lose their self-confidence and faith. It also seemed that with this chain reaction, a person could break one of the links in the chain and retain their faith and self-confidence. But which one of the three would be the best link to break?

Captain Bon knew the best one to break would be the fear of the unknown, but this would be the hardest to break. Everyone had fears, and everyone had to fight those fears if they were to become successful. But you couldn't avoid the fears. The fears would come, and to be successful, you had to face them.

Facing the fears was a way to break the chain, but it wouldn't be the first link that was broken. It would be the second link of doubt. By facing your fears, you can resolve not to allow them to beat you. As you face them, you are pushing doubt out of your mind and thus breaking the chain of the success pitfalls principles. This way, you never arrive at the last link in the chain.

Captain Bon also realized that if you didn't face the fears and doubts that entered your mind, it would be nearly impossible to stop the loss of self-confidence and faith. Now you can and should still battle this success pitfalls principle if you reach the last chain. Hope wouldn't be completely lost, but the battleground would be stacked against you. It would become a hard, uphill battle.

So how would you fight your fears and break the second link? Captain Bon felt that one could easily do so, but most people failed to do it. You just had to face the fear that would cause doubt. Facing the fears meant seeking them out and not waiting until they took hold of you. If you waited, the battle would just become harder, but if you looked for these fears, the battle was much easier. Seeking out your fears meant you had to be proactive. You were now on the offensive instead of the defense. This would put you in a position of power over your fears.

Captain Bon felt that by seeking out the fears within any part of the adventure, he would have an advantage. It would also allow him to prepare for what was to come and inspire some strategic plans to combat the fears of the unknown.

As he was planning his adventure to Mount La Felicidad, he knew that he had a limited understanding of the river and what he would face on it. He knew this could cause fear in himself as well as the team that would be with him. He looked for the fears he would face by reading all he could find that people had written about journeys to Mount La Felicidad. He also contacted people who had made the journey to find out more about the things that they had faced.

Captain Bon understood we learn more from failures than from successes, and so he also wanted to find the people who hadn't made it to

Mount La Felicidad. He knew smart people learned from their mistakes and failures, but brilliant people were able to learn from others' mistakes and failures. He wanted to be brilliant and prepared.

In reading and talking to others who had failed to make it to Mount La Felicidad, Captain Bon learned there wasn't anything to fear, but there were many things that he would have to prepare for along the way. He already knew about most of the details, but there were things he hadn't thought of, such as what type of bug spray to use to prevent infection and what tools he needed to repair the boat.

There were other things to be aware of, including the forks in the river and hostile villages to stay away from. Captain Bon learned from others about the signs to look for that would keep him away from these traps. These traps had ruined other adventures or had instilled fears in them that had caused the eventual failure of their adventures.

Looking for his fears helped him educate himself against possible failure. The lessons from others gave Captain Bon a great education. He was able to learn from their mistakes and build a plan to avoid the traps. This gave him the strength to fight his fears. It even exposed fears he hadn't thought of that would certainly attack him later.

In educating himself through others' experiences on the river, he was able to seek out the fears he would face. By talking to the adventurers who had failed to reach Mount La Felicidad, he learned through them the feelings they faced and how fear played a role in their failures. Captain Bon now understood the fears and could see how they would cause people to give up on their dreams. By understanding the feelings these people had, he could imagine himself in the grips of the same fear. Through his imagination, he could create a plan to fight the fear and get past it.

Though he knew that seeing it in his imagination wouldn't give him all the solutions he would need, it did give him an advantage that the people who had failed didn't have. It helped turn the unknown into the known, and he could face the known.

By seeking out what possible fears would come, Captain Bon was also able to prepare his team. This preparation helped build an alliance within the team. This alliance built the team's confidence that they could take on the river and make it to the mountain.

Captain Bon had looked at the success pitfalls principles that killed self-confidence and faith, and he found that life was hard and that fears would come. The only way to beat the fears and tough times was to face them and find the strength in yourself to push through. You will get help from others, but the strength must come from inside. Only you can force yourself to look for the fears and challenges that will come.

CHAPTER 17

CAPTAIN BON'S ADVENTURE
THE REST OF THE STORY

I GUESS YOU WOULD LIKE to hear the rest of Captain Bon's story. First, let's talk about the rest of your story. If you have done the exercises, you are now in the top ninetieth percentile. There is 10 percent left to total success. That may not seem like much, but like the rest of Captain Bon's story, you haven't gotten to the end of the adventure.

Now you are most likely saying, "I have read the book and story of Captain Bon. I have done the exercises. What can be left?" Well, what's left could be easy for you, or it could seem impossible. The only thing left between you and your dreams is *you*!

You are the only thing that can stand between you and your dreams now. If you have followed the principles to success and built your plan, organized your mastermind group, and followed the principles, you can succeed. But you still must make the moves. You still must put in the work, and most importantly, you have to have confidence in yourself. Even when times are hard and the world is against you, you must believe in yourself.

Believe that you can make it through anything. Even if you have failed a thousand times like Edison when he was working to create the light bulb, you will eventually succeed if you try one more time.

We have talked about many things in this book that will help you get to your dreams and desires, but nothing is more important than trying one more time. The art of trying one more time is about self-confidence, persistence, and determination. But it is more about driving past yourself. We all have it in us to get past anything in life, including ourselves, but many seem to stop when there is only 10 percent left to go in the journey.

When you think you can't go on, remember that you have nothing else to lose. Push through the pain and win for yourself. Each time you don't reach your desire, go for one more round and push through the pain, the humiliation, and whatever else is holding you back. Always try again.

But don't take the same path you did when you failed. Look at the failure, examine what went wrong and what action led to the failure, and then change that action. Find it in yourself to take that different approach and go for it one more time.

If this is your approach, you will eventually succeed and receive your desire. But don't stop there. Build a bigger dream with a grander desire and go after it. After all, that is a life lived well. That is a life worth living. It's a life that will be remembered by many and even studied as one for others to emulate. After all, isn't that what each of us is after? To be remembered past our time on this earth?

CAPTAIN BON'S STORY

Captain Bon and his team faced many challenges from the time they received the backing of Fred's company to right before they arrived at the mouth of the river. Some of the things they faced included multiple interviews and lunches with both employees at the outfitter and Fred's company. This was completely different for Bon and his team. They had never been in the spotlight before and wouldn't have thought that so many people would be interested in their adventure.

There were people of all ages and walks of life. Some were weekend warriors. Others were hunters, and then others were people with ordinary lives who liked the idea of a blue-collar person going after an adventure. Wherever they came from, each one had a genuine interest in the why behind the adventure. As Captain Bon told the story of his why, it only seemed to inspire and connect to the people at each of the functions.

As he spoke, Aaron, Kelly, and Fred all recalled their excitement when Bon first told them about his dream. A warmth came over Kelly that melted her heart. It was amazing to her that a man she hadn't known a year ago was now such a close friend and mentor. Bon had changed many people's lives with his adventure, but maybe none more than his own.

D-DAY

The team's preparation and hard work had come down to this day. It was now a warm July morning, and the sun was already peeking over the trees at five forty-five in the morning. From the feeling of stickiness that Bon already felt under his shirt, he knew it was going to be a warm day with high humidity for the start of their adventure.

Bon thought back over the last eleven months and all the preparation that had gone into making this day happen. He had acquired a great friend and mentor in Dennis, who had to help him put everything he had read and learned into a system so that he could accomplish his dreams. There had been times when he was down and out during the eleven months, but his mastermind group and team along with Theresa were always there to lift him and help him focus on the dream.

With every step, he had made progress one foot at a time, and now 80 percent of it all was behind him. A thought came to his mind like a ghost from the past. Señor Doubter was again trying to discourage Captain Bon one more time.

In his sneakiest voice, he reminded Captain Bon that even though he had accomplished much, the dangerous part was ahead of him. Now Señor Doubter wasn't saying, "You can't do this. What are you thinking?" It was a lot more devious than that. Señor Doubter used encouragement tactics this time as he whispered, "You have come a long way, Bon, and you have surprised me with what you have accomplished. There is much here for you to be proud of, but this next portion of your plan will be the toughest of all. If you don't make it to Mount La Felicidad, the adventure will still be a success, and then you can put all this behind you and go back to your comfortable life."

Not thinking about Señor Doubter's full statement, Captain Bon was feeling good, so he let down his guard against his old enemy. Then as if he had been hit in the face with a two-by-four, he realized that Señor Doubter was leading him down the river of settlement. He was telling him he had accomplished enough and didn't have to push through to reach the mountain. Well, that wasn't going to work for Captain Bon. He had come too far not to reach his dream.

Captain Bon spoke in his loudest and most earnest voice and said to Señor Doubter and the rest of the doubting universe, "I don't care if I have to make a thousand trips to this spot to eventually get to the mountain. I will make it eventually. I am determined, and short of dying—and I doubt that will happen—I will sit at the bottom of Mount La Felicidad. You can take that to the bank. So please leave." With that, Señor Doubter was gone, and Captain Bon set his eyes on the work ahead of his team and him.

UP THE RIVER WITH A PADDLE

It was now passing the time that the crew was supposed to head out from the base camp, but it wasn't as late as Captain Bon had feared. The sun was rising fast, and the temperature was climbing too. Though it seemed to be late, it was only six thirty-five. The team felt that time was flying, and if they didn't get moving, they would lose much of the morning, which was an easier time for traveling. Plus, they were eager to get underway, and so they did.

The first few days brought little in the way of any dangers, but everyone was sure they were coming. While the traveling was good on the river and the team could use the small onboard motor, they decided to travel until the last ray of sunlight shone through the trees. While this allowed them to get ahead of the mileage they had planned for the day, it also stressed their bodies. However, it helped their spirits too, so they felt it was a fair trade.

On the fourth day at around noon, the team decided to stop and do a little fishing to replenish their food supplies and take a break from the constant noise. The fishing was very good, and the three adventurers were having a fun time catching some food. Just then the sky opened up and started pouring down rain on the team. They hurried and got their rainwear out and decided to push off and continue ahead on their adventure.

After putting on their rain gear, they stored the fish they had caught in one of the ice chests and took their places in the boat to begin again on the river.

The rain continued all day and throughout the night. It made for a miserable night's sleep, but at least it kept the bugs away. They didn't have to put on any bug spray, which was nice, though if asked, all three would have preferred the bug spray instead of a night with constant rain.

Their tents kept the rain off them, but they weren't dry. It was like sleeping in a bathtub with two inches of water. It was not fun, and they had lots of wrinkles as a result.

The rain stopped early in the morning and didn't return for many days. Though it took the team two days to dry out their equipment and tents, things were going well and ahead of schedule.

Two days after the rain, the adventurers were a full three days ahead of their plans, and that was when tragedy struck.

In an area that was still supposed to be calm, they found rapids from the rain that was coming down the river from the mountain. The big fear was not so much the rocks as the whirling water created by the churning of the river.

The team decided they had to pick up the motor and use the paddles to guide their way through the rapids. It would be slower than using the motor, but it would be safer.

Now pushing toward the banks before the rapids, they worked to pick up the motor and pull out the paddles. The plan was for Bon and Aaron to work the paddles as Kelly acted as a lookout and guide. The team discussed their plan as they put on their life jackets. They hadn't been wearing them in the calm water (though they knew they should), but they didn't want to take a chance on what was to come.

As the three adventurers guided the boat down the river, the water became faster than they had expected. The river pushed the boat from side to side as Aaron and Bon work to paddle against the strong current and the rough waters. There were many rocks on each side of the boat, and the water was churning. The boat was being pushed faster now, and they were in danger of smashing into a large rock and sinking at any moment. The equipment in the boat was starting to move side to side and needed to be secured. They didn't want to take a chance of losing the equipment. If the team lost this equipment deep in the jungle, they would not make it out. They would be lost here without completing the adventure.

It was up to the three of them now to navigate through the dangers and get to a safe and calm area. Kelly and Aaron worked to stabilize the equipment, while Captain Bon steered the boat as best as he could. Once Aaron and Kelly were done securing the equipment, they went to the front of the boat and advised Bon of the dangers ahead. They would yell out instructions and warnings. Captain Bon heard, "Rock to the left. Steer right." Then they said, "Not too far right. We have a large rock a hundred feet off the right side. Prepare to shift back left."

It was crazy how the water now shifted back and forth from one bank to the other. As it did, it pushed the boat toward unforeseen rocks that the team knew were just under the water and would hit bottom with bangs and booms. Bon wasn't sure the boat would hold up much longer.

All of a sudden, the water calmed, and the boat stopped rocking. It seemed the team had made it through the hazards at last. It was great timing because the boat was heading for a hairpin turn. Turns like these were dangerous enough without fighting a swollen river and whirling rapids.

At that moment when the team let their guard down, the boat was pulled into a quick whirlpool. Bon fought as hard as he could, but he lost control of the oars. Now they were along for the roller-coaster ride. Shifting side to side and turned almost completely sideways, the boat struck a large rock and tipped to Kelly's side. She was thrown out and into the churning water.

Aaron and Bon did everything they could to get to Kelly; however, the boat was out of control, and the rapids were getting worse by the second. They were close to Kelly when the boat turned and struck her, pulling her underneath. At that second, Bon knew that if he didn't do something, he might lose his partner and friend. Without a second thought, he jumped into the water and swam as hard as he could toward Kelly. Everything in him was pushing his arms and legs to move as fast as they could.

Bon was able to reach Kelly. She was unconscious, and there was blood coming from her head. Holding on to Kelly like she was part of himself, Bon used his back and the life jacket to take the hits from the boulders in the water. They bobbed in the rapids for a while. Finally, they came to calm water, and Bon could see Aaron holding the boat in place just downstream. With the last of his energy, he swam toward the boat with Kelly in tow.

DAYS OF WORRY

As soon as Bon and Kelly were in the boat, Aaron rowed the boat toward the shore as Bon rested and tried to take care of Kelly. Once they anchored on the shore, Aaron got on the radio with Norris and the rest of the logistics team to get help for Kelly. Norris sent for one of his helpers named Tom, who was a medic in the National Guard. Tom walked Aaron and Bon through what they needed to do for Kelly. As they were checking her for broken bones, she came around and said, "Oh my god, my head hurts." Both Aaron and Bon released a deep breath that they had been holding since Kelly had fallen into the water.

Patching up Kelly's head with a poorly wrapped bandage, they made her as comfortable as possible. Tom walked them through the rest of the checks, but Kelly didn't want all the attention. Other than the cut and bump on her head, she was unharmed, but Tom advised that Aaron and Bon needed to watch her closely for signs of a concussion.

Through the night, Aaron and Bon took turns checking on Kelly. In the morning, the team decided to stay put for one more day, though Kelly protested. Kelly didn't want to be the reason for a delay and possibly not breaking the record for traveling the river. Aaron and Bon wouldn't dare take the chance of traveling until they knew Kelly was strong again. After all, they were only on day nine of what was to be a thirty-day trip, and they were still a day ahead of their schedule. Given that, why would they take any chances with Kelly's well-being?

The next ten days went well. Of course, they had to fight the current in the river, which slowed them down. They were now a day behind the original schedule they had planned, and food was running low. They should have been to the next food drop site by today, but again, they were behind on the timeline. Though they had built such things into their contingency plan.

They had enough food to last, but they were running low on water. As a result, the team had to ration the water for the next twenty-four hours. The only problem with rationing water was that the days were getting hotter and the current was working against them. They had to work to keep one another's spirits up, but they made it through to the drop and enjoyed a cool drink of water and a grand dinner.

Setting out the next day, the team had a revived spirit and a little luck too. The force of the current seemed to reduce, and water level of the river lowered too. It was now safe to use the motor again, and each of them thanked the heavens above for that news. With the use of the motor, the team was able to make up time and quickly get back on schedule.

THE FORK IN THE RIVER

Captain Bon, Aaron, and Kelly had been on the adventure for fifteen days when they came to a fork in the river. They checked their map, but it didn't show this fork. Which way should they go? They got together and discussed the situation as they always did when they were faced with a new problem. Each gave their thoughts about why the fork wasn't displayed on their map. Bon said maybe it was just a small runoff and would lead to a dead end, but then Kelly asked which one led to the dead end. Aaron said that the map they had could be out of date and that a canal may have been dug to support one of the mining villages that had popped up in the last year. One of these branches could circle to the main river upstream. They couldn't be sure.

Captain Bon asked the group, "What would the adventurers from the past do?"

Kelly's hero was Joan of Arc. She had been fighting the English, and now they had retreated. She had come to a fork in the road following their retreat and had to decide which way to go. She knew they had split up and had a bad feeling one group was circling back to attack her from the rear, but which group went which way? It was a hard decision to make. She decided to get information from her generals and trackers before proceeding. They advised her on the trails and the English's tactics. That was the answer. Find someone on the river to advise them on which way to go.

Aaron did the same in his imagination, except he was the explorer Marco Polo. He envisioned himself marching through the Alps, looking for a new land path to China. Marco Polo had to have come to many forks in his adventure. Aaron had read many books on Marco Polo and knew this to be true. What did Marco do when he found himself in these situations? Well, he did a few things. He consulted with his fellow explorers on what they thought was the best path. He sent riders ahead and kept the main explorer party in camp to rest until they could gather more information, and sometimes he sent explorers in both directions with a return time they had agreed to. This helped him prevent the team from wasting time and energy. That was the answer. Send one person ahead while the other two stayed and set up camp.

Captain Bon also considered the situation in his imagination. Now Captain Bon had special heroes in mind. His were Lewis and Clark. He thought about their adventure for President Jefferson to explore the territory of the Louisiana Purchase and to try to find a water route from Missouri to the Pacific Ocean. They must have come to this same sort of decision many times. How had they done it? Captain Bon considered in his imagination and thought of himself not as Lewis or Clark but as one of the explorers with them.

So how had Lewis and Clark explored such a vast land? How did they decide which direction to go? It came to him how they did it. They used the resources they had come across on the trip, including the native tribes. They asked about the road ahead as they passed through. They had scouts they would send ahead to look for the best path to take.

Then he realized that their team had not asked enough questions during their previous stops with the locals, but should they backtrack and ask questions now? Returning to the last village would mean losing two days. No, that wasn't the best plan, but there was a second option. They could send someone ahead to explore one side of the branch in the fork. One of them could quickly look this evening as the other two made camp. Our three adventurers talked it over and decided to send someone ahead to investigate what path would be best. This was the best option they had.

They decided that Aaron would be the one to take the small raft and explore the branch of the fork to the right. They also decided that he would travel up the branch for no more than two and a half hours before turning around. That way, he could be back before dark. Captain Bon and Kelly would set up camp and start cooking dinner while he was exploring.

Less than three hours later, Aaron returned to his partners with the news. He had traveled only an hour when he reached a small village. He spoke with the people there and learned that this new branch that was not on the map had been dug out within the last eighteen months. It now gave a roundabout to an area in the river where it was very rough, and there were large rocks that could damage boats. It would add an extra four hours to their trip; however, the water was calm, and they could restock their supplies at the village. All three agreed that this was the path to take and that their imaginations had given them the answer they needed just when they needed it.

WRAPPING UP

The river and all its tricks challenged the adventurers every step of the way for the next twelve days, but with courage and teamwork, they made it to the mountain. They worked together as if they were of one mind. They also used resources from the team members at the base camp to help them when things became tough. They received moral support over the radio and that was enough to help them push through the challenges they were facing at the time. Other times when supplies were running low, they would coordinate with the logistics team to have supplies airdropped along the river. Fresh clothes and special items were extremely helpful on the journey.

Many times, the supplies had to be dropped in areas that were a day or two from the team's location, but this only built a larger fire in their bellies and pushed them on to the next spot. It was always like waking up on Christmas morning and coming down to loads of presents under the tree. Every time the logistics team dropped a care package for them, it would have special notes in it. They had written notes for each of the adventurers to help motivate them and raise their spirits.

Even though the logistics team was not on the river with the three adventurers, they knew they played a big part in helping them reach the mountain. It was their responsibility and honor to support this team, and they took on this responsibility with honor and joy.

There were days when one or two of the team members felt it was foolish to go on. The river had beaten them down, and food was low. But

Captain Bon always built a fire in them by explaining how they would feel when they reached the mountain. Then they would have accomplished something only a handful of people had done.

Captain Bon's cheerleading came naturally to him. After all, that was how he had motivated himself in the first place to get off his butt and go after his dream. He had built himself up into a heightened state, and it had built a fire to push him forward. Each time he doubted that he could finish the journey, he used his cheerleader again to raise his spirits. He knew if he could build this fire in himself, he could build it in his team.

There were times, such as when they nearly lost both boats to the rapids and Kelly was hurt, that even he doubted they could make it, but he always believed that they could do whatever they set their minds to. That belief helped him get past these challenges. He used the same formula to help his teammates get past the rough challenges that might cause others to give up.

Now standing at the foot of Mount La Felicidad, he had realized his dream. His team had helped him achieve what only a year earlier he would have thought to be impossible. They had beaten the river with all its tricks and threats, and now they stood where only the great had stood before. They had accomplished the trip in less time than anyone before them. It had only been the twenty-eighth day. The previous record was thirty-one days. What an accomplishment! Now that was something else to be proud of. While they hoped to make it in at thirty days and beat the record, they had outdone even their expectations.

Through the adventure, the team had learned much about one another and themselves. Each member had learned that through the support and help of others, they could do the impossible. They had also learned that your mind could lie to you to save you from yourself. It works to preserve your body, and it tells the body it has done all it can do; however, they had come to learn that this was the biggest lie of all. They could push past the perceived limits of their minds. They could go further than they thought possible. And they could only push as far as they did because of the support they gave to one another. They had discovered that limits were only in their minds.

The team members did get tired, and they got discouraged too. But that normally did not happen at the same time for them all. Sometimes only one of them was down, and other times two had doubts. On one occasion, all three wavered, but through one another's support and encouragement along with the encouragement of the logistics team, they pushed past the fears and doubts. This was true teamwork in action, and each member of the team was grateful for the others not allowing them to quit.

All three members stood there for what seemed like an eternity without saying a word. They just took in the view of the mountain and thought about what they had gone through to get there. It was like a holy experience. This was something few in the world would ever get to experience. This adventure had begun more than a year ago with a dream from Captain Bon, and now the three of them had realized his dream.

Kelly saw a tear in Captain Bon's eye, and she figured it came from the joy of achieving his dream. Little did she know, however, that it was a tear not of joy but of sorrow. Captain Bon was sorry he hadn't accomplished this adventure earlier in his life. He had come to realize at this moment that he could have achieved this dream long before now and that the only thing that had stopped him had been himself. He thought of all the things he could have accomplished in his forty-nine years had he just had more faith in himself, and that thought brought tears to his eyes.

Now he understood that with a plan, determination, and help from others, he could achieve whatever he wanted. At that moment, his tears of sorrow turned to tears of joy. He just learned the most invaluable lesson of all. He had learned that the only limitations you have in life are the ones you put on yourself. Captain Bon understood now that when you stopped living in your life and started designing your life, you would get the things you wanted and not just the things that came to you.

Captain Bon thought about other limitations he had put on himself that had stopped him from accomplishing goals in life. Now he wasn't deluded. He didn't think he could win an ultramarathon, but he knew if he trained hard, he could finish with a respectable time. This would be his next challenge. He would train to compete in the Rocky Mountain ultramarathon.

Captain Bon had decided not to let himself or anyone else stand in the way of his dreams. He knew he would fail, but he also knew he would try one more time until he accomplished his dream. As with his adventure down the rivers to Mount La Felicidad, failures would become life lessons that would, in turn, teach him how to succeed.

With that thought, he grabbed both Kelly and Aaron and pulled them into a big bear hug, almost squeezing the life out of them from his excitement.

EXERCISE REVIEW

THE BUILDING OF A FOUR-DIMENSIONAL PERSON ON THE RIVER OF LIFE

IN THIS SECTION, YOU WILL find some of the exercises from the book. I hope you have enjoyed my story, but I hope you put the system to work in your life. You really can have everything you want, but you have to do the work. My greatest desire is to help people achieve their dreams, and I know if you do the work and put in the time, you can and will gain your desire.

Use the book and its system to get on the river to your mountain of dreams. You can reach it. It just takes courage. Remember, courage isn't the absence of fear but the strength to push through. You have this. Use the system and achieve the four-dimensional life that you deserve.

#

You are the designer, engineer, and CEO for your dreams, and you must develop your mind map. Remember, you are just breaking your pathway to your desire into manageable pieces.

Dream/Desire	Question	Actions	Feedback	New Actions
?	What help will we need?	Develop a plan with a list.	Need defined resources.	Develop a grocery list of resources needed.
Mastermind Group	What qualities do members need?	Develop a list of qualities needed in the group.	List of qualities is perfect but evaluate later.	Recheck list periodically.
Financial	How do we acquire financial support?	Develop a plan and presentation to pitch to investors and supporters.	The plan/presentation needs to explain better what the investors will get in return.	Rewrite plan to include investor return.
Adventure Route	What river will we take, and where will we set up to restock resources along that river?	Work with the team and the mastermind group to develop the route and support plan.	Get advice from past adventurers on your plan.	Request that past adventurers review your plan.

PASSIONS AND DISLIKES

Passions	Dislikes

YOUR PLAN

What is your plan for your desire? Have you defined your desire?
Decide.
First, evaluate.
Decide where to start.
Make a timeline.
Evaluate habits.
Organize a mastermind group or consult an expert.
Track your accomplishments.
Track your gains.
Evaluate your progress every fourteen days.
Adjust (if needed).

How to Get Your Desire

So how do we go after our desires? The system you have learned here will help you cement the desire in your subconscious mind. Many people will not admit to using this system or may not realize they have used it to become successful. But rest assured that they have used it in part or whole. This is not a complicated system, but it will take a little faith and dedication of time on your part.

1. Adopt a positive state of mind filled with the possibilities available to you and feelings of self-love and faith in your ability to succeed using your past success as an anchor to gain motivation.
2. Fix your exact desire in your mind.
3. Determine what you will give in return to gain your desire. As with anything in life, you can't get something without giving something. Whether it is your time, a special service you have to offer, a specialized knowledge you possess, or your money, you will have to decide what you are willing to give to get what you want.
4. Set a definite deadline to achieve your desire.
5. Create a definite plan on how you will get your desire. Begin working on it immediately. Do not wait until you have all the answers. If you wait, you will never have all the answers. If you start your plan and have faith in yourself and in the universe, the parts of your plan will come to you. Be on the watch for the opening doors and knowledge the universe will provide to you. They will come to you. The only problem in most people's lives is that they think they must succeed by their own will or thoughts instead of the all-powerful will and thoughts of the universe.
6. Write out a clear, concise statement of your desire, what you will give in return, a definite date, and your plan. After you have done this, sign the statement at the bottom. This will help in creating ownership in your statement.
7. Read your statement at least twice daily to feel you have already achieved your dream, preferably in the morning before you start your day and at night before you go to sleep. More important than just reading the statement is feeling like you have realized

the desire. See in your mind what you will be doing as you travel to your desire. Who will be on the trip with you? So often, people fail at this point due to the reasoning that if they do not get the desire, they will be let down or become a failure.

DESIRES IN EACH PART OF YOUR LIFE

Part of Life	Desire	Belief associated	Limiting or propelling	Needed Belief
Finance				
Health				
Career				
Relationship				

OUTLINE OF PARTS OF A PLAN

1. Summary
2. Overview / Activities to be Delivered
3. Whys/Objectives
4. Strategy / Desired Outcome
5. Financial
6. Staffing/Resource Requirements
7. Implementation/Timelines
8. Process for Monitoring Progress

PLEDGE OF ENGAGEMENT

Create your pledge of engagement by using the following example as a model:

I pledge my allegiance and forthcoming to this team. My part to play will advance the team as a whole and not just one person or group. I pledge that I will be openly honest and open-minded to others while not causing hurt to my fellow members. I will remember that I will make mistakes and that I do not retain all the necessary knowledge, and I know others will be the same. I understand that we are all in this adventure together and that the success of one is the success of all. So too, the failure of one is the failure of all. Together under God, we do make this pledge to each partner.

1. Your Pledge

_____
_____
_____
_____
_____
_____
_____
_____
_____
_____
_____
_____
_____
_____
_____
_____

CHOOSING THE RIGHT ADVISERS

You can ask the following questions:

- What are they after, or why do they want to help me get to my desire?
- How will my mastermind group get to their desires in life by helping me?
- Does my team tell me the truth or just what I want to hear?
- Are they the experts in the field of my desires?
- Does this individual or team work in harmony? Or do they fight?

- When working with this mastermind group, do our minds meld together to create solutions?
- Do the people in the mastermind group bring together the necessary accumulated experience to reach our desires?

DEVELOP YOUR PLAN

Now it's time to move forward and use the system you have learned to create a plan to meet your desired health and spiritual lifestyle as you build relationships with others. Remember the following steps:

1. Remember your dreams, desires, and decisions. It's time to create the dreams and desires you want for health and spirituality. What are your desires and your reasons for the lifestyle you want? Then make a true decision either way and move forward.

2. Imagination is your next step. Imagine what you will look like when you reach your desired lifestyle. What will your body look like? What compliments will you get? How will you feel about yourself? What will your spiritual relationship be? How will you use your spirituality to help you with your dreams and desires?

3. What is your subconscious mind saying about you getting into shape or about developing your spirituality? What are your beliefs and values? Are any of your beliefs and values holding you back? How did you come by these beliefs and values? Is it time to reevaluate your beliefs? Maybe it's time to build new beliefs.

4. Now you can build the plan to get the health and spirituality that you desire. You will build your plan and again see if it conflicts with your beliefs and values.

5. It's time to gather knowledge to help make your plan bulletproof. You will have to organize the specialized knowledge on creating a healthier and more spiritual lifestyle. You can collect this information by searching the internet, reading books, asking friends, or consulting experts. Seek out the knowledge that you need to build your road map and organize it so that you can use it all.

6. Now you need your mastermind group. The members of your group will help keep you going when times get hard. The group will give you feedback on the results you are getting. They will suggest exercises to do or spiritual lessons you need to learn. Just as with any other adventure you are working on, you need advisers to help you stay on course to accomplish your desires. Your mastermind group could include your spouse, a trainer, or a group of people who work out with you or raise your spiritual awareness. There are many people out there who can help you. You have to ask them.

7. You must care first about the people you are working out with before they will care about you. Work to help them before you ask them to help you.

8. Now put what you learned into your persistence and determination to keep moving and gaining on your dream. Remember, persistence and determination are about using willpower to help you create a habit and to get the help of your subconscious mind. Use the relationships you have built to help others with their persistence and determination, and they will help you with yours.

9. You will have to leverage and stretch yourself during any adventure in life, but you will have to do so with relationships, health, and spirituality as well. You must leverage your present self to do what is needed to realize your future self. Stretching yourself is a must when it comes to spiritual growth. There is a lot to learn about being spiritual and healthy. You will need to learn new things, and they may conflict with the person you were before. You must decide for yourself what your future will look like and what you will believe. This will take more stretching than you are used to, but it will help you grow internally. This holds for growth in relationships, health, and spirituality.

10. Have faith in yourself and develop your self-confidence. Even if you can't do one push-up today, you will be able to do many more in a month. Have faith that you can build your spiritual self and find the peace that you haven't had before. When you hit a hard spot in either your physical or spiritual journey, remind yourself that you will get past it just as you have gotten past other small

challenges. With relationships, you must have self-confidence so that you can open yourself up without being hurt. You must put your faith in other people and believe that they have your best interest at heart. There is always a chance of getting hurt, but with self-confidence and faith in others, you can build relationships that will serve you for a lifetime.

EXERCISE TO BUILD SELF-CONFIDENCE

1. Clear your mind of the problems facing you and of the world around you. The state of mind you are after is similar to meditation.
2. Think back over the things you had accomplished and pick one win that was challenging when you took it on.
3. Think and feel the emotions you had when you achieved the win.
4. Look in your imagination and figure out how you accomplished the win.
5. Feel the process you used for the win.
6. Associate the feeling of accomplishing the win you had with the present challenge you have.
7. Go after the new challenge with the assurance that you can win as you have in the past.
8. Anytime you are not feeling confident in yourself, return to these simple steps.
9. Remember one last thing: you only fail if you quit.

ABOUT THE AUTHOR

I AM NOT VERY FOND of writing about myself. That is why I wrote a story with a fictitious character. Though Captain Bon's life experiences come from me and others, I wanted to be able to entertain you as you learn. Another reason I prefer this type of approach is that through the story, you will become the main character. You will associate and relate to the experiences he has in life and how he gets past his challenges. If you imagine yourself as the character, you will see yourself changing your life through his adventure, and the lesson will be cemented in you.

I also know many people want to know more about the author so that they can relate or evaluate whether he or she knows and lives what he or she writes. With that in mind, I will tell you a little about who Christopher J. Bourg was in the past and who he is today.

I have been married twice, and I have two sons (Jake and Mason) of whom I am very proud. My wife, Tammy, is the love of my life and my best friend. She has given me the courage I never knew was in me, and I am forever grateful to her. With Tammy I have gained two more great children Joanna and Adam.

I am an industrial engineer by training but have not worked as an engineer very much of my life. I came from a very low-income family, and my father died when I was very young. I have held positions in multiple fields, including fabrication, inspection, industrial cleaning, and cement construction. I have been the guy pushing a broom and also been the senior Vice President of a large company. I've spent most of my career in research and development, as well as in training. I also have a great passion for safety, which I gained after two close friends died from accidents in the industry.

Through my career, I have traveled the world and worked in more than fifty different countries. Through these experiences, I have learned that people are people in each part of the world and that we are all the same. Some of us are good, and some of us are bad; however, for the most part, we are all good and bad.

Through my life, I have been blessed with mentors who have taken me under their wings and taught me. These mentors appeared in each step of my life, but I had to ask for help. They wanted to help, but again, I had to be open to them. I mention this because all too often in life the next great lessons or mentors are standing in front of us, but we are closed off to them. Please stay open-minded as you go through life.

When I was young, two of these mentors were family members, both with completely different backgrounds in life. One was a farmer and a jack-of-all-trades, and the other was a welder who eventually started his own business doing welding and fabrication. Both men taught me how to work hard and to work toward my goals in life. They never accepted that I couldn't do anything.

Whenever I complained that something was too hard or that I didn't know how to do it, they both would say, "If you want something out of life, you will have to work for it. Life owes you nothing and will give you nothing." Through this attitude, I learned to work hard and find the answers I needed to succeed.

I have read thousands of self-help books in my life and have attended hundreds of seminars. I can say I have learned something from each book and seminar, even if it was what not to do. I believe that you have to question everything. If you find something isn't congruent or doesn't work for you, then change it or stay away. But make sure that what isn't working isn't you; make sure that you aren't being lazy or avoiding the truth about yourself.

I have followed the work of three great men through my life, and each has helped me develop who I am. These three men are Napoleon Hill, John Maxwell, and Tony Robbins. Though I have studied others and have learned from their lives, these three have been my main resources. I am not telling you to follow just these three men. There are many great people you can learn from; however, these are my top three, and my style of teaching comes from them.

I started my company (OLC Resources) to help others reach their full potential in life. I hope that through my books and training, I can be a mentor to others the same way I have had mentors in the three men listed here. Through OLC Resources, I do training and life coaching for both individuals and companies. If you are interested in other books and courses or if you would like to attend a training seminar, please contact me at CJBourg@olcresources.com.

Look for my next book coming out "Getting out of Zombie Land".

Thanks for taking time to travel with me on this journey.

Christopher J Bourg

Printed in the United States
By Bookmasters